THE TAOS TRAPPERS

UNIVERSITY OF OKLAHOMA PRESS : NORMAN

DAVID J. WEBER

The Taos Trappers

The Fur Trade in the Far Southwest, 1540–1846

BY DAVID J. WEBER

(editor) *Prose Sketches and Poems Written in the Western Country*,
by Albert Pike (Albuquerque, 1967)
(editor and translator) *The Extranjeros: Selected Documents from
the Mexican Side of the Sante Fe Trail, 1825–1828* (Santa Fe, 1967)
(editor) David H. Coyner, *The Lost Trappers* (Albuquerque, 1970)
The Taos Trappers: The Fur Trade in the Far Southwest, 1540–1846
(Norman, 1971)

International Standard Book Number: 0–8061–0944–0

Library of Congress Catalog Card Number: 75–145508

Copyright in microfilm 1968 by David J. Weber, assigned to the
University of Oklahoma Press, 1970. New edition copyright 1971 by
the University of Oklahoma Press, Publishing Division of the University. Composed and printed at Norman, Oklahoma, U.S.A., by the
University of Oklahoma Press. First printing 1971.

To My Parents

Frances J. and Theodore C. Weber

*who educated me in
the broadest sense*

PREFACE

Dᴜʀɪɴɢ ᴛʜᴇ 1820's, when mountain men scoured the Far West in search of furs, the tiny village of Taos in northern New Mexico became the most important permanent market and supply depot for trappers between Fort Vancouver on the Pacific and St. Louis on the Mississippi. Beaver, the mainstay of the fur trade, were plentiful in those days. Beaver inhabited the high plateau and mountain country of the Far Southwest, and even frequented such unlikely rivers as the Río Grande and the Gila, whose waters flow less freely today. Taos, which became the center for furs trapped in this "arid" region of present-day New Mexico and Arizona, also lay within easy reach of the beaver-rich streams of the southern Rockies and the Great Basin. Partly because of this strategic location, Taos quickly became the home of figures as colorful and memorable as Kit Carson, "Peg-leg" Smith, Ewing Young, "Old Bill" Williams, Antoine Robidoux, and a host of others who made their living in the trapping and trading of furs.

Although the trapper's importance as a trail blazer and a harbinger of American manifest destiny has been long recognized and much chronicled, the story of the Taos trappers has never been told. Perhaps this is because theirs is not one story, but many stories. Large, single-minded fur companies never trapped successfully in the Southwest where the fur trade remained largely an individual or small-group affair. Records, then, are gathered in no convenient place. Usually illiterate or tight-lipped at best, the mountain man was not given to writing diaries or reminiscences. Taciturn trappers were even more secretive in Mexican New Mexico, which early forbade foreigners from trapping.

That the Taos-based trappers worked surreptitiously on a foreign frontier has served to obscure their activities, but Mexican archives have helped to put the researcher back on their track. Never before systematically mined by historians of the fur trade, Mexican archives have yielded a modest but rewarding return. They permit the correction of earlier errors of fact and interpretation; they cast some venerable "heroes" in a new and often unfavorable light; and they provide a fresh perspective and more balanced view of the fur trade in the region that is today our Far Southwest, but was then Mexico's northern frontier. Unquestionably further material will surface in uncatalogued and inaccessible archives in Mexico City, but enough sources are now available from both sides of the border to put together this first overview of the fur trade from New Mexico.

This study owes much to the helpful staffs of the archives and libraries cited in the bibliography. For extraordinary kindness, I am indebted to Sr. Rubio Ignacio Mañé, Director, and Sra. Beatrice Arteaga, Librarian, of the Archivo General de la Nación at Mexico City; Mrs. Frances Stadler, Archivist of the Missouri Historical Society at St. Louis; and especially to Dr. Myra Ellen Jenkins, Senior Archivist at the State Records Center, Santa Fe, New Mexico. My own institution has facilitated my work in every way possible and Mrs. Dorothy Ramsay and Mrs. Donna Hall, secretaries to the History Department, deserve special mention for seeing to the typing of the final manuscript. Of many friends and acquaintances who came to my rescue at critical moments in the preparation of this volume, I am particularly grateful to Robert Redding of San Diego State College; Marc Simmons of Cerrillos, New Mexico; Michael Mathes of the University of San Francisco; France Scholes, Sabine R. Ulibarrí, and Edwin Lieuwen of the University of New Mexico. The following specialists have critically read the entire manuscript, making invaluable corrections and suggestions: LeRoy R. Hafen, of Brigham Young University; Dale L. Morgan of the Bancroft Library; Janet Lecompte of Colorado Springs, who also generously shared her knowledge of the Arkansas Valley with me; and Donald C. Cutter of the University of New Mexico, who aroused my interest and directed my initial research in this area. I hope that the final product reflects, in small part, their efforts and attention. Finally, to my patient, cheerful, and talented wife, Carol, I am grateful for hours spent in typing manuscript, reading proof, and for enduring my preoccupation with things historical.

DAVID J. WEBER

San Diego State College

CONTENTS

ILLUSTRATIONS

ABBREVIATIONS

ARCHIVES

AGN   Archivo General de la Nación, Mexico City.
MANM   Mexican Archives of New Mexico, Santa Fe.
SANM   Spanish Archives of New Mexico, Santa Fe.

JOURNALS

BMHS   *Bulletin of the Missouri Historical Society*
HSSC   *Historical Society of Southern California*
CHSQ   *California Historical Society Quarterly*
HICM   *Hutchings' Illustrated California Magazine*
MHSB   *Missouri Historical Society Bulletin*
MHSC   *Missouri Historical Society Collections*
MHSGP   *Missouri Historical Society Glimpses of the Past*
NMHR   *New Mexico Historical Review*
OHSQ   *Oregon Historical Society Quarterly*
SHQ   *Southwestern Historical Quarterly*
UHQ   *Utah Historical Quarterly*

THE TAOS TRAPPERS

Taos was a place where corn grew and
women lived. Sooner or later every man
in the mountains came to Taos. They
came to it from as far north as the Red
and as far south as the Gila. They came
to it like buffalo to a salt lick across
thousands of dangerous miles. Taos
whiskey and Taos women were known
and talked about on every stream in the
Rockies. More than any other place,
Taos was the heart of the mountains.

—Harvey Fergusson, Wolf Song *(1927)*

I

AMERICANS who traveled the Santa Fe Trail in the 1820's and 1830's often took a short cut as they neared the New Mexico settlement. Leaving the trail at the Cimarron or at Octaté Creek, they followed what one contemporary called "a direct but rugged route" across the Sangre de Cristo Mountains into Taos.[1] Normally the wagons stayed on the main road to San Miguel and Santa Fe, for the short cut took one over rocky creek bottoms and through narrow ravines into the high pine country where Old Taos Pass crosses the mountains at an elevation of some nine thousand feet. Most men made the crossing on foot or on horseback, but even then it was tedious and difficult, especially in cold weather. Albert Pike, a young New England writer who crossed over Taos Pass in the winter of 1831–32, described how "the blue mist hung about the mountains, and gathered into icicles on our beards and blankets."[2] As the traveler scrambled down the western slope of the Sangre de Cristos, following the little Río Fernando de Taos, his efforts must have seemed worthwhile when civilization came into sight in the beautiful valley of Taos.

[1] Josiah Gregg, *Commerce of the Prairies* (ed. by Max L. Moorhead), 74.
[2] Albert Pike, *Prose Sketches and Poems Written in the Western Country* (ed. by David J. Weber), 19, 22–25. Use of this route was widespread. See, for example, Matthew C. Field, *Matt Field on the Santa Fe Trail* (ed. by John E. Sunder), 166–75.

TAOS

Running north and south, flanked by the deep gorge of the Río Grande to the west and mountains to the south, east, and north, Taos Valley was handsome to behold in any season. In winter it offered refuge from the spectacular snow-covered peaks that surround it, and in summer its green, irrigated fields of wheat must have seemed to the traveler fresh from the prairie like a bit of the East moved west. Santa Fe merchant Josiah Gregg pronounced that "no part of New Mexico equals this valley in amenity of soil, richness of produce and beauty of appearance,"[3] and most of his contemporaries agreed.[4]

An Anglo-American did not have to remain long before he discovered that he was very much a late-comer to the Taos Valley. Probably as early as the fourteenth century, Indians had begun building the magnificent multi-storied Pueblo of Taos, whose massive mud walls still bulk against Taos Mountain at the north end of the valley. Spaniards learned of this impressive pueblo in 1540 when one of Francisco Vásquez de Coronado's lieutenants visited there, but not until the mid-1600's did Spanish colonists settle that

[3] Gregg, *Commerce of the Prairies*, 104.
[4] Almost every American who wrote of the valley acclaimed its beauty: Ruxton, Field, Garrard, Sage, and Pattie, for example. See also Agustín de Escudero in H. Bailey Carroll and J. Villasana Haggard (trans. and eds.), *Three New Mexico Chronicles*, 86–87.

far to the north. Their settlement was short-lived. The famous Pueblo Revolt of 1680, inspired at Taos, drove the Spaniards out of the valley as well as from all other New Mexico settlements. Yet, after the area was reconquered, beginning in the second decade of the eighteenth century, emboldened colonists again ventured near Taos Pueblo to farm.[5]

After 1750, Comanches became a greater threat than the Pueblos and forced Spanish settlers in the valley to form a community for defense. This small village, apparently built near the present site of Taos, had to be abandoned in the 1770's, however, because it was not strong enough to resist Comanche attacks. Ironically, the colonists moved into the Pueblo with the Indians. By 1776 a new *plaza*, or settlement, was underway to the south of the Pueblo near the Río de las Trampas, where many Spanish colonists had their farms. Called Trampas for a time, the settlement was known as Ranchos de Taos by the 1820's when Anglo-Americans arrived; many found it an attractive place to live.[6]

Farther up the valley, about two miles south of Taos Pueblo, still another Spanish settlement came into being in the 1790's, when the Comanche threat had diminished. Named after a seventeenth-century pioneer in the area, this village was called Don Fernando de Taos. In the Mexican period, some called it Don Fernández de Taos, after a prominent local family, or corrupted the name further to San Fernández, or San Fernando de Taos. Although several other settlements had sprung up in the valley by the 1820's, most foreigners preferred to live at Don Fernando, which they called, simply, Taos, writing it phonetically as "Touse" or "Taus."[7]

To the newly arrived American the sight of Taos itself—a scat-

[5] Florence Hawley Ellis and J. J. Brody, "Ceramic Stratigraphy and Tribal History at Taos Pueblo," *American Antiquity*, Vol. XXIX, No. 3 (January, 1964), 316–27; Myra Ellen Jenkins, "Taos Pueblo and its Neighbors, 1540–1847," *New Mexico Historical Review*, Vol. XLI, No. 2 (April, 1966), 61, 89.

[6] Fray Francisco Atanasio Domínguez, *The Missions of New Mexico, 1776* (trans. and annot. by Eleanor B. Adams and Fray Angélico Chávez), 112–13; Jenkins, "Taos Pueblo," *NMHR*, Vol. XLI, No. 2 (April, 1966), 97–99. (See list of abbreviations, p. xv.)

[7] Jenkins, "Taos Pueblo," *NMHR*, Vol. XLI, No. 2 (April, 1966), 100; T. M. Pearce, *New Mexico Place Names: A Geographical Dictionary*, 169.

tering of mud houses dominated by two church towers, also of mud—served as a jolting reminder that he had left the American frontier behind. Indeed, on entering the village, a foreigner found himself, as did Albert Pike, in "a different world," where everything was "new, strange, and quaint," and often disappointing. A young town, Taos had not yet taken on the charm that it has today. Just like the capital at Santa Fe, the church, public buildings, and shops at Taos faced each other across a treeless plaza, alternately dusty and muddy, where animals and their excrement had to be dodged as one navigated the streets.[8]

To many Americans the town seemed nothing more than "a few dirty, irregular lanes, and a quantity of mud houses" or "rude hovels."[9] These adobe homes seemed architecturally tasteless. Their tiny windows, covered by wooden cross bars, reminded Americans of jails, and the great expanses of mud walls, which faced on the street, appeared foreboding and uninviting. The rough-hewn lumber of the *pórticos*, the roofs of mud, and windows of mica instead of glass, seemed to testify to the poverty of the land and the lack of ingenuity and initiative of its inhabitants. Inside a house the hard-packed dirt floors (found even in the most elegant residence), the scarcity of wooden furniture, and the use of blankets and animal skins as substitutes gave these homes a shabby and disagreeable appearance to the outsider. Crucifixes and saints' images on the walls added to the discomfort of the typical Protestant American almost as much as the strange spicy dishes urged upon him by his hosts.[10]

It is not surprising that a young trader and trapper, Ceran St. Vrain, was unimpressed during his first visit to Taos, in 1825. He

[8] Pike, *Prose Sketches*, 147–48; W. H. H. Allison, "Santa Fe as it Appeared During the Winter of the Years 1837 and 1838," *Old Santa Fe*, Vol. II, No. 2 (October, 1914), 177; minutes of the Ayuntamiento of Santa Fe, April 12, 1833, MS, University of New Mexico Library, Albuquerque.

[9] Pike, *Prose Sketches*, 47; LeRoy R. and Ann W. Hafen (eds.), *Rufus B. Sage: His Letters and Papers, 1836–1847, With an Annotated Reprint of His "Scenes in the Rocky Mountains . . . ,"* II, 83.

[10] Pike, *Prose Sketches*, 148, 102–103, 236–37; Hafen and Hafen, *Sage*, II, 83–84; Lewis H. Garrard, *Wah-to-yah and the Taos Trail* (introduction by A. B. Guthrie, Jr.), 175; Field, *Matt Field*, 182; James Ohio Pattie, *The Personal Narrative of James Ohio Pattie of Kentucky* (ed. by Timothy Flint), 39.

complained to his mother in St. Louis that he was "oblige[d] to spend the winter in this miserable place." Life could not have been too unbearable, however, for St. Vrain was already learning to speak Spanish and a year later would take a wife at Taos, making it his home for much of the remainder of his life.[11]

It was not just the village of Taos that Americans found "miserable," but its inhabitants as well. George Sibley, leader of a survey party, who also found himself "obliged" to spend the winter of 1825–26 in Taos, confided to his diary that he would have to leave the New Mexican family with whom he was staying and move into a rented house: "I am Sure I cannot easily Reconcile myself to the living of the poor inhabitants here."[12] Rufus Sage, a trapper who visited Taos briefly in 1842, concluded that "there are no people on the continent of America, whether civilized or uncivilized, with one or two exceptions, more miserable in condition or despicable in morals than the mongrel race inhabiting New Mexico." His sentiments were echoed by other trappers and traders who found New Mexicans depraved, indolent, untrustworthy, dishonest, cowardly, servile, ignorant, superstitious, and dirty—among other things. Some Americans even thought the Taos Indians superior to their Mexican neighbors.[13] Americans heaped most of their contempt upon public officials and priests, characterizing the latter as immoral, avaricious, and unduly influential in politics. Government officials were corrupt and ignorant, representing a political system which the Yankee found undemocratic and arbitrary. As Rufus Sage declared, Mexican government was "infinitely worse than none."[14]

Although these reactions were often little more than chauvinistic

[11] Taos, July, 1825, Chouteau Collection, Missouri Historical Society, St. Louis, Missouri; Harold H. Dunham, "Ceran St. Vrain," in LeRoy R. Hafen (ed.), *The Mountain Men and the Fur Trade of the Far West*, V, 300.

[12] Entry of October 30, 1825, in George Champlin Sibley, *The Road to Santa Fe: The Journal and Diaries of George Champlin Sibley* (ed. by Kate L. Gregg), 131.

[13] Hafen and Hafen, *Sage*, II, 83, 87. See also the reactions of Pattie, Pike, and Garrard. For a broader discussion of Anglo attitudes toward Mexicans at this time see Cecil Robinson, *With the Ears of Strangers: The Mexican in American Literature*, Pt. I.

[14] Hafen and Hafen, *Sage*, II, 124.

outbursts designed to please the American reading public's preconceptions of what a racially-mixed, Roman Catholic, Latin country should be like, American observers also identified problems of which New Mexicans, too, were painfully aware. Throughout its years as an appendage of the Spanish empire, from 1598 to 1821, New Mexico's development was hindered by its isolated position some fifteen hundred miles north of Mexico City, by the harshness of its climate and topography, and by successions of hostile tribes which kept the area in a state of continual defensive warfare. Between 1821 and 1846, while governed by the independent Republic of Mexico, New Mexico was too far from the center of power and Mexico in too much political turmoil itself to effect significant changes in her outlying provinces. Problems which had plagued the area while under Spain remained unaltered: an ill-equipped and ill-trained military, lack of public education, debt peonage, and the control of the economic and political life of the area by a handful of wealthy families. Public revenues would have been slight, too, except for the customs duties collected from American merchants.[15]

As backward and repulsive as New Mexico seemed to many visiting trappers and traders, the area had some redeeming features. One, clearly, was the hospitality of the people which made Taos and other villages a welcome refuge from the prairie or the mountains. As Albert Pike grudgingly admitted: "Whatever vices that people may possess, they are at least hospitable."[16] Most hospitable were New Mexico women, who were admired even by those Americans who despised Mexican men. Francis Parkman went so far as to term the women "Spanish" and the men "Mexicans." Some of the Americans' fascination focused on high skirts and loose blouses, which were unfamiliar sights on the American frontier. After being deprived of female companionship for many months, trappers and traders were willing to overlook behavior that might ordinarily displease them. Young Lewis Garrard even

[15] The best description of New Mexico during this period is by Lansing Bartlett Bloom, "New Mexico Under Mexican Administration, 1821–1846," *Old Santa Fe*, Vol. I, No. 1 (July, 1913), 9–49.
[16] Pike, *Prose Sketches*, xvi; Pattie, *Narrative*, 38.

suggested that cigarette smoking "does enhance the charms of the Mexican *señoritas*." It should not be surprising, then, that American trappers lived with or married these alluring creatures, and that mountain men made their homes and raised their families at settlements such as Taos. Even so, many relationships with Mexican women were clouded by a sense of impropriety. Garrard, a great admirer of New Mexican ladies, put the matter squarely. There was, he wrote, "much romance to a superficial observer in having a Mexican wife," but "the only attractions are of the baser sort. . . . We look in vain for true woman's attraction—modesty."[17]

Almost as talked about as Taos women was *aguardiente de Taos*, a whisky made from wheat which won notoriety as "Taos Lightning." This whisky, it was later remembered, "was as good as any, except that it lacked color and age"; it was imbibed as rapidly as it could be made. It seems to have enjoyed a reputation for excellence only in comparison with other Mexican *aguardiente*, however, for Americans thought it inferior to their own brands.[18]

To most trappers and fur traders, New Mexico's greatest asset was its strategic location, at the southern gateway to the Rockies. A trapper could sell beaver, obtain supplies, or pass a winter or summer in civilization without having to make the long trip back to the Missouri settlements. As the northernmost of New Mexico's villages, Taos profited most from this advantageous position. Trappers returning from the mountains would stop there first, and those setting out from Taos were within striking distance of the beaver-laden headwaters of the Arkansas, Río Grande, Platte, and San Juan rivers. This location, one historian has observed, "was enhanced by the navigational shortcomings of Southwestern streams."[19] Unlike fur traders on the Missouri River, those operating in the Southwest had to rely on overland transportation.

[17] Garrard, *Wah-to-yah*, 171; James M. Lacy, "New Mexico Women in Early American Writings," *New Mexico Historical Review*, Vol. XXXIV, No. 1 (January, 1959), 41–51; Hafen and Hafen, *Sage*, II, 86.

[18] Albert William Archibald to Francis Cragin, Trinidad, Colorado, December 25, 1907, Notebook XI, 40, Cragin Papers, Pioneers' Museum, Colorado Springs, Colorado; Garrard, *Wah-to-yah*, 166, 179.

[19] J. W. Smurr, in Paul Chrisler Phillips, *The Fur Trade*, II, 512.

Thus, a supply base near the Santa Fe Trail became a necessity, and Taos met this requirement too. For Americans who wanted to avoid New Mexico officials, Taos' remoteness, some seventy miles above Santa Fe over a rugged road, also seemed ideal. Furs could be taken out of Taos or supplies smuggled in over the Santa Fe Trail without attracting the attention of authorities. Throughout the Mexican period, Taos remained so free from officials that a custom house was never effectively established there, even though many Americans first entered New Mexico at that "port."[20]

Remarkably, then, the tiny village of Taos became the center of foreign-born residents of New Mexico, with the capital at Santa Fe "a far second," according to one authority.[21] In 1826, only five years after Americans had begun to trap out of New Mexico, Governor Antonio Narbona complained that Taos, because of its location "on the edge of our populated area," had become a "refuge which many take advantage of without giving knowledge of their presence." In 1833, a Santa Fe official complained when two Americans, ordered to leave New Mexico because of their bad behavior, fled to Taos, where "gather various foreigners who do not conduct themselves very well." Foreigners became so influential at Taos that they could intimidate or bribe the local alcalde for special favors.[22] Foreigners were even reputed to have "Americanized" the *Taoseños*. In 1840, Governor Manuel Armijo accused all citizens of Taos, except the priests, of traitorous inclinations—namely, being sympathetic to Texans.[23]

Long before the arrival of Americans, the isolated Taos Valley had been the scene of illicit trade and intrigue, and it was, in a

[20] Max L. Moorhead, *New Mexico's Royal Road: Trade and Travel on the Chihuahua Trail*, 134–35; Carroll and Haggard, *Three New Mexico Chronicles*, 66.

[21] Fray Angélico Chávez, "New Names in New Mexico, 1820–1850," *El Palacio*, Vol. LXIV, Nos. 9–10 (September-October, 1957), 292.

[22] David J. Weber (trans. and ed.), *The Extranjeros: Selected Documents from the Mexican Side of the Santa Fe Trail, 1825–1828*, 22, 42; copy of a letter regarding Alexander Le Grand, to the Department of the Interior, Santa Fe, March 14, 1833, Mexican Archives of New Mexico, Santa Fe, New Mexico.

[23] William C. Binkley, "New Mexico and the Texan Santa Fe Expedition," *Southwestern Historical Quarterly*, Vol. XXVII, No. 2 (October, 1923), 93.

sense, prepared for their coming. In 1746, for example, the Pueblos in the valley were reportedly carrying on illegal trade with Comanches and were even suspected of furnishing them with military information.[24] Utes, Apaches, and Comanches found the location of Taos as attractive as Americans would, and during the last half of the eighteenth century the valley became the scene of New Mexico's most important trade fair. Usually during July or August, Spanish settlers, government officials, and Pueblos from throughout the province would gather at Taos to trade with neighboring tribes—unless they were at war with them that year. On these occasions the "barbaric" Indians traded pelts, buffalo skins, chamois, and plunder (especially captives whom they had kidnapped from other tribes or from the New Mexicans), in exchange for horses, trinkets, knives, and other metal objects. A colorful marketplace, the Taos fair was also the scene of considerable tension. On one occasion, for example, Apaches, Utes, and Comanches all rode into Taos at the same time to trade. Since the three tribes were then at war with one another, this had a disquieting effect on the Spaniards and Pueblos. Apaches and Comanches in particular often failed to observe the courtesies of "civilized" trading, and would pause on the way out of town to pillage settlers in the valley. If an Indian felt that he had been cheated—which was not an infrequent occurrence—he often sought immediate and violent justice. Trading, then, could be a very risky business for an unscrupulous Spaniard, as well as for anyone standing too close to an aggrieved Comanche.[25]

Years of trading with neighboring tribes served to give the Taos Valley a "cosmopolitan" flavor which American trappers would find attractive and useful. By 1776, the Taoseños already were reputed to speak the languages of the Utes, Apaches, Comanches,

[24] Oakah L. Jones, *Pueblo Warriors and Spanish Conquest*, 117.

[25] Bishop Pedro Tamarón y Romeral, *Bishop Tamarón's Visitation of New Mexico, 1760* (ed. by Eleanor B. Adams), 58; Alfred Barnaby Thomas, *The Plains Indians and New Mexico, 1751–1778, A Collection of Documents . . .*, 68, 111–12, 136–37, 147; letter of Fray Trigo, 1754, and report of Fray Pedro Serrano, 1761, in Charles Wilson Hackett (ed.), *Historical Documents Relating to New Mexico, Nueva Vizcaya, and Approaches Thereto, to 1773*, III, 468, 486–87.

and Pueblos.[26] Thus, mountain men would find translators at Taos, some of whom could also serve as excellent guides, for Spaniards in New Mexico had developed a modest fur trade before 1821.

[26] Domínguez, *Missions of New Mexico*, 113.

II SPANISH FUR TRADE,

W<small>HEN</small>, in 1767, the Spanish military engineer Nicolás de Lafora wrote that New Mexicans "pay no attention to otter, beaver, ermines, and marten skins, which they have in abundance, because they do not know their value,"[2] he expressed simply and precisely a notion which Anglos have fostered into the twentieth century.[3] Spaniards, it has been supposed, were too ignorant and indolent to trap or trade fine furs. Thus, large-scale fur trading in the Southwest had to await the coming of American frontiersmen. Clearly, Spaniards in New Mexico paid scant attention to valuable fine furs, but a locally significant trade in coarse furs did develop during the colonial period and reasons for Spanish neglect of fine furs were various and complex. This neglect cannot be explained as ignorance.

From the very outset of exploration in New Mexico, Spaniards recognized the area's potential fur wealth, though they confined their wanderings to the plains and low plateaus, where fur-bearing

[1] This chapter follows closely my article "Spanish Fur Trade from New Mexico, 1540–1821," which appeared originally in *The Americas*, Vol. XXIV, No. 2 (October, 1967), 122–36, and is herein reprinted with the permission of the Academy of American Franciscan History.

[2] Nicolas de Lafora, *The Frontiers of New Spain: Nicolas de Lafora's Description, 1766–1768* (trans. and ed. by Lawrence Kinnaird), 95.

[3] J. W. Smurr in Phillips, *Fur Trade*, II, 471; Frank McNitt, *The Indian Traders*, 15-16.

1540–1821[1]

animals were least in evidence.[4] The first of the procession of conquistadors to penetrate the Southwest, led by the celebrated Francisco Vásquez de Coronado, had come in search of the fabulously wealthy "Seven Cities of Cíbola." A six-month journey north from New Spain, as Mexico was then called, brought him only to the baked-mud villages of Zuñi, where, in the summer of 1540, natives presented him with "well-dressed" buffalo hides and the skins of deer and rabbits. These Pueblo Indians had long used animal skins for clothing and footwear. When Coronado's men settled in for the winter along the Río Grande, they also relied on pelts for the same purposes, requisitioning them from the Pueblos and thereby making themselves increasingly unwelcome.[5]

In addition to their usefulness as clothing, hides and skins were apparently of some value to these first Spanish visitors as trade items. For example, Pedro de Castañeda, chronicler of the Coronado expedition, described his countrymen fighting over a pile of tanned hides which Teyas Indians had presented to them. This incident occurred in the warm months on the long trek east through the buffalo plains, when hides would have made impractical cloth-

[4] Alfred Barnaby Thomas, "Spanish Expeditions into Colorado," *Colorado Magazine*, Vol. I, No. 7 (November, 1924), 289.
[5] Herbert E. Bolton, *Coronado: Knight of Pueblos and Plains*, 130–31, 184, 265, 204–205, 225.

ing. Coronado's band was of course impressed by the buffalo. Castañeda opined that "excellent garments could be made from their wool," and observed that the Plains Indians were experts at skinning and tanning buffalo and deer skins. He also noted that Plains Indians traded surplus skins to the Pueblo Indians along the Río Grande, in exchange for corn, cloth, and pottery.[6] Perhaps Spaniards did the same thing with the skins they garnered on the buffalo plains and may also have taken some back to Mexico as curiosities. Yet Coronado found little else of value to impress the viceroy or the king, and exploration of New Mexico came to a halt for the next forty years.

Beginning in 1581, Spanish explorers returned to New Mexico. During the next decade expeditions such as those of Fray Agustín Rodríguez, Antonio de Espejo, and Gaspar Castaño de Sosa traveled north along the Río Grande or the Pecos toward the Pueblo villages. Like Coronado's men, they noted the use of buffalo and deer skins ("chamois") among Indians, and were particularly impressed by the quality of the buffalo hides and the possibility of using their hair as "wool." The quality of chamois and deerskins, one chronicler said, rivaled that of those which came from Flanders.[7] Members of Espejo's party brought buffalo hides down the Río Grande at least as far as La Junta, at the confluence of the Conchos and the Río Grande rivers, where they traded them with Indians for food.[8] Perhaps other contemporary exploring parties had done the same.

Thus, sixteenth-century Spanish explorers recognized the abundance and utility of furs in the Southwest, and even traded in them. It is not surprising, however, that during their quest for a new Mexico, a new Peru, or a sea passage to the wealth of the Orient, these Spaniards showed only modest enthusiasm for furs.

---

[6] Ibid., 257, 245, 247; George P. Hammond and Agapito Rey (trans. and eds.), Narratives of the Coronado Expedition, 1540–42, 292–93.

[7] George P. Hammond and Agapito Rey (trans. and eds.), The Rediscovery of New Mexico, 1580–1594: The Explorations of Chamuscado, Espejo, Castaño de Sosa, Morlete, and Leyva de Bonilla and Humaña, 78, 92, 114, 172, 228, 258, 278, 285, 217, 219.

[8] Ibid., 221; Jack D. Forbes, Apache, Navaho, and Spaniard, 65.

Unlike France or England, Spain had found more spectacular wealth than furs in the New World; she bent her energies to exploiting silver and gold and to finding even more.

This was demonstrated in 1598 when Juan de Oñate made the first attempt to colonize permanently the unproductive land of northern New Spain. Aware of the lack of visible mineral wealth in New Mexico, Oñate sent glowing reports of other resources of the new province back to the viceroy. He mentioned "the wealth from the wool and skins of the buffalo" and sent samples of their "beautiful wool" back to Mexico. But Spanish energy and manpower were needed to work the mines of New Spain, and in 1608 New Mexico was almost abandoned for lack of valuable mineral resources.[9] Soldiers, colonists, and missionaries would have been withdrawn from the area at that time had it not been for the presence of numerous Indian souls that required saving.

Thus, New Mexico came to be a mission province, having its political and economic life dominated by Franciscan friars for the next two centuries. But even in the hands of these able men, who showed a keen business sense in managing a hide trade from their Upper California missions, a significant trade in fine furs still did not develop in New Mexico. Although the friars and the colonists knew of the fur wealth of the area, a variety of circumstances prevented them from exploiting it.

In a report on New Mexico's economy in 1803, Governor Fernando Chacón revealed one problem. In New Mexico, he said, it was common to find

> furs of rabbit, furs of skunks of various species, and beavers for the making of hats. But this art is not practiced for no one is skilled or interested in it, as is true of that [trade] of leather dresser, tanner, saddler and others who work with all kinds of hides and pelts. These last are found in great numbers and in many types, to wit: elk, common deer, buck of the fallow

[9] George P. Hammond and Agapito Rey, *Don Juan de Oñate, Colonizer of New Mexico 1595–1628*, I, 483, 486; George P. Hammond, *Don Juan de Oñate and the Founding of New Mexico*, pp. 185, 176–77; Frank D. Reeve, *History of New Mexico*, I, 133.

deer, wild sheep, buffalo, bear, mountain lion, wolf, fox and coyote.[10]

Even without skilled artisans, New Mexico might have been able to export furs. But, as Pedro Bautista Pino, New Mexico's representative to the Spanish Cortes, observed in 1812, there were "no present means of exporting them without great freighting costs."[11]

The problem of transportation might have been overcome despite the great distance to Mexico City had there been an attractive market there. It would appear, however, that although leather goods were widely used in Mexico and Spain, their moderate climates precluded a widespread use of furs for warmth. Contemporaries were aware of the effect of this on the development of a fur trade in New Mexico. One visitor to New Mexico noted in 1818 that "because they have only a very small market for the furs which they receive . . . it follows that this commerce is unimportant."[12]

The development of a fur trade in New Mexico was still further hindered by the colonists' need to focus their energies on eking out a subsistence from the soil, and protecting themselves from marauding tribes. Leisure time for trapping was scarce, and would have been highly dangerous. Trading for furs from aborigines during occasional lulls in the normal condition of warfare was also difficult.

Apaches, Comanches, Navahos, and Pueblos apparently placed little value on small fur-bearing animals and had probably not developed the art of trapping. In most cases, these tribes were not even located near beaver streams.[13] Deer, elk, antelope, and buffalo

[10] Report of August 28, 1803, Doc. 1670a, in the Spanish Archives of New Mexico, State Records Center, Santa Fe, New Mexico.

[11] Carroll and Haggard, *Three New Mexico Chronicles*, 37. See also 134.

[12] See, for example, Isabel de Palencia, *The Regional Costumes of Spain*, and Charles Gibson, *The Aztecs Under Spanish Rule: A History of the Indians of the Valley of Mexico, 1519–1810*, 343; Alfred B. Thomas, "An Anonymous Description of New Mexico in 1818," *Southwestern Historical Quarterly*, Vol. XXXIII, No. 1 (July, 1929), 59; Arthur Preston Whitaker, *The Spanish-American Frontier: 1783–1795*, 44–45.

[13] Alpheus H. Favour discusses this in *Old Bill Williams, Mountain Man*, 83–84.

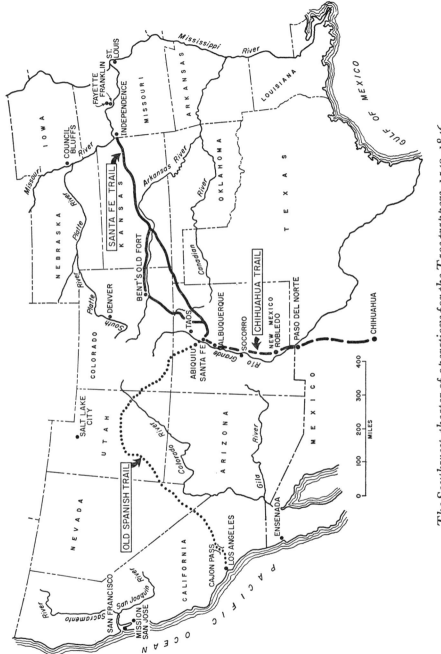

The Southwest, theater of operations for the Taos trappers, 1540–1846

were easier quarry and yielded greater amounts of fur, although not of high quality. It was a trade in the coarser furs of these readily obtainable animals to which the New Mexicans turned.

Throughout the seventeenth century, coarse furs were among New Mexico's few exportable resources and were of such local importance that the governors of the province entered and dominated the trade. New Mexico, like Spain and other of her colonies, had developed no strong middle or merchant class, [14] so that politicians controlled the area's slender economic life line.

Commerce and communication with the rest of New Spain depended largely on caravans which, during the seventeenth century, arrived at no less than three year intervals for the purpose of bringing supplies from Mexico City, some fifteen hundred miles away, to the missions along the Río Grande. The supply caravan usually had empty space on the return trip which the governors used to export local produce, buffalo and deer skins being among the most important items. Although Spanish law prohibited the governors from engaging in private business, most of them took advantage of their office to add to their personal wealth.[15] Their power was such that few could effectively challenge them.

In the seventeenth century, New Mexico governors obtained some animal skins through the *encomienda* system, whereby Pueblo Indians were obliged to make specific payments, in cash or in kind, to governmental officials. A monthly collection at Pecos Pueblo in 1662, for example, yielded sixty-six antelope skins, twenty-one white buckskins, eighteen buffalo hides, and sixteen large buckskins.[16] The Pueblos in turn probably came into possession of these furs through trade with Plains Indians, for Spanish occupation did not interrupt the exchange of maize and hides which the Pueblos had traditionally carried on with the roving tribes to the east. Navahos, to the northwest of the Pueblos, also traded "dressed

---

14 J. W. Smurr in Phillips, *Fur Trade*, II, 573.

15 Moorhead, *New Mexico's Royal Road*, 32; France V. Scholes, "Civil Government and Society in New Mexico in the Seventeenth Century," *New Mexico Historical Review*, Vol. X, No. 2 (April, 1935), 82.

16 Hearings in the case of Diego de Peñalosa, July 3, 1665, in Hackett, *Historical Documents*, III, 260.

chamois skins," game, and other items at the Pueblos at least as early as the sixteenth century.[17]

Much of the trade in hides that went on at the Pueblos was apparently encouraged by New Mexico's governors. The Franciscans had little to do with it, or so they said. In 1659, for example, some clerics admitted to trading in antelope skins, but explained that they used the resulting revenue for religious purposes, and noted that "it is in very few places that this [trading] occurs."[18] Their limited interest in hides may have been due less to a disdain for mundane matters than to the stiff competition which they faced from the governors.

According to the Franciscans, some of the governors used the missions as early-day trading posts, leaving knives with the friars which they were expected to trade for skins. Some governors seem to have taken this business quite seriously. One padre complained that Governor Francisco de la Mora y Ceballos (1632–35) "tried to make us his small merchants . . . so that we are buying such products as are in this unhappy land in exchange for his knives. The priests who have not consented to do this have been most unfortunate, for he has made cruel war upon them."[19] When Governor Luís de Rosas (1637–41) learned that Indians were not bringing a sufficient quantity of hides to trade for his knives at Pecos Pueblo, he reportedly became so angered that he blamed the friars for this failure and had one of them arrested. The friars claimed that Rosas' greed for animal skins was so great that he promised the Pecos Indians that they could return to their pagan customs if only they would furnish more hides.[20]

Not all New Mexico governors exploited the missionaries. Some governors, instead, sent trading parties out to the plains to barter directly for buffalo and antelope skins. Bernardo López de Mendi-

---

[17] Espejo's report in Hammond and Rey, *Rediscovery of New Mexico*, 224.

[18] Declaration of Fray Juan Ramírez and others to the Inquisition, Santo Domingo, September 8, 1659, in Hackett, *Historical Documents*, III, 192.

[19] Letter of Fray Estevan de Perea, Cuaras, October 30, 1665, to the Inquisition, in Hackett, *Historical Documents*, III, 130. See also France V. Scholes, *Church and State in New Mexico*, 105.

[20] Scholes, *Church and State*, 118.

zábal (1659–61) sent six men on a month-long trading venture in 1660, for example, and it may even be that Spaniards sent yearly trading parties into what is now West Texas during the latter half of the seventeenth century.[21] Aggressive governors often did their own trading. López de Mendizábal took the least pains to hide his economic activities. Upon appointment as governor, he purchased European manufactures and delicacies in Spain and brought them to New Mexico, where he set up a store in the Governor's Palace. Since specie was almost nonexistent in New Mexico, López de Mendizábal accepted local products, including hides, as payment.[22]

Governor Rosas, in the spring of 1638, personally led a group of five friars and forty soldiers to northern Sonora, where the friars hoped to convert the Ipotlapigua Indians. But Rosas turned the expedition into a profit-making venture by extorting feathers and hides from the Indians, thereby winning their enmity and losing a mission field for the padres.[23]

It is impossible, with the slender evidence available, to estimate the number of hides sent out of New Mexico during the seventeenth century. We do, however, have specific figures for some shipments. In the mission supply caravan which left Santa Fe in 1639, Governor Rosas exported 122 painted buffalo hides and 198 chamois skins.[24] In 1660, Governor López de Mendizábal sent 1,350 deerskins, as well as a quantity of buffalo hides, to Parral. This was only one of three large shipments he made during his brief term in office. At the end of his term, while López de Mendizábal waited for the completion of the customary investigation of the governor's conduct in office, the *residencia*, his embargoed belongings revealed a stock of about 1,200 antelope skins, in bundles of 100, 300, and 400. The full-sized skins were worth two pesos apiece. The smaller skins were valued at two per peso. López de Mendizábal also had

21 France V. Scholes, *Troublous Times in New Mexico, 1659–1670*, 44; Herbert E. Bolton, "The Spanish Occupation of Texas, 1519–1690," in Herbert E. Bolton, *Bolton and the Spanish Borderlands* (ed. by John Francis Bannon), 107.

22 Scholes, *Troublous Times*, 34.

23 Scholes, *Church and State*, 119.

24 Lansing B. Bloom, "A Trade-Invoice of 1638," *New Mexico Historical Review*, Vol. X, No. 3 (July, 1935), 244–45.

four bundles of elk skins worth twelve hundred pesos or about two pesos apiece.[25]

A few of the hides shipped to New Spain were in the form of completed products. Governor Rosas exported sixty-eight jackets via the 1639 caravan and López de Mendizábal included leather jackets, shirts, and breeches in his shipment. These were among the items made in workshops which the governors established in Santa Fe, using forced Indian labor.[26]

Some hides probably traveled the full length of the Camino Real. A few may even have gone as far as Spain. Alexander von Humboldt, in the late eighteenth century, observed that "thousands of mules arriving every week from Chihuahua and Durango, carry besides bars of silver, hides, tallow, some wines of El Passo del Norte, and flour."[27] Tanned hides were, along with silver, gold, and sugar, among the main exports of New Spain from Veracruz during the seventeenth century; they continued to be an important export item in the next. Most of these hides, however, were probably from the domestic cow.[28]

Toward the end of the seventeenth century, trade in animal skins, like nearly all other economic activity in New Mexico, came to an abrupt halt. In 1680 the devastating Pueblo Revolt forced Spaniards to retreat to the El Paso area. This proved to be only a temporary setback to the fur trade, however, for it resumed almost as soon as Spaniards returned and seems to have been more vigorous than ever in the eighteenth century.

In 1694, although the success of the reconquest by Diego de Vargas was still not assured, old channels of trade began to reopen.

[25] Scholes, *Troublous Times*, 44–45; declaration of Hernando Martín Serrano, Santa Fe, May 21, 1664, in the case against Diego Peñalosa in Hackett, *Historical Documents*, III, 248–49.

[26] Bloom, "A Trade-Invoice of 1638," *NMHR*, Vol. X, No. 3 (July, 1935), 244–45; Scholes, *Troublous Times*, 45; Scholes, "Civil Government," *NMHR*, Vol. X, No. 2 (April, 1935), 81–82.

[27] Alexander von Humboldt, *Political Essay on the Kingdom of New Spain*, IV, 14.

[28] Vicente Riva Palacio, *México a través de los siglos*, I, 512, 675, 677, 678; Humboldt, *Political Essay*, IV, 29–30, 37–38; Hubert H. Bancroft, *History of Mexico*, III, 642; Clarence H. Haring, *Trade and Navigation Between Spain and the Indies in the Time of the Hapsburgs*, 124.

In March of that year, a group of Apaches, eager to re-establish trade with the Spaniards, appeared at Pecos to arrange for an exchange of goods in October. In May, still more Apaches visited Pecos. As a sign of friendship, they presented three buffalo skins and an elk-hide camp tent to Governor de Vargas. They promised to return in the fall when the maize was ripe, "bringing buffalo, elk and buckskins for trade with the Spaniards." De Vargas seemed as eager as the Indians to resume trade, and he encouraged Utes also to bring goods to Santa Fe as they had done before. Commerce was soon resumed with Chihuahua and became, by 1724, a yearly event.[29]

In addition to trade with these familiar tribes, Spaniards gained an important new source of hides in the eighteenth century in the form of the Comanches. This Shoshonean people, previously unknown in New Mexico, had migrated from southern Wyoming and, with their linguistic cousins the Utes, soon displaced Apaches in trade with the Spaniards.[30] By midcentury Comanches had become accustomed—during times of peace at least—to attending the autumn "fair" at the Pueblo of Taos. They probably tanned many of the hides which they brought to Taos. Pedro Bautista Pino, writing in 1812, noted that "they tan hides extraordinarily well. Only the Comanches posses[s] the technical knowledge of how to tan hides with hair, as well as without hair, and in many other ways."[31] It is impossible to estimate the quantity of skins which changed hands on these occasions, or to tell what eventually became of them. Among the few available figures is an estimate that in 1786 at Pecos, where fairs were also frequently held, Comanches traded over six hundred hides.[32]

[29] J. Manuel Espinosa, *Crusaders of the Rio Grande*, 177, 183, 197, 336, n. 74.

[30] Alfred Barnaby Thomas (trans. and eds.), *Forgotten Frontiers: A Study of the Spanish Indian Policy of Don Juan Bautista de Anza, Governor of New Mexico, 1777–1787*, 26.

[31] Henri Folmer, "Contraband Trade Between Louisiana and New Mexico in the 18th Century," *New Mexico Historical Review*, Vol. XVI, No. 3 (July, 1941), 266; Carroll and Haggard, *Three New Mexico Chronicles*, 130.

[32] "An Account of the Events Concerning the Comanche Peace, 1785–86," Pedro Garrido y Durán, Chihuahua, December 21, 1776, in Thomas, *Forgotten Frontiers*, 306.

Trade with the fickle Comanches was sporadic, however, and even prohibited at times.[33] Beginning about 1750, the Utes had become a more dependable source of peltry. Utes had occasionally raided New Mexico villages during the first half of the century, but between 1747 and 1749 they had a falling out with the Comanches and joined the Spaniards against their now-common enemy.[34] Although Spaniards valued this peace for its own sake, they also prized the trade that accompanied it. Governor Tomás Vélez Gachupín instructed his successor in 1754 that friendship with the Utes meant trade in deerskins, which New Mexicans then took to Vizcaya and Sonora. "Without this trade," he wrote, the settlers "could not provide for themselves, for they have no other commerce than that of these skins." During periods of war with the Utes, trade came to an end and the New Mexicans were "without the possibility of clothing themselves and existing."[35]

Trade with Utes was important enough that New Mexicans were not content to wait for these Indians to come to them to trade, but began to venture into the southern Rockies and the Great Basin in search of pelts and Indian slaves. In doing so, these traders became the first Europeans to enter the heart of the Rockies. Spaniards who had earlier entered present-day Colorado had confined their explorations to the plains east of the Front Range of the Rockies and had been seeking Indians or French intruders rather than pelts.[36]

Spanish traders may have entered Ute country as early as the first decades of the eighteenth century, for in 1712 Governor Juan Ignacio Mogollón found it necessary to forbid traders, either Spanish or Indian, from going there. A royal order prohibited trade in Indian lands, but, according to Mogollón, New Mexicans were in the habit of making trading *entradas*, for they knew nothing of the royal decree.[37] The distance that these early traders had to travel to

---

[33] Jones, Jr., *Pueblo Warriors*, 117.

[34] Alfred Barnaby Thomas, *The Plains Indians and New Mexico, 1751–1778*, 29.

[35] Instructions of Tomás Vélez Cachupín, Governor and Captain General of New Mexico to his successor, August 12, 1754, in Thomas, *Plains Indians*, 130.

[36] Thomas, "Spanish Expeditions into Colorado," *Colorado Magazine*, Vol. I, No. 7 (November, 1924), 291–97.

[37] Jones, Jr., *Pueblo Warriors*, 86, and decree of December 16, 1712, in SANM, Doc. 185.

reach the Utes is not certain, but it must have been well into south-ern Colorado. In 1765, Juan María de Rivera led a trading party over the San Juan Range, in southwestern Colorado, and up to the Gunnison, traveling by way of the Dolores and Uncompahgre rivers. Even though two of his men crossed the Gunnison, they could locate no Utes and were forced to return to Santa Fe.[38] Others, almost certainly, followed within the next decade. In 1775, for example, three of Rivera's party, Andrés Muñiz, Pedro Mora, and Gregorio Sandoval, returned to the confluence of the Gunni-son and the Uncompahgre.[39]

It was one of these traders, Andrés Muñiz, who acted as a guide and interpreter for the well-known 1776 expedition of Frays Sil-vestre Vélez Escalante and Francisco Atanasio Domínguez, leading them with assurance as far as the Gunnison. That trading journeys into the Rockies were common before 1776 is illustrated by a state-ment of Fray Escalante who spoke of the fear that his interpreter, Andrés Muñiz, had of displeasing the "Sabuagana" Indians lest he "lose the ancient friendship which they maintain with them through the vile commerce in skins." Escalante commented that the traders were in the habit of staying among the Utes for "two, three or four months," motivated by "their greed for peltry," although the Friar suspected that "others go and remain with them for that [reason] of the flesh, obtaining there its brutal satisfaction." Domínguez and Escalante prohibited trade on their exploratory mission "in order that the heathen might understand that another and higher motive than this had brought us through these lands," but Andrés Muñiz and his brother, Antonio, among others, could not overcome "their greed for peltry" and brought trade goods along secretly.[40]

[38] Joseph H. Hill, "Spanish and Mexican Exploration and Trade Northwest from New Mexico into the Great Basin, 1765–1853," *Utah Historical Quarterly*, Vol. II, No. 1 (January, 1930), 4–6; "Diary and Itinerary" of Fray Silvestre Vélez de Escalante, in Herbert E. Bolton, *Pageant in the Wilderness: The Story of the Escalante Expedition to Interior Basin, 1776*, 152.

[39] Hill, "Spanish and Mexican Exploration and Trade," *UHQ*, Vol. II, No. 1 (January, 1930), 5, n. 5.

[40] "Diary and Itinerary" of Escalante, in Bolton, *Pageant in the Wilderness*, 215–16, 159.

From 1765, then, if not before, Spaniards traded regularly in Ute territory, often traveling great distances in search of pelts. In 1779, Governor Juan Bautista de Anza learned that Utes lived on the headwaters of the Río Grande and that "three civilians," who were doubtless traders, had explored to that point.[41] After Domínguez and Escalante found the way to the Ute villages on Lake Utah (Timpanogos) and the Sevier River, private trading parties probably also ranged that far. Documentation to support this contention is not available, however, until the early nineteenth century.[42] According to one contemporary account, José Rafael Sarracino traveled for three months through Ute territory in 1811, "in an effort to locate a Spanish settlement which the Yutas have always asserted lay beyond their territory, supposedly completely surrounded by wild Indians." Sarracino finally turned back at a large river.

> Among the Indians living there he found many articles manufactured by Spaniards such as knives, razors, and awls; he obtained the same information there, that the manufacturers of those articles lived across the river (somewhere between the north and west). . . . He brought back with him a large shipment of beautiful pelts which he had purchased very cheaply; for example, he traded one awl for a perfectly tanned deer hide.[43]

In 1813 a company of seven men under Mauricio Arze and a retired soldier, Lagos García, tried to trade with the Utes on the Sevier River and Lake "Timpanogos." As they told the story before the alcalde of Río Arriba, the Indians would trade only in slaves, thereby forcing the Spaniards to buy twelve captives. They managed, however, to acquire 109 pelts which represented "but a few." Making the round trip in four months, between March 16 and July

---

[41] Anza's Diary, in Thomas, *Forgotten Frontiers*, 126.

[42] Hill, "Spanish and Mexican Exploration and Trade," *UHQ*, Vol. II, No. 1 (January, 1930), 16–17; SANM, Doc. 1881; S. Lyman Tyler, "The Spaniard and the Ute," *Utah Historical Quarterly*, Vol. XXII, No. 4 (October, 1954), 356–57.

[43] Juan Bautista Pino, in Carroll and Haggard, *Three New Mexico Chronicles*, 134.

12, the Arze-García expedition had all of the earmarks of being routine. Its route is not known.[44]

Trade into Ute country remained illegal, as it had been in 1712, although it might have been possible to obtain a license from the governor. In 1775, Governor Pedro Fermín de Mendinueta found it necessary to publish a proclamation prohibiting any citizen, *genízaro*,[45] or Indian to trade in Ute territory, but to no effect. Again, in September, 1778, Acting Governor Francisco Trebol Navarro reissued this proclamation complaining that the traders, with "rash impudence and obstinate disobedience" had broken the law repeatedly. Particularly annoying, some alcaldes and their *tenientes* overlooked violations. The traders, according to Trebol Navarro, frequently mistreated the Utes and brought dishonor to the Spanish nation. There was danger that some incident would cause the Utes to break the peace. For fear of offending them, the traders allowed the heathen Utes to continue in their idolatrous behavior and thereby prejudiced their own convictions as well as the Christian religion. Exposure to these traders, superficial and bad Christians, made the Utes increasingly opposed to Spanish attempts at missionization. The acting governor apparently strengthened Mendinueta's original decree by threatening citizens with a loss of their goods and a ten-peso fine. Indians and *genízaros* were to receive ten lashes, while judges who tolerated the trade faced a ten-peso fine and removal from office. A portion of these fines was designated to pay the informant.[46] To Spanish officials in New Mexico, then, the interests of the fur trade were subordinate to military and religious goals. Illicit trade became common long before the coming of Americans.

[44] Hill, "Spanish and Mexican Exploration and Trade," summarizes this case, (SANM, Doc. 2511), *UHQ*, Vol. II, No. 1 (January, 1930), 16–19. Felipe Gómez, Josef Santiago Vigil, Gabriel Quintana, Josef Velásquez, and a retired soldier, Miguel Tenorio, were also along. I find no evidence in the document that the traders were on trial, as is suggested by S. Lyman Tyler, "The Spaniard and the Ute," *UHQ*, Vol. XXII, No. 4 (October, 1954), 359. See also Leland H. Creer, "Spanish-American Slave Trade in the Great Basin, 1800–1853," *New Mexico Historical Review*, Vol. XXIV, No. 3 (July, 1949), 173–76.
[45] In New Mexico, "a non-Pueblo Indian living in more or less Spanish fashion." See Domínguez, *Missions of New Mexico*, 42, n. 71.
[46] Bando of Governor Francisco Trebol Navarro, September 13, 1778, Santa Fe, SANM, Doc. 740.

Decrees and punishments notwithstanding, illegal *entradas* into the Ute country continued with furs and slaves as the main objectives. These *entradas* may have occurred as frequently as once a year, but we only know of those persons whom authorities apprehended. In 1783, for example, ten Spaniards and two Indians were brought to trial in Abiquiu for trading with Utes without permission.[47] Again in 1785 several Spaniards were tried in Abiquiu for trading "in the interior of the country of the Utes in violation of the repeated edicts." These men, Vicente and Francisco Serda, Vicente Luján, Juan Manuel Gómez, and Nicolás Cisneros, were fined and sentenced by Governor Juan Bautista de Anza.[48]

Aside from being illegal, the Spanish trade with Utes, if we may believe the testimony of some of the participants, was a small-scale, individual, and rather shabby affair. Of twenty-two men who were tried in Río Arriba in 1797 for trading with Utes without a license, all but two were illiterate. Although aware that this trade was illegal, most had gone because they were in debt. The amount of trade goods these men carried was incredibly small. Since New Mexico was deficient in manufactured items of all kinds, they took agricultural products—corn or flour (*harina*, probably also of corn). Some carried less than a *fanega* (about two and one half bushels) and a few carried more. "Hasencio" Lucero traded a *fanega* of corn for four chamois (*gamusas*) and two large elk skins. Pedro Sisneros, doing less well, found his *fanega* of corn worth only two large elk skins. Juan Griego carried about three fourths of a *fanega* of corn which he traded for one chamois, a saddle blanket (*sudadero*) and a piece of elk skin. For their trouble, all received short jail sentences and were fined.[49] The relatively small returns these men would have realized, and the tiny amount of trade goods invested, arouses the suspicion that they were not telling the entire truth, but were dealing in slaves, a commodity more profitable than

---

[47] Incomplete document, February 3, 1783, SANM, Doc. 855. Testimony was taken from eight persons: Encarnación Espinosa, Clemente Benavides, Jose A. Mariano Mondragón, Manuel Vigil, Pablo Gonzales, José Calletano Gonzales, Melchor López, Carlos Vigil.

[48] Case beginning on March 31, 1785, SANM, Doc. 920.

[49] Case of August 2 to September 2, 1797, SANM, Doc. 1393.

skins. Slaves were not discussed, however, at their trial. From the point of view of the Utes, it is not surprising that they later welcomed American mountain men and their superior trade goods. One Ute reportedly told an American trader in 1822 to "come over among us and you shall have as many beaver skins as you want." As the Indian described his country, it abounded in beaver: "The rivers are full of them. Their dams back up the water in the rivers." The Spaniards, he said, had less to offer American traders than did the Indians.[50]

During the first decades of the nineteenth century, Spanish restrictions against trading to the northwest of New Mexico in Ute country probably loosened. Such expeditions may even have been encouraged, for Spanish officials had changed their attitude toward the Indian trade by then. After the United States acquired Louisiana in 1803, Spanish officials had come more than ever to regard the fur trade as essential to securing the friendship of Plains Indians who could serve as a buffer against encroaching Americans. As Comandante General Nemesio Salcedo told Governor Alencaster in 1806, "The best means of maintaining the dependence of the Indian tribes is to facilitate trade and exchange of pelts and other articles."[51] Spanish officials in New Mexico, then, became increasingly committed to using the fur trade as a diplomatic tool, just as the French and British had so effectively done in their spheres of North America. In the late 1780's even the aloof Navahos were being encouraged to bring pelts, as well as woven goods, to the New Mexico settlements to trade.[52]

If trade was to be used as an effective tool of diplomacy, Spaniards needed to be as aggressive as Americans in seeking out Indians at their villages and not to wait for Indians to come to them. Particularly important were Plains Indians who occupied the vast

[50] Thomas James, *Three Years Among the Mexicans and the Indians*, 146. James's unconcealed anti-Spanish bias may be reflected in this conversation, rather than any Indian point of view.

[51] Salcedo to Alencaster, Chihuahua, January 16, 1806, SANM, Doc. 1953.

[52] Frank D. Reeve, "Navaho-Spanish Diplomacy, 1770–1790," *New Mexico Historical Review*, Vol. XXXV, No. 3 (July, 1960), 227; Revilla Gigedo to Fernando de la Concha, December 14, 1791, SANM, Doc. 1176, reference courtesy of Marc Simmons.

territory separating Spanish from American settlements. Foremost among these tribes in strategic importance were the "Lords of the Plains," the Comanches.

Since 1786, when Juan Bautista de Anza concluded a peace treaty with the Comanches, the way had been open for New Mexico traders to enter that tribe's once-hostile domain. *Comancheros*, as these traders to the Comanche came to be called, may have had seventeenth-century predecessors who traded on the plains of West Texas.[53] Trade in that direction did not really begin in earnest, however, until the early nineteenth century when Comanches gradually drifted east from the New Mexico settlements onto the Staked Plains of Texas, abandoning the Taos Fair. In 1805, Governor Joaquín Real de Alencaster reported that some Comanches had settled on the Canadian River. After that date Spanish documents reveal more frequent instances of trading expeditions into the Southern Plains.[54] In 1815, for example, twenty men under José Vigil received a license to trade with the Comanches and another party of twenty was licensed to trade with the Kiowas. Some Spaniards, determined to cut out the middleman, applied for a license that same year to hunt buffalo themselves.[55] Licenses for trading or hunting on the plains were obtained by petitioning the local alcalde, who sent the request on to the governor for final approval.[56] After 1821, Mexican officials in New Mexico retained control over hunting, trapping, and trading by using the same procedure.

During the last decades of Spanish control of New Mexico, plains tribes other than Comanches learned to expect visits from Spanish

[53] H. B. Carroll, "Some New Mexico-West Texas Relationships, 1541-1841," *West Texas Historical Association Year Book*, Vol. XIV (October, 1938), 97; Rupert Norval Richardson, *The Comanche Barrier to South Plains Settlement*, 19.

[54] Alencaster to Nemesio Salcedo, Santa Fe, November 20, 1805, SANM, Doc. 1925 (30), translated in Marc Simmons (trans. and ed.), *Border Comanches*, 33-34. For examples of trading parties visiting the Comanches see SANM, Docs. 2345, 2455, 2492, 2542, 2850.

[55] Pablo Lucero to Governor Alberto Maynez, Santa Fe, August 16, 1815, SANM, Doc. 2619. Spanish buffalo hunters are mentioned in SANM, Docs. 2089, 2345, 2566.

[56] Marc Simmons, *Spanish Government in New Mexico*, 185.

traders. Kiowas on the Arkansas, Pawnees whose villages were situated along the Platte, and Arapahos occupying the country between the south Platte and the Arkansas (and possibly into southern Wyoming), traded hides and pelts to Spaniards.[57] Trade for buffalo hides seems to have been particularly common in the Arkansas Valley, some New Mexico traders traveling as far east as the Kansas River. At the confluence of the Purgatoire and the Arkansas, where Bent's famous adobe fort would later be built, a regular rendezvous between Plains Indians and New Mexicans occurred. Spaniards trading in that area in 1818 referred to one location as the place of *La Nutria*—the place of the beaver.[58] To Indians, as well as to approaching Americans, it must have seemed that Spaniards were all over the plains.

The hides and pelts which wandering Spanish traders acquired, as well as those obtained through barter at various New Mexico settlements, had an importance for the primitive pastoral economy of New Mexico that can scarcely be overstated. Hides and pelts were used as clothing, as a medium of exchange, and on at least one occasion as food during a time of severe famine.[59] In 1806, Zebulon Pike noted that the floors of the Governor's Palace in Santa Fe were "covered with skins of buffalo, bear, and some other animal," and observed that a trade in "skins, some fur, [and] buffalo robes" existed between New Mexico and Sonora, Sinaloa, and Nueva

[57] Forrest D. Monahan, Jr., "The Kiowas and New Mexico, 1800–1845," *Journal of the West*, Vol. VII, No. 1 (January, 1969), 70–72; Zebulon Montgomery Pike, *The Journals of Zebulon Montgomery Pike with Letters and Related Documents*, (ed. by Donald Jackson), II, 37; Edwin James, *James's Account of S. H. Long's Expedition, 1819–1820*, Vol. XV, in *Early Western Travels*, (ed. by Reuben Gold Thwaites), 220–21; Herbert E. Bolton, "New Light on Manuel Lisa and the Spanish Fur Trade," *Southwestern Historical Quarterly*, Vol. XVII, No. 1 (July, 1913), 62.

[58] Thomas Maitland Marshall (ed.), "The Journals of Jules de Mun," reprinted from the *Missouri Historical Society Collections*, Vol. V, No. 3 (1928), 9; A. B. Thomas (ed.), "Documents Bearing Upon the Northern Frontier of New Mexico, 1818–1819," *New Mexico Historical Review*, Vol. IV, No. 2 (April, 1929), 148–49, 161.

[59] Letter from the *cabildo* of Santa Fe to the Viceroy of New Spain, Santa Fe, January 20 and May 26, 1702, in Espinosa, *Crusaders of the Rio Grande*, 337, n. 76; Petition of Fray Francisco de Ayeta, Mexico, May 10, 1679, in Hackett, *Historical Documents*, III, 302.

Vizcaya.[60] These skins, although of modest quantity, probably constituted New Mexico's chief export item at the end of the Spanish period. Nicolás de Lafora, visiting New Mexico in 1766, observed that "the trading of the inhabitants is limited to a few buckskins or buffalo hides, which they bundle and take annually to Chihuahua."[61]

In traveling to obtain the peltries which they found so valuable, Spaniards learned many of the secrets of the southern Rockies, the Great Basin, and the Great Plains. Alfred Barnaby Thomas, the foremost authority on Spanish exploration from New Mexico, once remarked that "the famous nineteenth century 'path finders' from Pike to Frémont but visited regions in the Rockies and on the Plains already opened by Spain's children, the pioneer of Western exploration."[62] But discovery in itself was not enough to hold the great northern frontier of New Spain and, later, Mexico. With the arrival of Anglo-Americans, increased exploitation accompanied exploration and the Spanish trade in peltries and hides was supplemented by the more valuable trade in fine furs. Spaniards had shown the way, but the secrets of the Rockies awaited rediscovery by that first great wave of America's westward movement, the mountain men.

[60] Pike, *Journals of Zebulon Montgomery Pike*, I, 392; II, 50.

[61] Lafora, *The Frontiers of New Spain*, 94.

[62] Alfred B. Thomas, "The First Santa Fe Expedition, 1792–1793," in *Chronicles of Oklahoma*, Vol. IX, No. 2 (June, 1931), 195.

III

If New Mexicans could not develop a viable fur trade while under Spanish dominion, foreigners who entered the territory were allowed to do no better. Spain's mercantile policy forbade foreigners from trading within her empire, including such remote places as New Mexico. Spain, then, would not have to compete with foreign merchandise or see New World resources find their way into the hands of rival powers. In New Mexico, Spain had nothing to fear from foreign merchants until the eighteenth century. Then, in succession, came trouble from Frenchmen and Americans who crossed into northern Mexico in search of trade and furs.

The initial threat to Spain's monopoly over New Mexico's commerce came from France, whose great North American empire was based almost entirely on the fur trade. From the time that Frenchmen moved into the Lower Mississippi Valley during the first two decades of the eighteenth century, New Mexico acted as a magnet to attract adventurous *voyageurs*. By 1720, Spanish officials in New Mexico and New Spain had become alarmed at rumors of the proximity of the French; it was even believed that a sizable contraband trade existed between New Mexico and French Louisiana.[1] Despite the great attractions of trade, imaginary mineral

---

[1] Folmer, "Contraband Trade," *NMHR*, Vol. XVI, No. 3 (July, 1941), 258–59;

INTRUDERS, 1739–1821

wealth, and an overland route to the Pacific, not until brothers
Pierre and Paul Mallet reached Taos in 1739 did French traders
succeed in crossing the plains from Louisiana to New Mexico.[2]

Released after a few months of friendly captivity, the doughty
Mallets were allowed to return home, which only encouraged
others to follow their example. Between 1749 and 1752 at least
four parties of Frenchmen entered New Mexico; perhaps there
were others. Like the Mallet brothers, these later arrivals were also
traders, though their ventures proved less profitable. New Mexico
officials confiscated their merchandise and prevented most of the
merchants from returning to Louisiana. This action not only reflected Spain's desire to keep foreign goods out of her markets, but
also reflected her fear that Frenchmen would supply Comanches
with arms and ammunition.[3] Still, New Mexicans might have welcomed French trade goods. Among the merchandise that New
Mexico officials seized in 1752, for example, were nine hats and nine

Alfred Barnaby Thomas (trans. and ed.), *After Coronado: Spanish Exploration
Northeast of New Mexico, 1696–1727*, 245 ff.

[2] Abraham P. Nasatir (ed.), *Before Lewis and Clark: Documents Illustrating
the History of the Missouri, 1785–1804*, I, 6–8, 28; Folmer, "Contraband Trade,"
NMHR, Vol. XVI, No. 3 (July, 1941), 261–63.

[3] Herbert E. Bolton, "French Intrusions into New Mexico, 1749–1752," in
Bolton and the Spanish Borderlands, 150–71; Folmer, "Contraband Trade,"
NMHR, Vol. XVI, No. 3 (July, 1941), 272; Nasatir, *Before Lewis and Clark*, I, 42.

pairs of shoes made of beaver skins.[4] These were probably scarce commodities in New Mexico—not for want of beaver, but for lack of artisans to fashion these items.

Interrogation of the captive traders revealed Spanish interest in the particulars of the fur trade in French Louisiana, and awareness of the proximity of the French gave new meaning to the limited New Mexico fur trade. In 1754, Governor Tomás Vélez Cachupín left instructions to his successor to maintain Comanche trade dependence on the Spanish colony. Otherwise, "an extremely useful branch of trade would be lost and the French of New Orleans would acquire it in toto."[5]

The story of these early French contacts with New Mexico, which has been told in considerable detail elsewhere,[6] is of only peripheral interest to this study, for these adventurous entrepreneurs displayed little interest in furs or the fur trade. With the cession of Louisiana to Spain in 1763, French attempts to penetrate the Spanish borderlands also came to an end, but many Americans with French surnames would later be New Mexico residents.

During the forty years that Spain held Louisiana, from 1763 to 1803, New Mexico enjoyed security from foreign intrusion and remained isolated, even within the Spanish Empire. Pedro Vial, a Frenchman exploring for Spain, found routes connecting Santa Fe and San Antonio, and Santa Fe and St. Louis, between 1786 and 1793, though no regular commerce developed over them.[7] Even though Spain's boundary with the United States, up to 1803, was at the distant Mississippi River, Spanish officials found reason to fear American expansion into New Mexico. In 1795, for example, the comandante general at Chihuahua, Pedro de Nava, warned New

[4] Affidavits drawn up concerning the French intrusion of 1752, in Thomas, *Plains Indians and New Mexico*, 95, 97, 99, 100, 101.

[5] Instruction of Tomás Vélez Cachupín to his successor, August 12, 1754, in Thomas, *Plains Indians and New Mexico*, 135.

[6] As in the previously cited articles by Bolton and Folmer and in Folmer's *Franco-Spanish Rivalry in North America, 1524–1763*, 291–310. See also Charles Wilson Hackett, "Policy of the Spanish Crown Regarding French Encroachments from Louisiana, 1721–1762," in *New Spain and the Anglo American West*, I, 107–45.

[7] Documents relating to Vial's remarkable journeys are in Noel M. Loomis and Abraham P. Nasatir, *Pedro Vial and the Roads to Santa Fe*.

Mexico Governor Fernando Chacón that "although American colonists live a great distance from that frontier [New Mexico] it is not impossible that they plan to go there."[8] The farsighted Baron de Carondelet, governor at New Orleans, worried that Americans, anxious to extend their fur trade, would attempt to win control of Plains Indians.[9] If Spaniards entertained these fears before 1803, how much more threatening Americans must have seemed after Louisiana exchanged hands and the boundary of the United States leapt westward toward the Rockies and the Arkansas River.

Indeed, after 1803 Spanish expressions of concern began to sound prophetic. In 1804 Charles Dehault Delassus, former Spanish lieutenant-governor of Louisiana, was still at St. Louis after it had become American. There he learned that "the [American] officials who are commanding here are continually informing themselves from the Indians of the Missouri and the white hunters and traders, whether they know the shortest routes to New Mexico or to Santa Fé." The Americans, he reported, intended to extend "their boundary lines to the Río Bravo," and he feared that "if the greatest precautions are not taken to stop this contraband, within a short time, one will see descending the Missouri, instead of furs, silver from the Mexican mines."[10] Delassus reflected the belief, which persisted for at least another decade, that the Missouri River provided easy access to New Mexico. The silver about which he worried, rather than furs, doubtless also interested those Americans who tried to reach Santa Fe during these years. It is interesting, however, that so many of these adventurers were involved in the fur trade. Delassus' report was not mere conjecture. He specifically warned that Baptiste La Lande, Lorenzo Durocher, and Jacques d'Eglise were trying to reach New Mexico. All succeeded.

The first of these foreigners to reach Santa Fe from American

[8] July 30, 1795, SANM, Doc. 1337. Quoted in Ramón Ruiz, "For God and Country, A Brief History of Spanish Defensive Efforts Along the Northeastern Frontier of New Mexico to 1820" (M.A. thesis, Claremont Graduate School, 1948), 95.

[9] Spanish fears of American expansion, and Carondelet's attitude, in particular, are well-described in Loomis and Nasatir, *Pedro Vial*, especially 138–41, 155, 157.

[10] Delassus to Marqués de Casa Calvo, St. Louis, August 10, 1804, quoted in Nasatir, *Before Lewis and Clark*, II, 742–45.

Louisiana was Baptiste La Lande, who, equipped with about two thousand dollars worth of merchandise, started across the plains in 1804 from Illinois. Once in Santa Fe he never returned to the Missouri and has been villified by historians as a scoundrel who betrayed his employer's confidence (apparently the prominent Kaskaskia fur trader, William Morrison). It seems clear, however, that Spanish authorities did not allow La Lande to leave New Mexico.[11]

Baptiste La Lande and one Jeanot Meteyer were to have been guided to New Mexico, according to Delassus' reports, by "Josef Gervaes," a man who "it is said knows the road very well." Gervaes had reputedly led the Pawnees, who sought to make peace, to Santa Fe in 1803 and again in the spring of 1804. After returning from this latter trip, he was to take La Lande and Meteyer to New Mexico.[12] It seems likely that he did just that. It could scarcely be a coincidence that in May, 1805, "Josef Charvet," a Frenchman, requested permission to settle in New Mexico and serve as an interpreter. He was soon assigned to the Pawnee villages,[13] becoming a trusted and important Spanish interpreter-scout.

Arriving soon after La Lande (if not with him) was a fellow French-American, Laurent Durocher. One of the founders of the well-known fur trading firm, the Missouri Company, Durocher was born in Canada in 1749, and was reported to be "somewhat old" when he set out for New Mexico from St. Louis in 1804 at age fifty-five.[14] Perhaps alarmed by the sudden arrival of La Lande

[11] Richard E. Oglesby, "Baptiste LaLande," in Hafen, *Mountain Men*, VI, 219–22. Evidence that La Lande was forcibly detained in New Mexico is in Donald A. Nuttall, "The American Threat to New Mexico, 1804–1821" (M.A. thesis, San Diego State, 1959), 65–67, and in Lansing B. Bloom, "The Death of Jacques D'Eglise," *New Mexico Historical Review*, Vol. II, No. 4 (October, 1927), 371.

[12] Delassus to Casa Calvo, St. Louis, August 10, 1804, quoted in Nasatir, *Before Lewis and Clark*, II, 743–44.

[13] Governor Joaquín del Real Alencaster, Santa Fe, to Nemesio Salcedo at Chihuahua, May 28, 1805, and September 1, 1805, SANM, Docs. 1838 and 1881 (7). In concluding that "Gervaes" and "Charvet" are the same man, I find myself in agreement with Nuttall, whose fine thesis, "The American Threat to New Mexico," became available to me after my initial writing of this chapter. See, 54, n. 16. Loomis and Nasatir, *Pedro Vial*, 172, n. 4, seem to disagree with us.

[14] Durocher was in Santa Fe sometime before May of 1805. Bloom, "The Death

and Durocher, Nemesio Salcedo, comandante general of the Interior Provinces of New Spain, ordered both Frenchmen to report to him at Chihuahua, which they did.[15] Back in New Mexico by October, 1805, the two traders tried to leave the country by accompanying Pedro Vial and José Chalvet on a planned expedition to visit the Pawnees and other tribes in the area of the Arkansas, Kansas, Platte, and Missouri rivers. Indians attacked them on the Arkansas, however, and drove them back to Santa Fe. In the summer of 1806, Durocher made another trip to Chihuahua and then drops from the historical record.[16] "Juan Bautista LaLanda," as he came to be known in New Mexico, acquired land in Taos, married at least three times and sired five known children before his death in February, 1821. There is no record of his involvement in the fur trade after 1805.[17]

Because Zebulon Pike met him in Santa Fe in 1807, James Purcell is also well known as one of the first Americans to reach New Mexico. In 1804, after two years of trapping out of St. Louis, Purcell was sent on a trading expedition to the Padoucas and Kiowas. As he told it, he went to Santa Fe in 1805 to obtain permission for these Indians to trade there.[18] When he arrived in June, 1805, two French trappers, Dionisio Lacroix and Andrés Terien, and two "Cuampes [Arapaho?]" chieftains were with him. Unlike Purcell, who was a carpenter, the two Frenchmen had no other trade except that of trapper. They explained that a Mr. Lauselle (Régis Loisel), who operated a trading post called the Blue Hill (*de la cuesta Azul*), had sent them to trade for beaver skins. After Kiowas captured them, they were freed under the protection of "Cuampes," and finally made it to Santa Fe with these Indians and

of Jacques D'Eglise," *NMHR*, Vol. II, No. 4 (October, 1927), 370–71, 374–75; Nasatir, *Before Lewis and Clark*, I, 225–26; II, 744.

[15] Bloom, "The Death of Jacques D'Eglise," *NMHR*, Vol. II, No. 4 (October, 1927), 375.

[16] Salcedo to Alencaster, January 16, 1806, SANM, Doc. 1953(2); Nuttall, "American Threat to New Mexico" (M.A. thesis, San Diego State, 1959), 65–66; Ysidro Rey, El Paso, to Alencaster, August 31, 1806, SANM, Doc. 2010.

[17] Year of 1847, First Book (A), Record of Land Established by Law, Federal Bureau of Land Management, Santa Fe, 19–21.

[18] Pike, *Journals of Zebulon Montgomery Pike*, II, 59–62. Pike referred to him as "Pursley."

the interpreter Pedro Vial.[19] James Purcell may have been with the Frenchmen from the beginning of their adventure. Probably because he had an occupation, Spanish officials allowed Purcell to remain in Santa Fe, but did not permit him to leave the country. He worked as a carpenter until 1821, when Mexico became independent of Spain, then he resumed his trading activities.[20] Lacroix and Terien were sent to Chihuahua in 1806, and probably never returned to New Mexico.[21]

Lacroix and Terien were not the only Frenchmen trapping and trading near the New Mexico settlements at that time. In July, 1806, Spanish carbineer Juan Lucero arrived at some Kiowa *rancherías*, perhaps on the Arkansas, where he found six Frenchmen and one American. One of the Frenchmen, whose name appears in Spanish documents as Juan Bautista La Casa, returned to Santa Fe with Lucero and was then sent on to Chihuahua.[22] Later that year, in October, when Lieutenant Facundo Melgares returned to Santa Fe after a futile search for Zebulon Pike, he brought with him two more Frenchmen, Andrés Sulier and Henrique Visonet, whom he had discovered among the Pawnees. Young men who knew no trade, they too were sent to Chihuahua.[23] In that same autumn an itinerant Missouri River fur trader, Jacques d'Eglise, succeeded in reaching New Mexico only to be murdered by two Spaniards near Santa Fe.[24]

[19] Salcedo to Alencaster, July 19, 1805, SANM, Doc. 1859; Nuttall, "American Threat to New Mexico" (M.A. thesis, San Diego State, 1959), 59–62, contains the best account of this episode and identifies Lacroix and Terien as the Frenchmen who were with Purcell.

[20] Alencaster to Salcedo, October 2, 1805, and Ysidro Rey to Alencaster, El Paso, August 31, 1806, SANM, Docs. 1900 and 2010; (Franklin) *Missouri Intelligencer*, April 3, 1824.

[21] Real Alencaster to Comandante Joseph Manrrique at San Elecario, September 1, 1806, SANM, Doc. 2010.

[22] Real Alencaster to Salcedo, August 30, 1806, SANM, Doc. 2006(1). Lucero was at the Kiowa ranchería on July 2 and had returned to Santa Fe by July 24; Real Alencaster, Santa Fe, to Comandante Joseph Manrrique, at San Elecario, September 1, 1806, SANM, Doc. 2010.

[23] Alencaster to Salcedo, October 8, 1806, and Alencaster to Manrrique at San Elecario, October 12, 1806, SANM, Docs. 2022 and 2023.

[24] Bloom, "Death of Jacques D'Eglise," *NMHR*, Vol. II, No. 4 (October, 1927), 369–79.

From La Lande to d'Eglise, foreign intruders had not profited commercially by venturing too close to the New Mexico settlements. It might be supposed that their failures would discourage similar ventures, but instead their visits only seemed to reflect Missouri Valley fur traders' increasing awareness of Santa Fe as a potential supply depot and market. Perhaps the person most aware of this potential was the aggressive, controversial Missouri River fur trader, Spanish-born Manuel Lisa.

In 1806 Manuel Lisa and Jacques Clamorgan outfitted a trading party to go to Santa Fe. Lisa, his attention temporarily diverted by the Upper Missouri, had to withdraw from active participation in the venture, but Clamorgan, three other Frenchmen, and a slave succeeded in reaching Santa Fe by way of the Pawnee villages on the Platte in December, 1807. After being sent to Chihuahua, Clamorgan was mysteriously allowed to sell his merchandise and return to St. Louis, via Texas, with a profit that he was unwilling to share with Lisa.[25]

In the meantime, from his new vantage point on the Upper Missouri, Manuel Lisa remained interested in Santa Fe. Like Delassus and other contemporaries, he believed that Santa Fe was a few days' journey from the area of the Upper Missouri and the Yellowstone. Thus, historian William Goetzmann has speculated that in the winter of 1807–1808, when John Colter made his famous trek to the Grand Tetons and Jackson's Hole in the employ of Lisa, Colter was probably "in search of the Spanish as well as Indians with beaver skins to trade, and this explains the great range of his trek south and west of the Teton Mountains."[26]

In the winter of 1808–1809, three of Lisa's men headed south from the Three Forks of the Missouri to trap the "River of the Spaniards," probably the Green River. If they hoped to meet New

[25] Joseph J. Hill, "An Unknown Expedition to Santa Fe in 1807," *Mississippi Valley Historical Review*, Vol. IV (March, 1920), 560–62; A. P. Nasatir, "Jacques Clamorgan: Colonial Promoter of the Northern Border of New Spain," *New Mexico Historical Review*, Vol. XVII, No. 1 (January, 1942), 111–12; Real Alencaster to Salcedo, Santa Fe, December 12, 1807, SANM, Doc. 2090; J. Clamorgan to the editor (St. Louis) *Missouri Gazette*, July 28, 1809.

[26] William H. Goetzmann, *Exploration and Empire: The Explorer and the Scientist in the Winning of the American West*, 20, 25.

Mexicans and discuss the possibility of trade, they, like Colter, met no success.[27] Jean Baptiste Champlain may have been a member of this 1808–1809 expedition, for as early as the spring of 1810 he displayed a remarkable knowledge of far northern Mexico. On April 21, 1810, Reuben Lewis wrote to his better-known brother, Meriwether:

> Mr. Shamplain [Champlain] tells me that the martin abound in the mountains dividing the waters of the Spanish River as it is called, on what is supposed to be the Rio del nort [Río Grande] from the waters of som of the Southern branches of the Collumbia, on a River falling into the Gulf of California. . . . Beaver abounds in the same country but it is so high that it is allmost perpetual snow.[28]

Meanwhile, a group of Spaniards who had been hunting buffalo in the fall of 1809 learned from Indians of foreign trappers on the upper Arkansas and brought this news back to Santa Fe. Members of a search party failed to locate the intruders, but Indians told them that five trappers had been frightened away at the news of the Spanish approach. Again, in autumn of 1810, rumor of Americans in the Arkansas Valley resulted in a search by Spanish troops. Finding no foreigners along the Arkansas, the soldiers continued to the Platte River where they heard that Americans frequently visited the Indians there.[29] No identification of these trappers and traders can be positively made, but it seems likely that they were some of Manuel Lisa's men. Already in 1810, a rumor was circulat-

---

[27] Richard E. Oglesby, *Manuel Lisa and the Opening of the Missouri Fur Trade*, 66–67. Oglesby identifies the "River of the Spaniards" as the Green River. The Spanish River, however, can mean either the Arkansas or the Green (See Phillips, *Fur Trade*, II, 267). In this case, because of the distance involved and Lisa's conception of Santa Fe as being much nearer, I agree with Oglesby, but subsequent events indicate that the Arkansas, even at this early date, is a possibility.

[28] Quoted by Oglesby, *Lisa*, 95.

[29] The documents upon which this discussion is based (SANM, Docs. 2308 and 2363) are analyzed in Eleanor L. Richie, "Background of the International Boundary Line of 1819 Along the Arkansas River in Colorado," *Colorado Magazine*, Vol. X, No. 4 (July, 1933) 173–74, and in Nuttall, "American Threat to New Mexico" (M.A. thesis, San Diego State, 1959), 115–16, 131–33.

ing in Louisiana that Lisa's hunters had come within two days' journey of Santa Fe.[30]

In 1811, Lisa, now a partner in the St. Louis Missouri Fur Company, sent Jean Baptiste Champlain on a trading expedition to the Arapahos, probably on the South Platte, but possibly on the Arkansas. Returning to Fort Mandan in the summer of 1811, Champlain reported to Lisa that the "Spaniards of Mexico" sent a trading party to the Arapahos each year. Lisa, therefore, equipped Champlain and Jean Batiste Lafargue to lead another expedition in the hope that they might open trade with Santa Fe.[31]

According to one of Champlain's men, Ezekiel Williams, they journeyed south and spent the fall and winter trapping on the Arkansas River. Harassed by Indians, they returned to the Platte by June, 1812, and there split up. Champlain, Williams, and eight others returned to the area of the Arkansas, perhaps still hoping to rendezvous with the Spaniards. Hearing from Indians that Lisa's fort "was broke up," four of their number headed for Santa Fe. In the fall of 1812, the remaining six launched another trapping expedition into the area of the upper Arkansas. Again attacked by Indians, only Champlain, Williams, and "Porteau" survived to spend the winter among the Arapahos on the Arkansas. The following March, 1813, Williams placed a canoe in the Arkansas and set out alone for civilization,[32] his companions apparently having been murdered.

Meanwhile, in September of 1812, having received no word from Champlain, Lisa dispatched Charles Sanguinet, "a man already familiar with the Arapahoes," to track him down.[33] Sanguinet

30 Walter B. Douglas, *Manuel Lisa* (ed. and annot. by Abraham P. Nasatir), 159–60.

31 Oglesby, *Lisa*, 66–67, 115; Douglas, *Lisa*, 155–60.

32 Williams to Joseph Charless, Boonslick, August 7, 1816, (St. Louis) *Missouri Gazette*, September 14, 1816, printed in (Walter B. Douglas) "Ezekiel Williams' Adventures in Colorado," *Missouri Historical Society Collections*, Vol. IV, No. 2 (1913), 202–208. Williams' dates in this letter are one year off. I have corrected them, retaining the months that he uses.

33 John C. Luttig, *Journal of a Fur-Trading Expedition on the Upper Missouri, 1812–1813* (ed. by Stella M. Drumm with preface and notes by Abraham P. Nasatir), 76.

carried a letter "To the Spaniards of New Mexico" in which Lisa, himself a Spaniard by birth, invited them to trade. Although Sanguinet somehow managed to deliver Lisa's letter, he was unable to locate Champlain and the trappers. Apparently on the Arkansas, the Arapahos informed him that Champlain and two others had been killed by Blackfeet and that "Lafargue and 5 others had run off" to New Mexico.[34]

Lafargue seems to have made it through to Santa Fe with three companions, later identified as "Vesina, Grenie, and Roi."[35] In March, 1812, José Antonio Casados of Taos, and two other Spaniards, met four Frenchmen on the "Llano" or "Llara" River and directed them to New Mexico. At Santa Fe the foreigners were interrogated then sent on to Chihuahua and finally to Arizpe, where they remained imprisoned at least until 1815.[36] These four must have been Lafargue and company. Lafargue is said to have been released and returned to St. Louis in 1817 with the Chouteau–de Mun party,[37] but nothing more is known of his companions.

The adventures of Ezekiel Williams, while trapping for Lisa and Champlain, achieved notoriety in 1847 with the publication of David H. Coyner's fanciful *Lost Trappers*. Although characterized by one authority as "the completest fabrication that was ever published under the guise of history,"[38] Coyner's story contains some elements of truth. The preposterous adventures of "James Workman" and "Samuel Spencer," for example, were probably based on the imprisonment of Lafargue and his companions. Workman and Spencer, whose names do not appear among Lisa's

[34] Luttig, *Journal*, 102–103. Lisa's letter appears on 142–43. The letter first appeared in Bolton, "New Light on Manuel Lisa and the Spanish Fur Trade," *SHQ*, Vol. XVII, No. 1 (July, 1913), 61–66. Although the Arapahos reported that Blackfeet killed Champlain, Snake Indians had heard that the deed was done by the Arapahos. See entry of October 18, 1812, in Robert Stuart's "Journal' in *On the Oregon Trail: Robert Stuart's Journal of Discovery*, (ed. by Kenneth A. Spaulding), 119.

[35] Letter of Joseph Philibert in the (St. Louis) *Missouri Gazette*, July 29, 1815.

[36] José Antonio Casados to Ignacio Elías Gonzales, Santa Fe, April 11, 1813, SANM, Doc. 2484; Bolton, "New Light on Manuel Lisa," *SHQ*, Vol. XVII, No. 1 (July, 1913), 61, n. 2.

[37] Luttig, *Journal*, 103, n. 151.

[38] Hiram Martin Chittenden, *The American Fur Trade of the Far West*, II, 651.

engagés, were reported by the inventive Coyner to have made their way across the Rockies to the Colorado River, where they met a Spanish caravan on its way to California! In Coyner's version, they later returned to Santa Fe and there remained, at least until 1821.[39]

The murder of Jean Baptiste Champlain also struck a death blow to Manual Lisa's attempts to tap the fur wealth and markets of northern Mexico. Had Lisa succeeded in forming a trade connection with Santa Fe, he might have circumvented the St. Louis merchants and established a new headquarters for his trappers near the southern Rockies. But, even had Lisa's men succeeded in reaching Santa Fe, it appears that his plan would have failed anyway, for Spanish officials, never impressed by Lisa's Spanish birth, strongly distrusted him.[40] Following the death of Champlain, Lisa confined his activities to the Missouri.

Still, other trappers who had no connection with Lisa continued to penetrate the hazy border of New Mexico. In November, 1814, Josef Charvet ("José Sarvet"), still in the employ of Spain as an interpreter-scout, brought four Frenchmen into Santa Fe. According to their testimony, they had been trapping for beaver for six years on the Platte and other rivers. Indians from the "nacion Cuampe" had attacked them and killed three of their companions, but these four had escaped by hiding in the woods along the river bottom. The Frenchmen were unable to escape from New Mexico officials, however, who promptly sent them on to Chihuahua.[41]

At the same time that trappers were drifting into Santa Fe from the Upper Missouri and the Platte, others tried to reach it more directly from St. Louis. Three Americans, Joseph McLanahan, Reuben Smith, and James Patterson, made the first attempt. Accompanied by a Spanish guide, Emanuel Blanco, and two Negro

---

[39] Coyner, *Lost Trappers*, 166–72. The list of Lisa's engagés appears in Luttig's *Journal*, 157–58. For a discussion of the validity of Coyner's account, see Frederick E. Voelker, "Ezekiel Williams of Boon's Lick," *Bulletin of the Missouri Historical Society*, Vol. VIII, No. 1 (October, 1951), 17–51.

[40] Oglesby, *Lisa*, 67; Douglas, *Lisa*, 159–60 (notes by Nasatir).

[41] Governor Alberto Maynez [?] to Comandante-General Bernardo Bonavía, Durango, November 20, 1814, SANM, Doc. 2565; Nuttall, "American Threat to New Mexico" (M.A. thesis, San Diego State, 1959), 145, settles the question of the dating of this document.

slaves, they were discovered hunting and trading in Comanche country near the Red River in 1810. Taken to Santa Fe, the Americans professed interest in becoming Spanish citizens, but the merchandise they carried made Governor José Manrrique rightly suspect that they had come to trade, and they, too, found themselves in Chihuahua, imprisoned until 1812.[42]

As these merchants were being released in 1812, another trading party was forming in St. Louis, apparently under the illusion that Father Miguel Hidalgo's famous revolution near Mexico City had removed both Spanish authority and trade restrictions from New Mexico. Nine men, Robert McKnight, James Baird, and Samuel Chambers among them, soon found themselves only slightly more successful than Hidalgo (who had been executed). Arriving in Santa Fe in June, 1812, at about the same time as Lisa's men under Lafargue reached there, they too were taken captive and languished in confinement of various sorts until 1820.[43]

Both of these St. Louis–based expeditions were trading parties, with little interest in furs. They demonstrate, however, the interest that Americans had in reaching Santa Fe. While yet in St. Louis, McKnight wrote: "We discover at this Early Period a jealousy arising in this place respecting the trade to that Country [New Mexico]. We beg you be silent on the subject—like Charity."[44] But for Spanish opposition, the Santa Fe Trail might have been born a decade earlier.

Although he had been fortunate in getting back to Missouri alive, the "Lost Trapper," Ezekiel Williams, was not yet through with the mountains. In May, 1814, he left the Boonslick country with two partners, Morris May and Braxton Cooper, to recover

---

[42] James, *Three Years Among the Mexicans and the Indians*, 286–92; Manrrique to Salcedo, Santa Fe, July 20, 1810, SANM, Doc. 2342. Spanish reaction to these merchants is more thoroughly discussed in Nuttall, "American Threat to New Mexico" (M.A. thesis, San Diego State, 1959), 117–30.

[43] Regarding this group, a number of sources exist. See particularly, Rex W. Strickland, "James Baird," in Hafen, *Mountain Men*, III, 27–37, and Frank B. Golley, "James Baird, Early Santa Fe Trader," *Missouri Historical Society Bulletin*, Vol. XV, No. 3 (April, 1959), 171–93; (St. Louis) *Missouri Gazette*, July 29, 1815.

[44] Letter, McKnight and Brady to M. McDonogh, St. Louis, May 21, 1812, Santa Fe Envelope, Missouri Historical Society, St. Louis.

furs he had cached on the Arkansas. Also along were eighteen Frenchmen of a company under Joseph Philibert. Williams succeeded in retrieving part of his furs and returned to Missouri,[45] while the Frenchmen continued up the Arkansas. In September Philibert "fixed his hunting camp about four leagues north of the place where Captain Pike was taken by the Spaniards [also on the Río Grande?]." Soon two of his men who were out "seeking beaver dams" came across a group of Spanish hunters who took them to Santa Fe as prisoners. Then, according to Philibert, the governor sent two hundred and fifty men, who captured the remainder of the party, taking merchandise and beaver as well. By his own account, Philibert and his men were released from confinement by orders from Durango and remained the rest of the winter in Taos.[46]

Philibert claimed that "the whole affair was a ruinous business," but Spanish officials had treated him unusually well, for that same autumn they had sent four other foreign trappers on to Chihuahua. In view of this extraordinary leniency, and since no other source substantiates Philibert's story (which appeared in a St. Louis newspaper in July, 1815), one suspects that he was just spinning a good yarn. If so, it turned out to be prophetic.

Following his "release" in the spring of 1815, Philibert left most of his men on the Arkansas and returned to the Missouri settlements for trade goods, and horses to carry in his furs. In September, 1815, when Philibert started west again, he joined with Auguste P. Chouteau and Jules de Mun, who had also outfitted a trading party planning to ascend the Arkansas. Along the way, Philibert sold them "his furs, goods, horses, etc., and the time of his men,"[47] and then continued to travel with them. Far up the Arkansas, within sight of the Front Range of the Rockies, they came across four

[45] Voelker, "Ezekiel Williams of Boon's Lick," *BMHS*, Vol. VIII, No. 1 (October, 1951), 26–27; Douglas, "Ezekiel Williams' Adventures in Colorado," *MHSC*, Vol. IV, No. 2 (1913), 205.

[46] (St. Louis) *Missouri Gazette*, July 29, 1815.

[47] Jules de Mun to Governor William Clark, St. Louis, November 25, 1817, in Marshall, "The Journals of Jules de Mun," *MHSC*, Vol. V, No. 3 (1928), 7. Some members of the Chouteau–de Mun party identified in the statement of Jean Batiste Brizar *et al.*, are conveniently listed in Robert Glass Cleland, *This Reckless Breed of Men: The Trappers and Fur Traders of the Southwest*, 124–25.

more American trappers, including Caleb Greenwood, a former Lisa man.[48] These men had left St. Louis on September 7, some three days ahead of de Mun. Their presence on the Arkansas, along with the combined Philibert–Chouteau–de Mun group, indicates a surprising amount of American activity on the edge of New Spain's far northern frontier.[49]

Philibert's men were supposed to be waiting at a rendezvous site at Huerfano Creek, near the Arkansas, but when the Chouteau–de Mun group reached there on December 8, 1815, they discovered that the men had run short on supplies and "had gone over to the Spaniards." Thus, in early January, de Mun took eight men and went in search of the trappers, whom he found wintering safely at Taos. De Mun continued to Santa Fe, arriving in mid-January. There he asked elderly, courteous, Interim-Governor Alberto Maynez for a license to trap on various tributaries of the Río Grande, for, as de Mun later wrote, he had noticed on his way to Santa Fe that these streams "abounded with beaver." Maynez forwarded de Mun's request, along with news of the arrival of nine "Frenchmen" at Taos, to the comandante general at Chihuahua. Meanwhile, de Mun was allowed to return to Taos, where he gathered together his engagés, added two Spaniards to his group, and returned to St. Louis by way of the Arkansas in order to re-equip.[50]

De Mun returned to New Mexico on two more occasions from his camp in the Arkansas Valley. Each time Spanish officials denied him permission to trap and escorted him out of their territory. Following de Mun's initial visit, Governor Maynez had received orders from the comandante general that foreigners "ought to be viewed with distrust and suspicion, making them return to their country by the way they came." This order had been circulated

[48] Luttig, *Journal*, 157.

[49] Marshall, "The Journals of Jules de Mun," *MHSC*, Vol. V, No. 3 (1928), 41–42; Charles Kelly and Dale Morgan, *Old Greenwood: The Story of Caleb Greenwood; Trapper, Pathfinder, and Early Pioneer*, 49–60.

[50] De Mun to Clark, November 25, 1817, in Marshall, "The Journals of Jules de Mun," *MHSC*, Vol. V, No. 3 (1928), 7–8; Alberto Maynez, Index of Correspondence to the Comandante General at Chihuahua, January 18, 1816, SANM, Doc. 2639.

among the alcaldes of San Miguel del Vado, Abiquiu, and Taos, in May, 1816, and explains much of the new hostility shown de Mun and his men.[51] In addition, a new governor, Pedro María Allande, proved to be far less gracious than Maynez had been. In late summer or early fall of 1816, when de Mun tried to get permission to trap, he was not allowed to proceed farther south than Río Colorado, a new settlement to the north of Taos. The next spring, in March, 1817, when de Mun again tried to talk to the governor, he learned that the Spaniards believed the Americans to be building a fort at the junction of Río de las Animas and the Arkansas, near the site where Bent's Fort would later be built. When Spanish troops proved the report to be false, they released de Mun. In May, however, soldiers returned to his camp on the Arkansas, arrested all twenty-six men present, and took them to Santa Fe. There, de Mun later reported, after forty-four days in prison, the Americans were called to give testimony before Governor Allande, who lost his temper, talked of shooting the men, and insisted that the Mississippi Valley was the correct boundary of New Spain. Indeed, until the Adams-Onís Treaty of 1819 settled the western boundary of Louisiana, Allande's claim was no more preposterous than United States claims that Louisiana extended to the Río Grande and included all of Texas.

Allande released the trappers, but kept their furs and equipment. De Mun reported the loss as $30,380.74½, representing "the fruits of two years' labor and perils." Neither de Mun nor Chouteau lived to see the day, in 1850, when their claims against the United States government for this loss were finally paid.[52]

The harsh treatment accorded Chouteau and de Mun must have served warning to others who might have trapped or traded too near New Mexico settlements. With the exception of David Meriwether, who was trading among Pawnees when he was lured to

[51] Bernardo Bonavía to Governor *interino* Maynez, Durango, February 13, 1816, SANM, Doc. 2646. Bonavía does not mention trapping.

[52] De Mun to Clark, November 25, 1817, in Marshall, "The Journals of Jules de Mun," *MHSC*, Vol. V, No. 3 (1928), 8–16, and George S. Ulibarri, "The Chouteau-Demun Expedition to New Mexico, 1815–17," *New Mexico Historical Review*, Vol. XXXVI, No. 4 (October, 1961), 263–73.

Santa Fe in 1820 by stories of gold and silver,[53] no other American broke the tranquility of Spain's commercial monopoly over New Mexico before 1821.

Chouteau and de Mun's expedition represents the high point of American attempts to trap Mexican territory and is of particular significance since it anticipated the shape of the southwestern fur trade of the next decades. By establishing base camps in the Arkansas Valley near the present-day Purgatoire River, Chouteau and de Mun foreshadowed Bent's famous fort, as well as others which would be built in that same area in the 1830's. Supplying themselves by land, directly from St. Louis, they not only broke the trader's tradition of staying near a navigable water course, but anticipated the use to which trappers would put the Santa Fe Trail. Furthermore, from their camp at the edge of the southern Rockies, Chouteau and de Mun planned to penetrate the mountains to trade with Crow Indians, whom they believed were located at the headwaters of the Columbia River. Had Spanish soldiers not interrupted them, they might have crossed to the Colorado River basin several years before William Ashley started a stampede in that direction in 1824.[54]

But there is no need to dwell on that which might have been. Chouteau and de Mun, even in failure, managed to provide some of their *engagés* with a close and apparently unforgettable view of the beaver-rich streams of northern New Mexico and the southern Rockies. Joseph Bijeau, or Bissonette, for example, an experienced trapper who had been with Manuel Lisa on the Upper Missouri in 1812,[55] was among Chouteau and de Mun's group. In 1820, when Bissonette returned to the Rockies as a guide and interpreter for Major Stephen H. Long's government exploring party, he revealed unusual geographical knowledge. According to Long's chronicler, Edwin James, Bissonette was familiar with the

[53] David Meriwether, *My Life in the Mountains and on the Plains: The Newly Discovered Autobiography of David Meriwether* (ed. by Robert A. Griffen), 78-79, 81-82, 90.
[54] The best analysis of Chouteau's and de Mun's activities is in *The West of William H. Ashley, 1822-1838* (ed. by Dale L. Morgan), xliii-xlvii.
[55] Luttig, *Journal*, 158.

area between the North Fork of the Platte and the Arkansas, and had frequented the Rockies "where beaver are particularly abundant." Bissonette gave James a general but remarkable description of "the region lying west of the first range of the Rocky Mountains, and between the sources of the Yellow Stone on the North and Santa Fé on the South." Bissonette had been in North Park, near the headwaters of the North Platte River, and also provided Major Long with an account of trading with Indians near the site of present-day Denver, in 1816.[56] Clearly, he had acquired much of his familiarity with the Rockies while with Chouteau and de Mun. Bissonette had even seen Santa Fe, chiefly through the bars of the *calabozo*, and returned to settle there in the 1820's.

Étienne Provost and probably François Leclerc also gained their first view of northern New Mexico while with Chouteau and de Mun. Provost and Leclerc would be among the first American trappers to work out of New Mexico after Spain lost the area in 1821, and from Taos they would launch a significant expedition into the Great Basin in 1824.

Foreign intruders learned more of New Mexico than the location of beaver streams, however. They saw there a ragtag militia, poorly equipped regulars, nonexistent fortifications, and low morale. They surmised that it would be easy to win alliances with nearby Indians and reported on the great ease of travel from St. Louis over the plains to Santa Fe. As Jules de Mun pointed out, the journey could be made in thirty-five to forty days and "no difficulty would be encountered in making a way for carriages or artillery, except at the passages of the rivers." De Mun's knowledge of the territory, along with Zebulon Pike's writings, became the basis of a report prepared for the French government in 1818.[57] Other intruders probably expressed similar views to their neighbors and acquaint-

56 James, *James's Account of the S. H. Long Expedition*, XVI, 226–58; LeRoy R. Hafen, "A Brief History of the Fur Trade of the Far West," in Hafen, *Mountain Men*, I, 62–63.

57 De Mun's views, as Loomis and Nasatir (*Pedro Vial*, 257), point out, formed the basis for Louis de Mun's report, published by Alfred B. Thomas as "An Anonymous Description of New Mexico, 1818," *Southwestern Historical Quarterly*, Vol. XXXIII (July, 1929) 50–74.

ances when they returned to the American settlements. Thus, the process of shaping American attitudes of superiority toward Mexico, and New Mexico in particular, began some three decades before the Mexican War. Trappers and traders continued to help this process along.

As long as Spain held New Mexico, however, attempts by American trappers and traders to harvest the furs of the southern Rockies were thwarted. Historian William Goetzmann has observed that, in contrast to the English who tried to trap out beaver in the Oregon area in order to discourage Americans from entering their territory, the Spaniards "chose to leave the beaver in the streams and instead embarked on a plan to sweep the country of American adventurers."[58] Although some trappers might have succeeded in obtaining supplies or wintering in Taos, Abiquiu, or more remote villages, neither the French nor the Americans were able to penetrate effectively the Spanish trade barrier. With the coming of Mexican independence the situation would change. The handful of men like Bissonette and Provost would soon be joined by others who would come to know the New Mexico settlements, the Rockies, and the Southwest even more intimately. A considerable contribution would be made by the trappers from Taos.

[58] Goetzmann, *Exploration and Empire*, 55. Spanish military reaction to American traders is best, but not adequately, described in Ruiz, "God and Country," (M.A. thesis, Claremont Graduate School, 1948), Chapter VII.

IV FURS ON THE TRAIL,

Mexico had effectively achieved its independence from Spain by the spring of 1821, following General Agustín de Iturbide's publication of the famous Plan of Iguala on February 24. Although news of the Plan had spread rapidly throughout Mexico, more remote provinces were slow to learn of it. Not until September, 1821, did word reach Santa Fe.[1] Then, quietly, and with no significant opposition, New Mexico officials endorsed independence and abruptly reversed Spanish policy by allowing foreign merchants to enter New Mexico villages. This action toward Americans is understandable, for Chihuahua merchants had long imposed monopoly prices on merchandise shipped to New Mexico, leaving the province in constant debt and short of manufactured goods.[2] Through occasional contact with Americans, New Mexicans were doubtless aware of advantages which trade with the United States could bring. Thus, among its first acts following independence, the New Mexico deputation voted to extend to American citizens a status equal to Mexican citizens of the Province, so long as they paid municipal taxes and "other charges."[3]

[1] Bloom, "New Mexico Under Mexican Administration," *Old Santa Fe*, Vol. I, No. 1 (July, 1913), 141.
[2] Moorhead, *New Mexico's Royal Road*, 51–54.
[3] Bloom, "New Mexico Under Mexican Administration," *Old Santa Fe*, Vol. I, No. 1 (July, 1913), 152.

1821–1823

Since the publication of Zebulon Pike's *Journals* in 1810, if not before, American frontiersmen knew the great trading potential of the strangled New Mexico markets. Despite the costly failure of American attempts to trade and trap in New Mexico before 1821, Americans still remained eager to tap Spanish markets. Moreover, the depression of 1819 had left the Missouri frontier with a serious shortage of specie which forced many merchants out into Indian country where they could trade for furs those goods that would no longer bring much cash in the settlements. Farmers too, had to supplement their income by hunting, trapping, and trading.[4] So it was, in the fall of 1821, that three groups of Americans were trading and hunting on the periphery of New Mexico. Each would be pleasantly surprised at being welcomed to long-forbidden New Mexico settlements.

The first of these three groups to learn of Mexican independence was led by William Becknell, remembered as the father of the Santa Fe trade. Near the Arkansas, New Mexican troops had told Becknell of Mexico's change of sovereignty, and persuaded him to go to Santa Fe, which he reached on November 16, 1821.[5]

[4] Morgan, *Ashley*, li, lii; Moorhead, *New Mexico's Royal Road*, 59.
[5] William Becknell, "Journal of Two Expeditions From Boone's Lick to Santa Fe," is most conveniently available in Archer B. Hulbert (ed.), *Southwest on the Turquoise Trail*, 63.

Becknell had recruited some seventeen men by promising the opportunity of "trading for Horses and Mules, and catching Wild Animals of every description." When these men met at Ezekiel Williams' Missouri farm to plan the hunt,[6] it seems likely that they discussed beaver and arranged to take traps along. Once in New Mexico, Becknell quickly sold his trade goods and started back to Missouri for more. Most of his men, however, decided to stay behind at the village of San Miguel del Vado, where the Santa Fe Trail would soon cross the Pecos River.[7] Perhaps they spent the winter trapping. Certainly plentiful beaver in nearby streams did not escape their attention, for a few years later Becknell himself would lead a trapping party out of Taos.

On December 1, 1821, two weeks after Becknell's arrival in New Mexico, John McKnight and Thomas James, a former trapper for the St. Louis Fur Company,[8] brought a party of trappers and traders to Santa Fe. Their journey had been nearly fatal. As James later wrote, Indians acting under instructions from the governor at Santa Fe would not let the Americans pass. Just as hostilities seemed imminent, however, a group of New Mexicans arrived with the welcome news that they "were now independent and free; and brothers to the Americans"; crisis was thus averted. From Santa Fe, John McKnight went to Durango in search of his brother, Robert, who had been held captive since his failure to crash the New Mexico market in 1812. Reunited, the brothers were back at Santa Fe by April, 1822. Meanwhile, after being denied permission to go to Sonora to sell his goods, Thomas James had set up shop in Santa Fe while his men divided into small bands and "engaged in trapping." Some of his trappers, who "had gone far into the interior of Mexico," apparently did not return to the United States with James. In June of 1822, he gathered together

[6] See notices in the (Franklin) *Missouri Intelligencer* of June 25, 1821 and August 14, 1821, both signed by William Becknell.

[7] Becknell, "Journal of Two Expeditions," in Hulbert, *Southwest on the Turquoise Trail*, 65.

[8] Contract between the St. Louis Fur Company and Thomas James, March 29, 1809, in James, *Three Years Among the Mexicans*, 271. A biography of James is Frederick E. Voelker, "Thomas James," in Hafen, *Mountain Men*, IV, 153–67.

his remaining men and left Taos, crossing over the Sangre de Cristos onto the plains.[9]

In early 1822, a third group of Americans found its way into New Mexico. This was led by Hugh Glenn, an Indian trader who was heading west in an attempt to regain a modest fortune lost in the panic of 1819. From his trading post among the Osage Indians, Glenn and nineteen others had trapped and traded their way up the Arkansas River in the fall of 1821.[10] They saw little sign of beaver, however, until they were well into present-day Colorado. By late December they had reached the area of Huerfano Creek, east of what is now Pueblo. There, as Jacob Fowler, the chronicler of the expedition, recorded, they met some "Spanierds." Glenn and four others accompanied these New Mexicans to Santa Fe, while Fowler stayed behind with the rest of the party to spend the month trapping. The season was not at its best, and Fowler soon complained that "the Weather is So Cold I beleve the bever will not Come out." To everyone's relief, by the end of the month word arrived from Glenn that "the Governor and People Head Recd Him on the Most Frendly terms and thus our feer from that quarter Ware all Removed." Glenn had obtained permission to "trap and traid" in New Mexico, and soon he and Fowler reunited near "touse."[11]

Fowler and his companions enjoyed the comforts of Taos only briefly, for Glenn soon divided his men into three trapping units, while he remained in the settlements to sell merchandise. As Fowler noted in his journal, furs were not to be their only objective in trapping again: "We Intend to go as Soon as poseble to Cetch Bever to live on as there is no other game In this part of the Cuntry

[9] James, *Three Years Among the Mexicans*, 121–25, 151–56, 160–67.

[10] A biographical sketch by Harry R. Stevens, "Hugh Glenn," appears in Hafen, *Mountain Men*, II, 161–74. Included in the party were Jacob and Robert Fowler, Baptiste Roy, Baptiste Peno, George Douglas, Nat Pryor, Richard Walters, Eli Ward, Jesse Van Bibber, Dudley Maxwell, Baptiste Moran, and men named Paul (a Negro slave), Bono, Barbo, Taylor, Simpson, Slover, and Findley. See Jacob Fowler, *The Journal of Jacob Fowler* (ed. by Elliott Coues), 4–5.

[11] Fowler, *Journal of Jacob Fowler*, 55, 61, 71, 83, 94, 95, 105. A biographical sketch by Raymond W. Settle, "Jacob Fowler," appears in Hafen, *Mountain Men*, III, 119–30.

—." On February 10, two groups, one led by Isaac Slover[12] and the other by Jesse Van Bibber, headed north toward the San Luis Valley. Fowler, with three men, planned to follow the Río Grande south, but the forbidding rocky cliffs of the river's gorge near Taos discouraged them, and they hurried north to join their companions in the San Luis Valley. By May 3, all three groups had returned to Taos after a seemingly successful hunt. Fowler, in his laconic style, expressed no satisfaction with the results of the hunt, but since beaver were plentiful it seems reasonable to conclude that it was a success. A creek near Taos had been disappointing; Fowler noted that "the Bever Have been all taken out by Some trapers—." Perhaps these were members of the Becknell or James-McKnight parties, or perhaps Spaniards had trapped there on occasion. After lounging around Taos for a month, Glenn's group crossed the Sangre de Cristos via Taos Pass and returned to St. Louis.[13] There, Glenn and his trappers sold over eleven hundred pounds of beaver fur to Ramsay Crooks of the American Fur Company for $4,999.64,[14] a good season's showing.

For two of these first three groups who visited newly independent Santa Fe, trapping seems to have been more profitable than selling merchandise. In fact, only Becknell seems to have found trading profitable in the Mexican settlements; a later observer reported that Becknell sold his goods at "a very handsome profit."[15] The other two groups, however, were less fortunate. Thomas James complained that "I continued my trading, though without much success on account of the scarcity of money." Hugh Glenn must have shared James's experience, for he had to borrow one hundred dollars from James while they were in Santa Fe. That they found little cash in New Mexico is not surprising. Decades of an unfavorable balance of trade with Chihuahua had sapped the province of specie so that even the governor, Facundo Melgares, felt the squeeze; he too owed Thomas James eighty dollars.[16]

[12] Fowler, *Journal of Jacob Fowler*, 106, 114; Cleland, *This Reckless Breed*, 217.
[13] Fowler, *Journal of Jacob Fowler*, 108–25, 137–38, 142.
[14] David Lavender, *The Fist in the Wilderness*, 334; Stevens, "Hugh Glenn," 173.
[15] Gregg, *Commerce of the Prairies*, 13.

The shortage of hard cash in New Mexico remained throughout the 1820's. Yet Americans continued to haul merchandise over the Santa Fe Trail. This apparent paradox is explained in part by the extension of the Santa Fe Trail south to Chihuahua, where the market could absorb a greater amount of American goods; but the lure of newly opened beaver streams also explains why so many Americans made the arduous journey to New Mexico. Some of the merchandise they brought was used to outfit trappers, and some was probably destined for a growing Indian trade. Alphonso Wetmore, who first visited Santa Fe in 1824, noted that at Santa Fe and Taos "American mountain companies are annually fitted out . . . and our traders take into account this branch of the business in laying in their goods."[17] The trader who exchanged goods in New Mexico for beaver fur instead of money found it to his advantage. A New Mexico official, writing in 1832, explained that "since exports of beaver are not taxed by the national government, Americans try to take back on their return trip, instead of money, beaver skins."[18]

Indeed, the opening of New Mexico to foreigners in 1821 coincided with renewed interest in the fur trade along the American frontier. In 1821 the price of furs was rising and in March, 1822, the United States government abolished its "factories," or trading posts. Established in 1796 to protect Indians from unscrupulous traders, the factory system had become a competitor to private trade and its passing brought a sigh of relief from the frontier. The demise of the factories stimulated a flurry of activity as men, money, and trade goods flowed into Missouri River towns.[19] Although the Missouri saw most of this enlivened trading activity

[16] James, *Three Year Among the Mexicans*, 157, 158; Moorhead, *New Mexico's Royal Road*, 50, 62–63.

[17] Frank McNitt, *The Indian Traders*, 15; Alphonso Wetmore to Secretary of War, Lewis Cass, Franklin, Missouri, October 11, 1831, in Hulbert, *Southwest on the Turquoise Trail*, 179.

[18] Antonio Barreiro, *Ojeada sobre Nuevo Mejico*, in Carroll and Haggard, *Three New Mexico Chronicles*, 108.

[19] The purpose of the factories, and reasons for their failure, are discussed in Chittenden, *American Fur Trade*, I, 12–16; *St. Louis Enquirer*, in Morgan, *Ashley*, 19.

during the next years, some venturesome trappers and traders moved through Indian territory into northernmost Mexico. Josiah Gregg, a prominent Santa Fe trader of the 1830's, estimated that some one hundred and twenty Americans took the trail to Santa Fe during 1822 and 1823.[20] Many of these men were drawn to New Mexico by the rapidly spreading news of virgin beaver streams abundant in the area.

The Glenn-Fowler party, returning to St. Louis in the late spring of 1822, passed two other groups heading west. On June 12, Jacob Fowler recorded meeting "Conl Cooppers party from Boons lick on their Way to the Spanish Settlement With Some goods and Some traps to take Bever," and on July 1, Fowler passed "Becknal and His party."[21]

"Conl Cooper" was Colonel Benjamin Cooper of Boonslick, whose party of fifteen men, including his nephews Stephen and Braxton, had responded to the favorable reports of William Becknell. Cooper's group left Missouri in mid-May, a few days ahead of Becknell's second Santa Fe expedition. If Cooper put the traps he brought to any use it is not known. When the October 8, 1822, issue of the *Missouri Intelligencer* noted Cooper's return from Santa Fe, it did not mention beaver fur as being among his profits. Still, some of his group probably lingered in Taos for the winter, hoping to trap.[22]

William Becknell also returned to the Missouri settlements in the fall of 1822, and there is no doubt that some of the twenty-one men who had accompanied him to New Mexico stayed to trap. Two of these, a tall Tennessee carpenter named Ewing Young, and Kentucky-born William Wolfskill, each in their twenties, began a profitable and lasting relationship which kept them in the vanguard of the Taos trappers. Wolfskill and Young stayed in Santa Fe until autumn came and beaver fur began to thicken, then they trapped on the Pecos River.[23] They were probably not alone.

[20] Gregg, *Commerce of the Prairies*, 332.
[21] Fowler, *Journal of Jacob Fowler*, 154, 157.
[22] Kenneth L. Holmes, "The Benjamin Cooper Expeditions to Santa Fe in 1822 and 1823," *New Mexico Historical Review*, Vol. XXXVIII, No. 2 (April, 1963), 139–50.

While Young and Wolfskill trapped the Pecos, still another group of Missourians was traveling toward New Mexico—dangerously late in the season. On September 3, 1822, the *Missouri Intelligencer* of Franklin reported that "a Company of about fifty persons, principally from St. Louis and its vicinity are now in town, on their way to Santa Fe. Their purpose is to hunt and obtain furs." Reports of the number included in this group vary (one account set the number at twenty and another estimated forty), but it is known that it included the firm of "James Baird and Company," formed on July 23, 1822, and comprising five partners: Baird, William and Paul Anderson, Wilson McGunnegle, and John Foughlin.[24] James Baird was a man of considerable experience in Mexico. As one of the unlucky members of the abortive 1812 commercial expedition to Santa Fe, he had spent eight years in various degrees of confinement in Chihuahua. Released in September, 1820, Baird lingered in Chihuahua for over a year before beginning his journey back to the United States. Once home, he made plans for an immediate return. His second venture into Mexico was financed in part by Ramsay Crooks of the American Fur Company and Oliver N. Bostwick of a St. Louis mercantile firm associated with the Missouri River fur trade.[25]

Of Baird's four partners, relatively little is known. At this time William and Paul Anderson were just beginning a long association with the fur trade in New Mexico, where they would become known as Julian and Pablo Anderson. They were probably the same Paul and William Anderson who advertised themselves as commission merchants in St. Louis in 1818 and 1819.[26] John "Foughlin" may be the John Loughlin who was later involved in the Santa Fe trade. In 1828, for example, Loughlin and "Pablo" Anderson received *guías*, or trade permits, to travel down the

23 H. D. Barrows, "The Story of an Old Pioneer," *Wilmington* (California) *Journal*, October 20, 1866.

24 *St. Louis Enquirer*, September 2, 1822, December 1, 1823, and (St. Louis) *Missouri Republican*, August 20, 1823.

25 Strickland, "James Baird," in Hafen, *Mountain Men*, III, 29–30; Lavender, *The Fist in the Wilderness*, 334–35; Crooks to Samuel Abbott, St. Louis, July 31, 1822, in Chouteau Collection, Missouri Historical Society, St. Louis, Missouri.

26 Ad in the (St. Louis) *Missouri Gazette*, June 5, 1818, and April 28, 1819.

Chihuahua Trail together.[27] Wilson McGunnegle had been an employee of the Missouri Fur Company and, in 1821, had been entrusted with a shipment of goods and dispatches bound for Fort Lisa on the Upper Missouri. He was thought to have "the making of a smart young man," and had been recommended as a clerk, but his career with the Missouri Fur Company was brief. The trip to New Mexico with Baird and Company seems to have been McGunnegle's only foray into New Mexico, although he was recommended to be secretary for a survey of the Santa Fe Trail in 1825. He died in 1829.[28]

It is interesting that Samuel Chambers also accompanied Baird and Company back to Santa Fe. Chambers is a curious and obscure figure. He seems to have been a member of Wilson Price Hunt's famous overland Astorians in 1810, going no farther with the group than St. Louis. In 1812, he joined the ill-fated McKnight expedition to Santa Fe and, like James Baird, suffered captivity until 1820. In 1822, or soon after, Chambers settled in Taos as a trader and was still traveling the Chihuahua Trail as late as 1835.[29]

Baird and Company did not leave St. Louis until late August, and early snows stopped them on the Arkansas far from their destination. The freezing winter killed their mules, forcing the men to cache their merchandise and make their way to Taos on foot. Even before reaching Taos on February 2, 1823, Baird dropped out of the firm which now called itself "Andersons, Foughlin, and McGunnegle."[30] Purchasing more livestock, McGunnegle and the two Andersons returned to the Arkansas with

[27] Weber, *The Extranjeros*, 33.

[28] See Thomas Hempstead to Joshua Pilcher on the Missouri River, St. Louis, September 11, 1821, September 21, 1821, September 9, 1821, Hempstead Letterbooks, Coe Collection, Yale University Library, New Haven, Connecticut; Sibley, *Road to Santa Fe*, 228; Morgan, *Ashley*, 259, n. 32.

[29] Kenneth W. Porter, "Roll of Overland Astorians, 1810–1812," *Oregon Historical Quarterly*, Vol. XXXIV, No. 2 (June, 1933), 106; Sibley, *Road to Santa Fe*, 157; Chávez, "New Names," *El Palacio*, Vol. LXIV, Nos. 9–12 (September–December, 1957), 301, 371; *Guía* for Samuel Chambers, October 16, 1835, in Mexican Archives of New Mexico, State Records Center, Santa Fe, New Mexico; William Waldo, "Recollections of a Septuagenarian," Missouri Historical Society, *Glimpses of the Past*, Vol. V, Nos. 4–6 (April–June, 1938), 78.

[30] *St. Louis Enquirer*, December 1, 1823.

a few "Spaniards" in order to "lift" the caches. Their plan did not immediately succeed, though, for the ubiquitous Pawnees robbed them of their animals, killed one of the Spaniards, and forced their return to Taos, again on foot—"a pedestrian tour of fifteen days." Later in the spring the contents of the caches were finally rescued, leaving gaping holes near the river's edge to remind travelers of the incident.[31]

Still, these difficulties did not prevent some of Baird and Company's men from trapping in New Mexico as originally planned. According to William Parker, who later wrote a letter describing the group's experiences, plans were made immediately upon arrival at Taos to continue even farther west. The objective, Parker explained, was trapping grounds some four hundred miles to the west of Santa Fe "which lay in that wild Mountainous tract of country that interrupts the Most westerly Spanish Settlements, And the Gulph of California—." When the trappers reached this place, however, a force of one hundred men under a Spanish captain arrested them and took them back to Taos. There, Parker wrote, "We were set at liberty, treated with much politeness and hospitality, but were informed, that it was a violation of the law of the land, and the rights of the Citizens of the Government for foreigners to take the beaver from any of the waters within the Empire—."[32]

Parker's letter is significant because it reveals that Americans were moving west out of the Río Grande Valley into the drainage of the Colorado River Basin as early as 1823. Yet, this spare letter is intriguing in that no other contemporary document refers to the incident. There is no evidence that Mexican troops were operating as far as four hundred miles west of Santa Fe, but some, who were pursuing Navahos from mid-June to the end of August, 1823, might have intercepted the American trappers in the San

31 Letter from Wilson McGunnegle, Taos, June 20, 1823, in the (St. Louis) *Missouri Republican*, September 3, 1823. Additional proof that the Andersons were along comes from a well-known Santa Fe trader, Alphonso Wetmore, whose *Gazetteer of the State of Missouri* referred to these holes as "Anderson's Caches on the Arkansas," 269.

32 William Parker to Mr. Harm Ian Huidekaper[?], September 9, 1824, Fur Trade Papers, Missouri Historical Society.

Juan River, near the Chuska Mountains, some two hundred miles west of Santa Fe. Still, the extant journals of this campaign make no mention of finding foreigners.[33]

William Parker's indication that New Mexican officials felt some antipathy toward American trappers in 1823 is also significant as a portent of things to come. There is no evidence that any law against foreign trappers existed in Mexico at this time, but officials may have been enforcing Spanish laws. When "Andersons, Foughlin, and McGunnegle" returned to Missouri, they circulated a story which was similar to Parker's, but less sympathetic to Mexican officials. The *St. Louis Enquirer* commented on November 8, 1823:

> The greatest obstacle to the success of these gentlemen, was the jealous and tantalizing conduct of the Spaniards, who, under the pretence of saving them from the Indians would go and order them in from their trapping stations, when at the time it was believed that Indians were more friendly to the American party than they were to the Spaniards.

Mexican solicitude for the welfare of the Americans was probably motivated less by envy than by a genuine concern for their well-being. At least five Americans, according to Wilson McGunnegle, had already lost their lives to "friendly" Indians within sixty miles of Taos. Three of these five, Jesse Van Bibber, Dudley Maxwell, and a man called Findley, had been with Hugh Glenn's group and had stayed on in New Mexico, apparently to trap.[34]

In addition to complaints about their treatment at the hands of "Spaniards," James Baird's former partners managed to bring some furs back from New Mexico. One St. Louis fur merchant learned, in the fall of 1823, that the St. Louis firm of "Tracy and Wahren-

[33] David M. Brugge, "Vizcarra's Navaho Campaign of 1823," *Arizona and the West*, Vol. VI, No. 3 (Autumn, 1964), 233–44.
[34] Letter of Wilson McGunnegle, June 20, 1823, Taos, in the (St. Louis) *Missouri Republican*, September 3, 1823. McGunnegle's report is substantiated in the "Reports of the Fur Trade and Inland Trade to New Mexico 1831," *Missouri Historical Society Glimpses of the Past*, Vol. IX, Nos. 1–2 (January-June, 1942), 35.

dorff have again received some beavers from McGunnigle [*sic*] and Anderson. The amount is not large, but it is said that each of them is bringing some from the mountains." Whatever the amount of furs, it was not large enough to hold the firm together. Just before leaving Taos, on September 1, 1823, the Andersons, Foughlin, and McGunnegle dissolved their partnership.[35]

The year 1823 saw a decline in the Santa Fe trade; only one expedition is known to have left Missouri that year.[36] Led again by Colonel Benjamin Cooper, this group included Joel Walker, who later told of meeting his more famous brother, Joseph Reddeford Walker, along the trail. Joseph, according to Joel, "had started the year before trapping," and "had returned to the Arkansas river for goods cached there the previous year when on his way to Santa Fe." Evidently, Joseph was returning to the cache with some of Baird's men when the brothers met.[37] The Cooper party of 1823 found trade profitable, returning with "about 400 Jacks, Jennies, and mules, a quantity of beaver, and a considerable sum in specie." The *Missouri Intelligencer*, in the fall of 1823, noted that "the beaver and the livestock will bear a profit by transportation to some of the older states."[38] Cooper's successful second expedition enjoyed national news coverage in *Niles' Weekly Register*. The story even reached Mexico's secretary of foreign relations through the embassy in Washington.[39] This publicity may have

35 Bartholomew Berthold to B. Pratte and Co., St. Louis, November 14, 1823, Chouteau Collection. Portions of this letter are translated in Ashley, *Ashley*, 61–62. See also an ad in the *St. Louis Enquirer*, December 1, 1823.

36 Chittenden, *American Fur Trade*, II, 505.

37 Joel Walker's reminiscences are most conveniently available in Joel P. Walker, *A Pioneer of Pioneers, Narrative of Adventures Thro' Alabama, Florida, New Mexico, Oregon, California, Etc.*, 7. See Holmes, "The Benjamin Cooper Expeditions to Santa Fe in 1822 and 1823," *NMHR*, Vol. XXXVIII, No. 2 (April, 1963), 144–48, for further analysis. Joseph Walker's biographer, Douglas Watson, suggests that he came to New Mexico in 1820. See *West Wind: The Story of Joseph Reddeford Walker, Knight of the Golden Horseshoe*, 8, 9. Cleland, *Reckless Breed*, 277, puts the date at 1821. Joel Walker suggests the year 1822, which seems most likely.

38 Article from the (Franklin) *Missouri Intelligencer* in the (Jackson, Missouri) *Independent Patriot*, November 29, 1823.

39 Holmes, "Benjamin Cooper Expeditions," *NMHR*, Vol. XXXVIII, No. 2 (April, 1963), 149–50.

promoted the further penetration of New Mexico by American traders and trappers and may have given impetus to a Mexican decree of 1824 that banned trapping by non-nationals in New Mexico.

Doubtless other trappers and fur traders, whose activities have not yet come to light, found their way into New Mexico during these first years. Louis Robidoux, for example, once swore under oath that he had been living in Taos since the winter of 1823–24.[40] Étienne Provost and his partner, Leclerc, were also in New Mexico in 1823 and perhaps earlier. In the following year, 1824, Provost and Leclerc would play a significant role in the fur trade of the Far Southwest, but of their earlier activities, almost nothing is known.[41]

By 1823, after only two years of commercial contact with Santa Fe, Americans had already begun to mine the fine furs that the Spaniards had scarcely touched and had begun to incorporate the fur trade into their mercantile trade. Thus, the Santa Fe trade and the fur trade developed hand in hand, setting a pattern which would last for another decade. Merchants who brought goods to Santa Fe or Taos in the spring often returned home in the fall with furs among their profits, while others lingered through the fall and winter to trap. As one scholar put it, "The Santa Fe trade was in a sense an off shoot of the fur trade, and during the first fifteen years of the overland commerce practically every returning caravan had considerable quantities of fur."[42]

In 1823, however, the fur trade from New Mexico had scarcely begun. Only a handful of men were operating out of Taos and Santa Fe. Although their activities remain shadowy, most trappers

[40] Testimony of Luis Robidoux in the case of the embargoed merchandise of Francisco Robidoux, December 9, 1825, MANM.

[41] LeRoy R. Hafen, "Etienne Provost, Mountain Man and Utah Pioneer," *Utah Historical Quarterly*, Vol. XXXVI, No. 2 (Spring, 1968), 101; William Marshall Anderson, *The Rocky Mountain Journals of William Marshall Anderson* (ed. by Dale L. Morgan and Eleanor Towles Harris), 343.

[42] F. F. Stephens, "Missouri and the Santa Fe Trade," *Missouri Historical Review*, Vol. XI, No. 3 (April, 1917), 303–304. See also Robert Luther Duffus, *The Santa Fe Trail*, 100, and Edgar B. Wesley "The Fur Trade of the Southwest" (M.A. thesis, Washington University, 1925), 3–4.

certainly centered their operations on the virgin streams of the Pecos and Río Grande valleys. The beaver supply in this convenient area was already being depleted, however, and by 1824 trappers would imitate William Parker and head still farther west.

V TO THE COLORADO,

In 1824, trappers working out of Taos and Santa Fe somehow attracted the attention of officials in Mexico City. On June 26 of that year an agency of the central government ordered the governor of New Mexico to prevent foreigners from trapping in his territory.[1] Unfortunately this order cannot be described with greater precision, for no copy has yet been found. It was, in fact, lost from the New Mexico archives as early as 1825. Still, there is no doubt of its existence.

According to a contemporary description, the "regulations provided that only settlers should hunt the beaver; to this end, after paying a municipal tax, they were given a written hunting license which recorded the number of hunters in the party, the manner of hunting, the weapons to be used—fire arms, traps, or snares—and the number of days to be spent on the expedition."[2]

If this order was designed to protect a natural resource from wholesale foreign exploitation, it had slight effect at first. The *Missouri Intelligencer* at Franklin, usually sensitive to problems affecting the Santa Fe trade, does not even mention it. Josiah

[1] Summary of proceedings against Ewing Young, 1827, in papers pertaining to Young's arrest, Archivo de Relaciones Exteriores, Mexico, D.F., Doc. H[242.2 (73:72)]-2. Legajo 12-12-12.
[2] José Agustín de Escudero, in Carroll and Haggard, *Three New Mexico Chronicles*, 105.

1824–1825

Gregg, who traded at Santa Fe in the 1830's, explained why. Since native New Mexicans did not trap, Gregg said, both governors Bartolomé Baca and Antonio Narbona gave licenses to foreigners in the name of Mexican citizens, provided the foreigner took along "a certain proportion of Mexicans to learn the art of trapping."[3] Thus, up to the spring of 1826, when Narbona underwent a change of heart, foreigners continued to trap Mexican waters without opposition. In fact, they dramatically expanded their operations, beginning with a massive movement into the Colorado River Basin in the fall of 1824.

A pioneer venture into this area had been made in the spring of 1824 by William Wolfskill, Ewing Young, and Isaac Slover (of the 1822 Glenn-Slover party), who after outfitting a party in Taos in February, trapped their way west on the San Juan River. Their return to Taos in June, 1824, laden with furs,[4] was probably sufficient in itself to motivate an exodus from the Río Grande Basin, although the awakening hostility of the Mexican government toward foreign trappers may have given additional impetus to the westward move. But most important, three seasons of concentrated

[3] Gregg, *Commerce of the Prairies*, 160.
[4] Barrows, "The Story of an Old Pioneer," *Wilmington* (California) *Journal*, October 20, 1866.

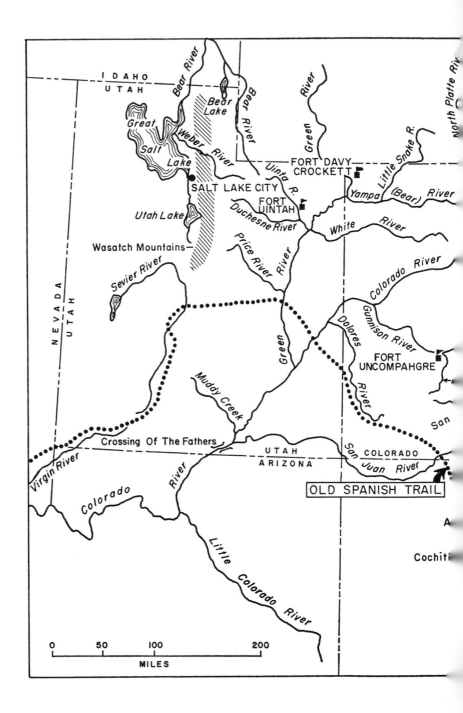

The area of fur-trading activities northwest of Taos

trapping on the Río Grande and its tributaries must have depleted the local beaver and forced the trappers west out of necessity.

Many of the trappers who were to beat new trails to the Colorado Basin were among the eighty-three men who arrived in Santa Fe toward the evening of July 28, 1824, with the annual caravan from Missouri.[5] Most of these men remain nameless, but it is certain that Paul Anderson, formerly of "Andersons, Foughlin and McGunnegle," had returned, for he was elected first lieutenant of the caravan. Other leaders of the caravan were its captain, Alexander Le Grand, and Augustus Storrs.[6]

Upon returning to the Missouri settlements in the fall of 1824, Storrs penned a letter to Senator Thomas Hart Benton of Missouri which provided his contemporaries, and posterity as well, with a valuable glimpse at the workings of the New Mexico fur trade. Storrs described it as a "business, which, is exclusively enjoyed by American citizens." He explained that trappers had worked the Río Grande and nearby mountains up to the previous winter when some "descended the western slope of our continent," (apparently a reference to Wolfskill, Young, and Slover). During the present season the number of trappers in New Mexico had tripled. These men, traveling in one large force, had left Taos on August 1, planning to travel "westward thirty days' journey, probably seven hundred miles." Then, Storrs wrote, they would divide into contingents of three or four in order to trap.[7] Storrs seems to have been describing the plans of a group, or combination of groups, led by Étienne Provost and François Leclerc, Thomas L. Smith, William Huddart, and Antoine Robidoux, all of whom led trapping expeditions west from New Mexico in the early fall of 1824. These New Mexico-based trappers would find themselves competing with British trappers and other American trappers from the Missouri frontier; the season of 1824–25 saw groups converge from three

[5] "M. M. Marmaduke Journal," in Hulbert, *Southwest on the Turquoise Trail*, 69, 70, 75.
[6] "Extract of a letter from one of the company to the editor," Camp, 10 miles south of Fort Osage, May 25, 1824, in the *Missouri Intelligencer*, June 5, 1824.
[7] Storrs, "Answers to Certain Queries," in *Santa Fé Trail First Reports: 1825*, 33–35.

directions on the basins of the Salt Lake and the Colorado River. Those from Taos formed the vanguard of this movement.

One of the first trapping parties to head northwest from Taos in the fall of 1824 was led by Thomas Long Smith, a young man of twenty-three who had not yet earned the sobriquet of "Peg-leg." Described a few years later as "a middle sized, stout man, with a bold, rather handsome and expressive countenance,"[8] Smith had been born into a large family on the Kentucky frontier and had run away from home at age fifteen. Even before his arrival in New Mexico, Smith had become an experienced trapper and trader, working for two years among the Sioux and Osage Indians. In the spring of 1824, he joined the large Santa Fe caravan under Alexander Le Grand, taking along "a hunting horse and few mules packed with goods suitable for the market, besides Indians trinkets, beads, buttons, awls and paints."[9] From Santa Fe, Smith quickly found his way to Taos, which became his home, in between adventures, for the next decade or so. From there, in September of 1824, Smith set out for his first hunt in the Rockies.

As Smith later told it, he left Taos that fall with eighty men. Allowing for some exaggeration, this sizable group might have represented the combined parties of William Huddart and other free trappers to whom Augustus Storrs alluded. On the headwaters of the Río Grande, Smith, Maurice "Le Duke" (LeDuc), men named Hopper and Marlow,[10] and three Mexicans separated from the larger body. Proceeding west through the rugged San Juan Range, they crossed the continental divide and found their way to

[8] Pike, *Prose Sketches*, 281.

[9] "Sketches From the Life of Peg-leg Smith," *Hutchings' Illustrated California Magazine*, Vol. V, No. 5 (November, 1860), 203–204. The account in *Hutchings'*, it seems to me, is the most reliable for these years. Smith's reminiscences were also dictated and published on two other occasions: "The Story of an Old Trapper, Life and Adventures of the late Peg-leg Smith," *San Francisco Evening Bulletin*, October 26, 1866, and "Peg-Leg Smith—A Short Sketch of His Life," (San Francisco) *Daily Alta California*, March 8, 1858. He has become the subject of a biography by Sardis W. Templeton, *The Lame Captain: The Life and Adventures of Pegleg Smith*, which should be used with caution. A short biography by Alfred Glen Humphreys, "Thomas L. (Peg-leg) Smith," appears in Hafen, *Mountain Men*, IV, 311–30.

[10] Dale Morgan suggests that Hopper's first name may be Charles, in *Ashley*, 279. If he is referring to Charles Hopper of California fame, this seems unlikely.

one of the affluents of "Grand River," as the Gunnison was then called.[11] This stream, which they traveled toward the Gunnison, may have been the Uncompahgre or the San Miguel, but we may never know, for Smith modestly called it Smith's Fork.[12] At least one of the three New Mexicans who accompanied him probably knew the stream by another name, however, for it seems likely that Smith was being guided over a variant of the well-known route to the Ute country which Spaniards had used for a half-century.

After Smith and his seven companions trapped their way some fifty miles down the Gunnison, they concluded that the group was too large to trap profitably: "Whilst Hopper, Marlow and the three Mexicans went off westward for Green river," Smith and Maurice LeDuc continued down the Gunnison, where some Utes soon robbed them of five horses. Fearful of further robberies, Smith and LeDuc left the Gunnison and headed south. Crossing the San Juan River and a "high range of mountains," they reached Navaho country. There they traded "trinkets for sheep and goat skins, also serapes of superior quality manufactured by the Indians and so closely woven as to be almost impervious to water." They were back at Taos by mid-December.[13]

At Taos, Smith busied himself that winter by building a distillery with James Baird, Samuel Chambers, and a man named Stevens as partners. Although this appears to be the first American-made distillery in Taos, Smith and his cohorts have never received proper recognition as pioneer industrialists. Others soon paid them the high tribute of emulation, however, making their monopoly short-lived. The effects of "Taos Lightning," as the locally produced

[11] Grand River of today was then called the Blue. See the Ferris map of 1836 in Carl I. Wheat, *Mapping the Transmississippi West*, II, facing 156. Smith's account also makes it clear that he was on the Gunnison.

[12] "Sketches From the Life of Peg-leg Smith," *HICM*, Vol. V, No. 5 (November, 1860), 204. Smith's account in the *San Francisco Evening Bulletin* also refers to Smith's Fork as "a stream emptying into Grand river." Yet, in 1832, on a trapping expedition led by Smith, today's Eagle River, which flows into the Río Grande, was also dubbed Smith's Fork. He must have had a fondness for place names.

[13] "Sketches From the Life of Peg-leg Smith," *HICM*, Vol. V, No. 5 (November, 1860), 204–206. The *San Francisco Evening Bulletin* article says this journey took eighteen months.

whisky came to be called, could be attested to throughout the Rockies by a generation of mountain men.[14]

In February, as Smith remembered, Hopper "with his little band from Green river arrived." By that time virgin streams in the Green River country were probably scarce, for, on his return to Taos, Hopper had been "accompanied by Antonio Rubedoux, John Roland and some twenty-five men of Provost's company,"[15] all of whom had been trapping to the northwest of New Mexico. In addition to these trappers, a group led by William Huddart had also been in the Green River country that season. A Missourian, Huddart had probably first come to New Mexico with Benjamin Cooper in 1823. His companions on that trip long remembered how Huddart, crazed by thirst, stuck his head inside a freshly killed buffalo to drink its blood; the story continued to be told on the trail for at least another decade.[16] Huddart had started for the Green from Taos on August 24, 1824, with fourteen men, at about the same time that Thomas Smith remembered leaving Taos. Perhaps their parties joined together on the first leg of the trip. We know very little, however, of Huddart's experience in the mountains and would know nothing if it were not for a brief account that he gave the *Missouri Intelligencer* upon his return to Franklin in April, 1825. The newspaper reported that Huddart and his men had

left Taos for the purpose of trapping for beaver, and travelled west thirty days. On Green River (probably the Río Colorado of the West) the company separated, and nine ascended the river. Our informant was among those who remained; and in a few days they accidentally fell in with five other Americans, among whom was Mr. Rubideau. Two days after this junction [meeting], a large party of Aripehoes [*sic*] attacked them, killed one person by the name of Nowlin, and robbed the others. The party of six then concluded to return to Taos, and left

14 David J. Weber (ed.), "A Letter from Taos, 1826: William Workman," *New Mexico Historical Review*, Vol. XLI, No. 2 (April, 1966), 156.
15 "Sketches From the Life of Peg-leg Smith," *HICM*, Vol. V, No. 7 (January, 1861), 318–19.
16 Holmes, "Benjamin Cooper's Expeditions," *NMHR*, Vol. XXXVIII, No. 2 (April, 1963), 148–49.

Mr. Rubideau and his men in the mountains without a single horse or mule.[17]

Huddart's account not only furnishes us a view of his activities, but also suggests the wide-ranging interests of the Robidoux brothers. The "Mr. Rubideau" whom Huddart met on the Green was probably Antoine. Thirty years old, the fifth of seven brothers, Antoine was a tall, slender, and handsome figure whom many found courteous and charming.[18] Early in 1824, Antoine had taken "a small assortment of goods" up the Missouri River from St. Louis to Fort Atkinson, where his arrival as "young Robidoux" was recorded by the post sutler on February 15.[19] Four days later he received a permit to travel through Indian Territory from Fort Atkinson "in the direction of Santa Fe." From there, Antoine must have continued west to the Green River, where Huddart saw him. By February, 1825, Peg-leg Smith later recalled, "Antonio Rubedoux" had come into Taos from the Green River.[20] For the next two decades Antoine Robidoux would be associated with the fur trade from New Mexico.

In addition to Huddart, Smith, and Robidoux, the perplexing Étienne Provost and his even more enigmatic partner, François Leclerc,[21] also operated in the Colorado Basin in the season of 1824–25. Provost and Leclerc seem to have journeyed farther north and west than their contemporaries from New Mexico, and we are able to piece together some of their activities from the accounts of

[17] *Missouri Intelligencer*, April 19, 1825. Confusion about Huddart's name has existed, unnecessarily, since the publication of Dale's *Ashley-Smith Explorations* which called him Heddest (151–52, n. 292). The *Intelligencer* spells his name Huddart and a list of letters in the Franklin Post Office, published in the *Intelligencer* of July 9, 1825, contains a letter addressed to "Wm. Huddart."

[18] William S. Wallace, *Antoine Robidoux, 1794–1860*, 4–5, 48.

[19] Edgar B. Wesley (ed.), "Diary of James Kennerly, 1823–1826," *Missouri Historical Society Collections*, Vol. VI, No. 1 (October, 1928), 54. Wesley says this is François, but I concur with Dale Morgan (*Ashley*, 154) that this was Antoine.

[20] Permit signed by Colonel Henry Leavenworth, Fort Atkinson, February 19, 1824, Ritch Papers, No. 79, Huntington Library, San Marino, California; "Sketches from the Life of Peg-leg Smith," *HICM*, Vol. V, No. 7 (January, 1861), 319.

[21] For a discussion of the complex problem of identifying Leclerc, see Morgan, *Ashley*, 278, n. 151.

other American and Canadian trappers in the area. That Provost used New Mexico as a base was advantageous, for he had had considerable experience in the area while trapping and trading with Jules de Mun and Auguste Chouteau—including an inside look at Santa Fe, where, along with the rest of that unfortunate party, he had spent a month and a half in the local jail. In 1823 Provost returned to New Mexico for awhile, perhaps to trap, but we know nothing of his motives that year. In the late summer or early fall of 1824, Provost and Leclerc left Taos for the Green River. Their route very likely followed the Spanish Trail or a northerly variant. Perhaps Mexican traders guided Provost; there is no doubt that Mexicans went with him. Provost's party, contemporaries reported, consisted of twenty or thirty men.[22]

Antoine Robidoux may have been among those trappers who accompanied Provost, for both were of the clannish French fur trade fraternity on the Missouri River and both seemed to use Council Bluffs as an outfitting point for their journeys to New Mexico.[23] Robidoux may have traveled to the Green with Provost and then, as was customary, split off from the main party to trap. After his meeting with Huddart and their near-tragic encounter with Indians, Huddart reported leaving Robidoux in the mountains without any pack animals. Yet, Peg-leg Smith remembered that in February Robidoux showed up at Taos with some of Provost's men. Robidoux, it seems likely, had returned to the main party after the Indian attack and then had come back to Taos with some of Provost's men.

Meanwhile, after establishing a base camp at the mouth of the White River where it joins the Green, Provost had divided his men to trap and trade. Provost pushed westward with a group of ten

22 Peter Skene Ogden, *Peter Skene Ogden's Snake Country Journals, 1824–25 and 1825–26,* (ed. by E. E. Rich), 51, 233; William Ashley, "Diary," entry of May 17, 1825, in Morgan, *Ashley,* 112. Dale Morgan has found that men named Pino, Adams, and La Bonte belonged to Provost's party and has surmised from various evidence that White, Polite [Paulet?], Morin, Beauchemin, and Pumbar [Pombert?] may also have been along. See *Ashley,* 283, n. 180 and 290–91, n. 217 and n. 218, wherein Morgan tries to identify Pino, LaBonte, Adams, and White.

23 Provost and Leclerc seemingly returned to Fort Atkinson in the summer of 1823. Robidoux's license to go to Santa Fe was issued there in February, 1824.

through the Wasatch Mountains into the basin of the Great Salt Lake, probably to trade with Utes as Spaniards had done before him. By October, 1824, Provost had reached today's Jordan River and may have been the first white man to see the Great Salt Lake.[24] On the Jordan, the Snake Chief "Bad Gocha" invited Provost and his men to smoke the peace pipe and lay down their arms. For eight of the trappers, acceptance was a fatal mistake. Only Provost and one other escaped the ensuing slaughter.[25] With considerable justification, the Americans later blamed Hudson's Bay Company trappers for inciting the Indians. Peter Skene Ogden, who made his well-known first Snake country expedition that same season, reported to the Company that the Snakes had retaliated against the Americans because a Hudson's Bay man had killed a Snake chief. Thus, Ogden explained, the Americans were "greatly irritated . . . against us, and they would most willingly shoot us if they dared."[26]

The massacre seems not to have seriously interrupted Provost's plans for the winter, for he remained in the mountains while some of his men returned to Taos, apparently for supplies. François Leclerc was probably in this group and may not have returned to the mountains that season. Perhaps Leclerc was again at Taos in 1826, but little can be said of Leclerc with certainty.[27]

From his base camp at the mouth of the White River, Provost split his remaining men into small groups to trap the Green and its tributaries. Four men, for example, descended the Green in a canoe, a voyage that they later reported, in a classic understatement, was "very dangerous." Game was so scarce that they had to eat the skins of beaver that they trapped along the way. The four also reported that Indians in the area were "hostile desposed and have killed and robed 15 or 20 men who were from the neighborhood of St. Louis."[28] Perhaps the trappers had heard indirectly of Robi-

[24] Anderson, *William Marshall Anderson*, 344; Hafen, "Etienne Provost," *UHQ*, Vol. XXXVI, No. 2 (Spring, 1968), 103.

[25] Warren A. Ferris, *Life in the Rocky Mountains . . . February 1830, to November, 1835*, Paul C. Phillips (ed.), 308–309, and Dale L. Morgan, "New Light on Ashley and Jedediah Smith," *The Pacific Historian*, Vol. XII, No. 1 (Winter, 1968), 18–19.

[26] Peter Skene Ogden to the Governor, Chief Factors and Chief Traders [of the Hudson's Bay Company], East Fork, Missouri, July 10, 1825, in Frederick

doux's or Huddart's misfortunes. Provost himself led a group into the Wasatch Mountains, where, in Weber Canyon in May, he was surprised to run across Peter Skene Ogden and his Hudson's Bay Company trappers. As Ogden reported to his employers:

> On the 23 a party of 15 Canadians and Spanjards headed by one Provost and Francois an Iroquois Chief who deserted from our party two Years since joined us, we were surprized of seeing them, and still more so when they informed me, that the Spanish Settlement where they had received their Supplies was not more then 15 days march with loaded horses. This place is called *Taas* distant about 100 miles from *St Fe* and is now supplied with goods from St Louis overland in waggons by the Americans.

Provost thus added significantly to the geographical knowledge of the Hudson's Bay Company officials and Ogden did not soon forget the proximity of Taos to the Rockies.[29] Nevertheless, relations between the Americans and the British remained hostile.

On June 7, two weeks after meeting Ogden, Provost ran across William Ashley near present-day Fruitland, Utah. A successful businessman, politician, and experienced Missouri River fur trader, Ashley's entrance into the Rockies that season was destined to change the entire character of the Rocky Mountain trade. At the time he met Provost, however, Ashley was short of pack animals and welcomed Provost's assistance in transporting supplies. It was the Taos trappers who told Ashley that the name of the river he

Merk, "Snake Country Expedition, 1824–25," *Oregon Historical Society Quarterly*, Vol. XXXV, No. 2 (June, 1934), 109.

27 Morgan finds a record of François Leclerc in St. Louis in September of 1825. See *Ashley*, 279, n. 151; A "Francisco Le-Clair" was one of five Frenchmen who requested permission, on June 5, 1826, to marry Taos women. Chávez, "New Names," *El Palacio*, Vol. LXIV, Nos. 9–10 (September–October, 1957), 303. There is no record of his marriage.

28 William Ashley's "Diary," May 17, 1825, in Morgan, *Ashley*, 112. See also 279, n. 153 and 280, n. 161.

29 Ogden to the Governor, Chief Factors and Chief Traders, East Fork, Missouri, July 10, 1825, in Merk, "Snake Country Expedition," 109; Ogden to the Governor, . . . October 10, 1826, quoted in George Simpson, *Fur Trade and Empire: George Simpson's Journal* (ed. by Frederick Merk), 284.

was on was the Green, the Spanish Río Verde.[30] He had been calling it the Shetskedee, while its present-day name was already in common usage among Becknell, Huddart, and others trapping out of New Mexico. Thanks to Ashley, however, merchants in New Mexico were denied at least a part of the harvest of Provost's months in the mountains, for in July, 1825, Ashley inaugurated his famous rendezvous system on Henry's Fork of the Green River. Without returning to the settlements, Provost, like other trappers, was able to obtain sugar, coffee, and tobacco from Ashley, as well as beads and colored cloth for the Indian trade. It is curious that beaver from Provost's party brought only $2.50 per pound, while Ashley bought beaver for $3.00 from his own men. Provost's skins, many of which he apparently obtained from Utes, may have been inferior.[31]

The rendezvous seems to have lured Provost permanently from his Taos base. He remained in the mountains until September, 1826, when he returned to Missouri. The promise of his adventurous early career remained unfulfilled, for no outstanding achievement distinguished his later life. Although he continued his involvement in the fur trade, there is no evidence that he saw New Mexico again before his death in 1850.[32]

Late in the fall of 1824, the Father of the Santa Fe Trail, William Becknell, attempted to follow the snow-covered tracks of Smith, Huddart, Robidoux, and Provost toward the northwest. Even before leaving Missouri, Becknell told one of his neighbors of his plans to trap his way into the mountains and "to visit the Oregon" before returning. But Becknell got off to a late start. His party of sixteen did not leave Franklin, Missouri, until sometime after August 19.[33]

[30] Entry of June 7, 1825 in Morgan, *Ashley*, 116, 283, n. 180 and 284, n. 183.

[31] *Ibid.*, 119, 290–91, n. 217. Ashley's account book shows only the amount of beaver that four Provost men sold.

[32] For the little that is known of Provost's later years, see Anderson, *William Marshall Anderson*, 344–51, and Hafen, "Etienne Provost," *UHQ*, Vol. XXXVI, No. 2 (Spring, 1968), 105–12.

[33] Alphonso Wetmore to Hon. John Scott, Franklin, Missouri, August 19, 1824, 18 Cong. 2 sess., *House Doc.* 79 (Ser. 116), in *Santa Fe Trail First Reports*, 68.

Becknell may have been the first American to receive a Mexican license to trap. In a letter of October 29, 1824, to "His Excelannce govirnor of New Mexico Barlota Marie Barker [Bartolomé Baca]," Becknell said, "Sew I recvd the licance you granted me by the onrabel prest of Santa Cruse Manuel Radar[34] and will Comply with your orders and obey them punctaly." In any case, Becknell does not appear to be concealing his impending trip from Governor Baca. He mentions that, "I shall be in next June if nothing Hapins to us," and "I shal Cum an see you when I Cum in from the woods the winter is aprochin so near I cant [find] time to Cum now."[35] Indeed, winter was approaching. Not until November 5 did he and nine others set out from Santa Cruz de la Cañada, just above Santa Fe, "with a view of trapping on the Green River, several hundred miles from Santa Fe." He too probably followed the Old Spanish Trail, but his late departure was costly: "The depth of the snow and the intense cold of the season rendered trapping almost impracticable." Becknell and his men set up winter quarters, perhaps in the area of present-day Mesa Verde National Monument, where he found pieces of pottery, the remains of furnaces and of "many small stone houses, some of which have one story beneath the surface of the earth." After a miserable winter in the "inhospitable wilderness," Becknell reached a New Mexican village on April 5. Although discouraged, he was still "disposed to make another experiment," but there is no further record of his participation in the fur trade of the Far Southwest.[36]

Remarkably, by the end of 1824, no fewer than six groups—those of Wolfskill, Smith, Huddart, Robidoux, Provost, and Becknell—had attempted to trap in the Colorado Basin from a New Mexico base. All six had probably followed known trails, there being more continuity between the routes of Spanish traders and those of American trappers than is usually realized.[37] Even at this early date,

[34] This was Manuel Rada, of Santa Cruz de la Cañada; see Bloom, "New Mexico Under Mexican Administration," *Old Santa Fe*, Vol. I, No. 3 (January, 1914), 236.
[35] Becknell to Baca, October 29, 1824, in Ritch Papers, No. 80.
[36] William Becknell to Mr. Patten, n.d., *Missouri Intelligencer*, June 25, 1825.
[37] Hafen and Hafen, *Old Spanish Trail*, discuss the specific routes of various trappers' trails to the Green River country. See especially, 101, n. 24. See also Goetzmann, *Exploration and Empire*, 67–68.

trappers operating out of New Mexico had visions of reaching Oregon via Santa Fe. We have seen that Becknell had such ambitions. Peter Skene Ogden had learned from the American trappers themselves, that they had not only opened a wagon route from St. Louis to Taos, but that "they intend reaching to Columbia also with Waggons [which is] not impossible so far as I have seen."[38]

The great expectations of the New Mexico–based trappers were not to be realized; their bold thrust into the upper Colorado and Salt Lake basins ended almost before it had begun. For the next decade, this area would be the scene of ruthless competition between the British Hudson's Bay Company and Americans represented by Ashley and his successors. Despite their pioneering efforts, several years passed before the Taos mountain men would again be serious competitors for the furs of the area. Ashley's rendezvous system provided a more popular and effective base than Taos, and his return to St. Louis in the autumn of 1825 with a cargo of beaver valued at close to fifty thousand dollars completely overshadowed the returns from Santa Fe.[39]

Ironically, much of the Green River country and the popular trapping grounds to the east of the Great Salt Lake were in an area legally under Mexican sovereignty. The first four mountain rendezvous, held respectively on Henry's Fork, in Cache Valley, and twice on Bear Lake, all took place in Mexican territory, just below the forty-second parallel.[40] But the trappers, and even the Mexican government, had only the haziest notion of their location in respect to international boundaries. The various administrations in Mexico City during the first decades of independence, occupied with the tasks of shaping a new nation and maintaining themselves in power, rarely turned their attention to beaver hunters roaming the uncharted northern frontier.[41]

[38] Ogden to the Governor, Chief Factors and Chief Traders, June 27, 1825, in Merk, "Snake Country Expedition," *OHSQ*, Vol. XXXV, No. 2 (June, 1934), 116.

[39] See Morgan, *Ashley*, 136–37.

[40] See the map in Hafen, *Mountain Men*, I, and his introduction to the series.

[41] For example, Despatches From U.S. Consuls in Mexico City, 1822–1906, Vols. I and II and Notes From the Mexican Legation in the U.S. to the Department

Although the rendezvous system eclipsed New Mexico as a source of supplies and a market for beaver from the central Rockies, Taos remained an important outfitting point for mountain men. Checked in their expansion to the northwest by Ashley, the trappers from Taos soon discovered new beaver streams in other directions.

of State, Vol. I, both in the National Archives, Washington, D.C., do not concern themselves with the activities of American trappers.

VI ENTER THE FRENCH,

WHILE trappers from Taos found their way to the Green and Colorado rivers in the fall of 1824, word of New Mexico's fur wealth continued to reach the Missouri settlements and excite the attention of experienced Missouri River traders.

In November, 1824, Augustus Storrs reported to Senator Thomas Hart Benton of Missouri that the furs on the return caravan from Santa Fe, of which he had been a member, valued some $10,044. This, Storrs later admitted, was only a small part of the profits taken from New Mexico in 1824, because the figure did not account for three other companies operating there that year.[1] The same month that Storrs made his report to Benton, Jean Pierre Cabanné of Bernard Pratte and Company learned that a Mr. Anderson, doubtless Paul or William, and a man named Hubert, had recently brought thirty packs of beaver back from Santa Fe.[2] A few months later, in January, 1825, the *Missouri Advocate* of St.

[1] Storrs, "Answers to Certain Queries," in *Santa Fé Trail First Reports: 1825*, 16; Storrs to Governor Antonio Narbona, Santa Fe, September 25, 1825, Doc. H/200(72:73)/1, L-E-55, Tomo I, Archivo de Relaciones Exteriores, Mexico, D. F.

[2] Cabanné to Pierre Chouteau, Establishment at the Bluffs, November 8, 1824, Chouteau Collection. Portions of this document are translated in Morgan, *Ashley*, 99. In Morgan's translation Cabanné says that the Santa Fe traders returned with "50 packs." The original document, however, seems to indicate a return of "50 percent."

1824–1825

Charles reported that "north of Santa Fe the country is said to abound with beaver and several Missourians have returned richly rewarded for the labor."[3]

Beaver from New Mexico found anxious buyers in 1824. In late October, William B. Astor, president *pro tem* of the New York–based American Fur Company, learned of the arrival at St. Louis of "some persons with Beaver" from Santa Fe. Immediately, Astor wrote to his St. Louis agent, Oliver N. Bostwick, "If it is as I presume Rocky Mountain buy it by all means, for the article is in demand and will pay well."[4] Astor seems to have used the term "Rocky Mountain" beaver synonymously with "drab" or light-colored beaver which was very much in demand that season. Apparently most of the beaver in the southern Rockies had what Ramsay Crooks called "pale fur," and the demand for this color vacillated with the whims of fashion.[5]

Buyers other than Astor also had their eyes on the beaver from New Mexico. Oliver Bostwick was soon reprimanded by Astor, who wrote:

[3] Quoted in Kenneth L. Homes, *Ewing Young: Master Trapper*, 20–21.

[4] Astor to Bostwick, New York, October 30, 1824, Chouteau Collection.

[5] Astor to Bostwick, New York, November 11, 1824, and Ramsay Crooks to Pierre Chouteau, Jr., New York, February 23, 1841, both in Chouteau Collection.

I regret you allowed our opponents to get into their hands the 1500 [pounds of] Beaver from New Mexico—the connection between them and the owners of the Beaver may have given them a preference over you; but I do hope, and shall be glad to hear, that you exerted yourself to effect the purchase, and only failed because it was impossible to succeed—[6]

Among those with a reported interest in Santa Fe beaver was William Ashley, whose efforts to ascend the Missouri had been frustrated in the previous year by the Arikaras. Rumor in the fall of 1824 had it that Ashley would soon start for New Mexico. J. P. Cabanné remarked, "I would be quite surprised if he did not go to Taos, to try obtaining the right, perhaps exclusive, to hunt," and James Kennerly, the sutler at Fort Atkinson, noted, "Genl Ashly passed this place some 20 or 30 days ago, with a party of men for the spanish country and I believe for the purpose of Traping and hunting near the mountains."[7]

Ashley, as we have seen, managed to reach the new source of fur wealth by a more northerly route, avoiding New Mexico settlements entirely, but the interest of Bernard Pratte and Company in Santa Fe transcended mere rumor. Known as the "French Company," Pratte and his partners had been one of the principal trading firms on the Missouri River since 1821. By 1824, crusty, fifty-year-old Jean Pierre Cabanné, one of the partners in the firm, was looking toward Santa Fe, eager to secure "an arrangement" with Provost, Leclerc, or James Baird, apparently for sending out a party of trappers.[8] But in its ventures into New Mexico, Bernard Pratte and Company were one step behind its own employee, Joseph Robidoux, and his ubiquitous brothers.

The brothers Robidoux—Joseph III, François, Isidore, Antoine, Louis, and Michel—had been born to the fur trade on the Missouri

[6] Astor to Bostwick, New York, November 11, 1824, Chouteau Collection.

[7] Cabanné to P. Chouteau, November 8, 1824, in Morgan, *Ashley*, 99 (original in Chouteau Collection); Kennerly to P. Chouteau, Jr., at Philadelphia, Fort Atkinson, December 1, 1824, quoted in Morgan, *Ashley*, 99 (original in Chouteau Collection).

[8] Cabanné to Pierre Chouteau, Establishment at the Bluffs, November 8, 1824, Chouteau Collection; portions translated in Morgan, *Ashley*, 99.

River. When their father, Joseph II, died in 1809, the family business continued under the leadership of the eldest brother, Joseph III, as an *ad hoc* organization.[9] By 1822, Joseph Robidoux was in the employ of the French Company as a factor at the Oto post, near Fort Atkinson. He remained with Pratte and Company into the period under consideration, when employer and employee rivaled one another for a share of the New Mexico fur trade. Clearly, as one scholar has commented, "the comings and goings of 'Robidoux' parties during the 1820's and 1830's are perplexing,"[10] and perhaps they always will be.

Although it has been suggested that Joseph Robidoux sent trade goods to Santa Fe as early as 1822,[11] solid evidence of this is unavailable. That Joseph Robidoux sent a party to New Mexico in 1823 seems more likely. If so, Louis Robidoux probably led this group, for in December, 1825, he swore under oath that he had been living in Taos for the previous two years.[12]

By the early fall of 1824, it will be remembered, Antoine Robidoux had found his way to the Green River from a New Mexico base. But he was not the only member of the family to reach northern Mexico that season. Even while Antoine was traveling toward the Colorado Basin, his brother Joseph had launched another expedition to Santa Fe. This included two more of the brothers, François and Isidore, nine other "traders to Mexico," and Manuel Alvarez, a Spaniard who migrated to the United States by way of Cuba and who would soon become an important figure in the fur trade of the Southwest.[13]

Although still employed by Bernard Pratte and Company, Joseph

[9] See Wallace, *Antoine Robidoux*, 4-7. A seventh brother died in infancy.

[10] Morgan, *Ashley*, 154, 243, n. 157.

[11] *Ibid.*, 154. Orral M. Robidoux, *Memorial to the Robidoux Brothers*, 168-69.

[12] David J. Weber, "Louis Robidoux," in Hafen, *Mountain Men*, VIII.

[13] Letter of introduction from the Governor of Missouri, Alexander McNair, September 3, 1824, in Manuel Alvarez, petition for naturalization and other documents, New Mexico Land Grant Papers, Microfilm (University of New Mexico Library, Albuquerque), Reel 6, No. 1132. Also included were: Antonio LaMarche, José Martin, Joseph Gervais, Astasio (Anastasio?) Lasalle, Charles Hotte, François Laroque, François Quenelle, Joseph Decary, and Antoine Baucheam.

Robidoux had privately equipped this trading party, purchasing some of his merchandise from the Company. Irascible J. P. Cabanné was particularly vexed. Robidoux had reached Cabanné's post near Council Bluffs on September 14, "full of ardor, and interested only with his trip to the mountains," and had raided Cabanné's warehouse to equip his twelve traders. "What an annoyance! I want to oppose his trip by trying to tell him how indelicate his conduct is, and even blamable, in wanting to appropriate to himself a branch of the business which we are certainly not going to give up."[14] Cabanné did just that. Joseph Robidoux complained to Pierre Chouteau, Jr., another partner in Bernard Pratte and Company, that "Cabanné reproached me for hunting two hares at the same time, by taking away from you this business branch—because I was your employee." As Joseph Robidoux told it, Cabanné had first showed "repugnance" for his ventures into New Mexico. Only when the Robidouxs had succeeded did Cabanné become interested. "Well," Robidoux told Chouteau, "I flatter myself to be in a position to tell you that it is not my fault if you do not own the whole. It's your turn to say your 'mea culpa'."[15] There is no evidence that either Chouteau or Cabanné asked Robidoux's forgiveness. Cabanné, too short of manpower to send a competing party to New Mexico and aware that the furs would be gone by the time he raised a party, did the best he could—he bought a one-third interest in Robidoux's party.[16]

The bickering and bargaining ended, François and Isidore Robidoux, Manuel Alvarez, and the others set out from Council Bluffs. The post sutler, James Kennerly, noted in his diary of September 30, "Robidoux party started for St. Afee to day."[17] François Robi-

[14] Cabanné to Pierre Chouteau, Jr., Establishment at the Bluffs, October 11, 1824, Chouteau Collection.

[15] Joseph Robidoux to Pierre Chouteau, Jr., March 15, 1825, Chouteau Collection. Portions of this document are translated in Morgan, *Ashley*, 154. Joseph mentions the return of Michel Robidoux with thirty packs of beaver, from Santa Fe. There is no record of his entrance into New Mexico at this time, but this furnishes another example of the mysterious and wide-ranging activities of the Robidouxs.

[16] Cabanné to Chouteau, October 11, 1824, Chouteau Collection.

doux, presumably accompanied by the remainder of the trading party, arrived in Taos, on this his first visit, on November 25.[18] There the alcalde, for reasons not yet clear, confiscated his merchandise. In March, 1825, Governor Bartolomé Baca ordered it returned and instructed the alcalde that Robidoux was prohibited to trade arms with the Indians, but he and any other Americans were not to be detained if they wished to trade legitimate goods with the Indians, or if they wished to trap beaver in the rivers of the Territory of New Mexico.[19] Thus, it was probably at this time that, in the name of the tariff collector, Juan Bautista Vigil, Robidoux received the trapping license from Governor Baca which is mentioned in later documents.[20]

François Robidoux may have had a group trapping during this winter of 1824–25, even though he had not yet received official permission. At least the furs of the area had not escaped his attention. In the spring of 1825, his brother Joseph, still on the Missouri, remarked: "You have the letter that Francois, my brother wrote to us. I don't believe he makes any mistake as to the beaver over there."[21]

François Robidoux saw more than beaver in New Mexico, and through his eyes we see that Taos was even then enjoying the "civilizing influence" of the mountain men. In a letter to the alcalde of Taos, he complained of a "slanderous acusation" which was sent to

[17] Wesley (ed.), "Diary of James Kennerly, 1823–26," *MHSC*, Vol. VI, No. 1 (October, 1928), 75. Wesley identifies this as a party led by Antoine Robidoux. Other historians have agreed with him. See, for example, Joseph J. Hill, "Antoine Robidoux, Kingpin in the Colorado River Fur Trade," *Colorado Magazine*, Vol. VII, No. 4 (July, 1930), 126; Wallace, *Antoine Robidoux*, 10. This seems unlikely from the documentation now at hand and, if William Huddart's account may be relied on, he met Antoine Robidoux on the Green River at the very time he is alleged to have been leaving the Bluffs.
[18] Testimony of Francisco Robidoux, December 9, 1825, MANM; Francisco Robidoux to the Alcalde of Taos, January 14, 1825, Ritch Papers, No. 82.
[19] Baca to the Alcalde of Taos, March 3, 1825, MANM.
[20] *Borrador* (rough draft) of a letter written by Agustín Durán, March 1, 1827, MANM. This license was granted sometime before Baca ceased to be governor in September of 1825.
[21] Joseph Robidoux to Pierre Chouteau, Jr., Council Bluffs, March 15, 1825, quoted and translated in Morgan, *Ashley*, 154 (original in Chouteau Collection).

the government of the territory and which reflected on "the good reputation of the residents of this plaza and on that of the foreign inhabitants of it." He protested:

> During my stay in this plaza since the 25th of November until today, there has not been committed, on the part of my people or myself, any disorder, scandal nor any controversy with these honorable neighbors. Moreover, my people, as well as myself, in our business dealings and community and political relationships, have always exhibited the greatest harmony and brotherhood. . . . We have always respected the laws, and the authorities, and the well established customs.

One suspects that François protested too much. Nevertheless, he had good reason to concern himself with these community affairs, for by the spring of 1825 Taos was fast becoming his home. There, on January 30 of the following year, Luisa Romero would bear him a daughter.[22]

When Antoine Robidoux returned from the Green River in the spring of 1825, he very likely encountered his two brothers at Taos. Then Antoine and Isidore apparently returned to Missouri, where their names, as well as that of Michel Robidoux, appear on a passport of June 29, 1825, allowing them to travel through Indian country back to the "Republic of New Mexico."[23]

Although this passport bore a June 29 date, they waited until fall to make the tedious trip. Again they traveled by way of Council Bluffs, doubtless to report in to brother Joseph and pick up trade goods. While at the Bluffs, another member of the family returned from New Mexico, for on August 30 James Kennerly recorded the arrival of "Robideaus party from Tous." The new arrivals, probably led by François, brought back furs which were turned over to Joseph Robidoux and shipped down the river to St. Louis (after Cabanné took his share of one third). On September 14, after a two-week respite, four of the brothers, Antoine,

---

[22] F. Robidoux, January 14, 1825, Ritch Papers, No. 82, Chávez, "New Names," *El Palacio*, Vol. LXIV, Nos. 11–12 (November-December, 1957), 373.

[23] Permit signed by William Clark, Superintendent of Indian Affairs, June 29, 1825, Ritch Papers, No. 83.

François, Michel, and Louis, started again for Taos, arriving in early November.[24]

The enterprises of Joseph Robidoux and his brothers in New Mexico did not go unnoticed by Bernard Pratte and Company. Yet, in order to minimize Robidoux's effectiveness as a competitor, they kept him in their employ. From Cabanné's point of view, this strategy had clearly failed. In the spring of 1825, he complained to Pierre Chouteau, Jr.,

> I ask you in the name of the friendship that is between us, no more Robidoux! This man will bring about our ruin! His competition is no more to be feared than any other's; disabuse yourself, my friend, it is buying him at too high a price.[25]

Nevertheless, the relationship continued.

Bernard Pratte and Company, however, had not abandoned the New Mexico trade to Robidoux. In the fall of 1824, apparently unknown to his partner Cabanné, General Pratte had equipped a small party to capture some of the furs of New Mexico. Although the leader of this venture, Ceran St. Vrain, was only twenty-two years old, he enjoyed a position of considerable trust, for he had lived, since his mid-teens, in the general's household.[26] From December, 1822, until October, 1824, St. Vrain had worked for B. Pratte and Company, drawing twenty dollars a month. In autumn, 1824, he formed a partnership with François Guerin, in which B. Pratte and Company owned one-third of the stock.[27]

St. Vrain's small party did not leave St. Louis until November.

[24] Wesley, "Diary of James Kennerly," *MHSC*, Vol. VI, No. 1 (October, 1928), 78–80. A notation in the "Account which shows the transfer of the funds of the Public Treasury . . . . On January 12, 1826," MANM, mentions that the four "Americanos Rovidour" had paid customs duties the previous fall. The four brothers were identified by Governor Narbona, in a report of February 1, 1826, as Francisco, Miguel, Antonio, and Luis "Ribidu." See Weber, *Extranjeros*, 22.

[25] J. P. Cabanné to Pierre Chouteau, Jr., at St. Louis, Council Bluffs, April 28, 1825 (translation with original document), Chouteau Collection.

[26] Harold H. Dunham, "Ceran St. Vrain," in Hafen, *Mountain Men*, V, 298.

[27] St. Vrain's account in Book D and Book M of Pratte and Company, Chouteau Collection, a copy of which was graciously furnished to me by Janet Lecompte of Colorado Springs.

Winter probably caught them on the trail, although they might have lingered deliberately on the Arkansas to trap. In either case, their arrival in New Mexico was not noted until late March, when Tomás Sena, the alcalde at San Miguel del Vado, a small town on the Santa Fe Trail near Santa Fe, informed Governor Baca that two Frenchmen and three Americans had arrived there; their trip to the capital would be delayed because their livestock had been stolen. Three days later, Sena informed the governor that two of the Americans had gone to trap, while the remaining two Frenchmen and one American continued on to Santa Fe.[28] Baca immediately responded, ordering that the American and two Frenchmen were not to sell any of their merchandise until they had reported to Santa Fe and paid the customs duties. Nor were the others to be allowed to hunt beaver. Baca explained to Sena that an order to that effect had been received from the Mexican federal government and had been circulated among the alcaldes, but had somehow been lost. He instructed Sena to prevent the foreigners from trapping.[29] St. Vrain eventually found his way to Taos, where he and Guerin hoped to sell their merchandise to trappers, but business was slow. St. Vrain discharged one of his employees named "Lafleche," sending him back to St. Louis with twenty-five beaver skins which Bernard Pratte bought for three dollars apiece. Then Guerin sold his share of the partnership to St. Vrain "for reasons two teajus to mention." On his return to St. Louis, Guerin carried a letter for Pratte from St. Vrain which explained that he was remaining in Taos: "We have Sold but verry fue goods and goods is at a verry reduced price at present, I am in hopes that when the hunters come in from there hunt that I well Sell out to Provoe and Leclere."[30] But Provost seems to have sold at least part of his furs to William Ashley and to have obtained supplies at the July rendezvous far to the north. St. Vrain was forced to seek his fortune elsewhere. In July he wrote to his mother,

[28] Tomás Sena to Baca, March 21, 1825, and Sena to Baca, March 24, 1825, MANM.
[29] Baca to Sena, March 25, 1825, MANM.
[30] St. Vrain's Account, Book M of Pratte and Company, Chouteau Collection; Ceran St. Vrain to Bernard Pratte, April 27, 1824 [1825], Chouteau Collection.

I have equipt Sum men to goe traping, thinking that it will be the moste proffatable for me, I have Sold the greater part of my goods [at] a verry good profite if I am fortunate enought to be paid, the men that I have Equipt is all the best Knihed [kind] of hunters, if they make a good hunt, I will doe verey good business.[31]

The trappers whom St. Vrain staked in the summer of 1825 may have been a group which included Peg-leg Smith. Indeed, Smith later remembered that "St. Vrain of St. Louis, a merchant of Taos," had outfitted him and nine others "to trap the St. Juan, Dolores, St. Miguel and other tributaries of Grand river."[32]

After outfitting Smith, or perhaps some other party, St. Vrain himself gave trapping a try. Sometime in the fall of 1825, he led a party of "18 or 20" men to the area of Utah Lake. It must have been a long winter, for the group did not return until early July of the following year. This hunt was apparently outfitted by Pratte and Company's newest representative in New Mexico, Sylvestre Pratte.[33]

By themselves, St. Vrain's small-scale operations in New Mexico would do little credit to Bernard Pratte's powerful company. Jean Pierre Cabanné, eager to launch a more significant expedition into northern Mexico, made plans for a larger party to leave for Santa Fe in the spring of 1825. Selected to lead this group was Sylvestre S. Pratte, the eldest son of the general. Born in St. Louis in 1799, Sylvestre Pratte had been employed by his father's company on the Missouri River at least as early as 1820. When Joseph Robidoux beat Cabanné to New Mexico in the fall of 1824, Sylvestre Pratte

[31] Ceran St. Vrain to his mother, Taos, July, 1825, Chouteau Collection. Michel S. Cerré probably carried this letter, Morgan, *Ashley*, 281.

[32] Smith's perplexing accounts reveal little else about the trapping activities of these men. See "Sketches from the Life of Peg-leg Smith," *HICM*, Vol. V, No. 7 (January, 1861), 319.

[33] S. S. Pratte, testimony in the case involving the seizure of his furs, November 30, 1826, MANM. St. Vrain is widely believed to have returned to the United States by the spring of 1826 (see, for example, Dunham, "Ceran St. Vrain," in Hafen, *Mountain Men*, 300–301), but there is no primary evidence to support this contention.

was responsible in part for Cabanné's shortage of manpower, for, believing "that the mountains would remain exclusively Robidoux's and that the company did not desire to send there anymore," Pratte had taken a number of *engagés* with him to trap and winter on the James River. Thus, instead of competing with Joseph Robidoux, Cabanné had been forced to buy a one-third interest in his venture. Certainly this episode contributed to Cabanné's future disenchantment with Sylvestre Pratte.

Cabanné grew restless as his spring departure date for the Santa Fe party was delayed. On June 5 he wrote to Pierre Chouteau, Jr., at St. Louis, "If Pratte or Papin have not already left, hasten their departure; I have several engagés here; not only do they cause me a great deal of trouble and increase expenses, but they may very well become impatient waiting."[34] On July 26, Pratte finally reached Council Bluffs, and Cabanné lamented: "The expedition for the Mountains, if it had left 1 ½ months ago, as it should, would probably have good results and what I said about 80 packs will make me seem an overexcited mind. . . . I will not think of the Mountains again." Probably angered at Pratte for the delay, Cabanné now charged that Pratte's performance on the James River during the previous season had not been satisfactory. He asked Pierre Chouteau, Jr., "How can a young man who seems to be guided by a sense of good have so little success in what he undertakes?"[35] Cabanné repeated these sentiments two months later and predicted that, with Sylvestre Pratte as its leader, "the expedition to the Mountains will undoubtedly be unsuccessful." Bernard Pratte was, he thought, "much to be pitied, for having children who, by their incapability, show themselves so little worthy of him."[36] Cabanné's gloomy predictions of failure would prove to be true.

Pratte's delay in leaving had one unexpected advantage that would not be appreciated for another generation. It enabled the young Kentuckian, James Ohio Pattie, to join the expedition and

[34] David J. Weber, "Sylvestre S. Pratte," in Hafen, *Mountain Men*, VI, 359–61.
[35] Cabanné to Pierre Chouteau, Jr., "Near the Bluffs," July 27, 1825, Chouteau Collection.
[36] Cabanné to Chouteau, September 16, 1825, Chouteau Collection.

record some of its adventures in his famous and controversial *Narrative*.[37] Pattie and his father, Sylvester, both bereaved at the loss of James Ohio's mother, had left their farm and large family behind to travel to St. Louis and outfit themselves for a trapping and trading venture on the Missouri River. They were forbidden to proceed upriver beyond Council Bluffs, however, for they had no license to enter into the Indian trade. So, when they stopped at Cabanné's post and learned of Pratte's plans, they decided to accompany him to New Mexico.

Finally, on July 30, Pratte left the Council Bluffs area with 116 men (according to Pattie). But they did not reach Taos until October 26, only a few days before the Robidoux brothers, for Pratte paused on the way to trade buffalo robes with Pawnees and beaver and deerskins with Utes on the Arkansas.[38]

Interestingly, both Pratte and the Robidoux brothers made Taos their first stop and never took their merchandise into Santa Fe. This seems to have been the pattern for those who used the Taos Trail to enter New Mexico. Although the border guard, Rafael Luna, and the Taos alcalde, Severino Martínez, were empowered to intercept Americans and examine their invoices and merchandise, it seems to have been customary at this time to send to Santa Fe for the customs collector to come to Taos for the final assessment. The traders were reluctant to carry their goods on to Santa Fe if they did not intend to market them there because, as they complained, the road was too rough.[39] Sylvestre Pratte, although a novice in New Mexico, relied on the common expedient of burying some of his goods on the eastern side of the Taos mountains before

37 James Ohio Pattie, *The Personal Narrative of James O. Pattie* (ed. by Timothy Flint) was first published in 1831. Pattie's accuracy, especially his chronology, has often been impugned by historians. Only recently did Dale Morgan discover conclusive evidence that Pattie left Council Bluffs in 1825 instead of 1824, the date given in the *Narrative*. Morgan, *Ashley*, 206, n. 337.

38 Pattie, *Narrative*, 11–38. Pattie's dates are corroborated by Kennerly's diary, which mentions the arrival of "young Pratte" at Cabanné's post on July 26, in Sibley, *Road to Santa Fe*, 114.

39 Juan Bautista Vigil, instructions to Rafael Luna and Severino Martínez, Santa Fe, April 20, 1825, MANM; testimony of James Baird in the case involving the embargo of the merchandise of Francisco Robidoux, December 9, 1825, MANM.

entering the settlement to avoid paying duty.[40] The Robidouxs, when they arrived, probably did the same thing. Pratte then journeyed to Santa Fe to hire the services of the tariff collector, Juan Bautista Vigil y Alarid, apparently taking James Baird along to act as an interpreter. Vigil took some time reaching Taos, where one contemporary recorded in his diary on November 8 that Vigil "has been expected every day for a Week past." He finally arrived at Taos on November 12.[41]

Pratte's merchandise entered New Mexico with no apparent difficulty, while the more experienced François Robidoux had his goods promptly confiscated by Juan Bautista Vigil, for they lacked the proper *factura* or invoice. François—Francisco to the Mexicans —told Vigil that his brother Michel would be along in two hours with the proper papers, but Vigil returned to Santa Fe and left Robidoux's goods under lock and key at the house of Alcalde Martínez. François Robidoux and Manuel Alvarez, then an employee of Robidoux, proceeded to Santa Fe, reportedly to petition the governor for the release of the goods. Instead, as Alvarez told it, they found themselves at Vigil's house where the payment of a one hundred-peso debt secured the immediate release of the merchandise. That this was a debt, rather than a direct bribe, seems clear from the documentation, for even François Robidoux admitted to this. Perhaps the one hundred pesos represented a fee which Robidoux had neglected to pay to Vigil in return for Vigil's securing a trapping license for Robidoux the previous spring, or perhaps it represented a share of Robidoux's trapping proceeds. Whatever the particulars, Vigil had used his power as a public official to settle a private matter. For this, and other indiscretions, he soon lost his job as tariff collector[42] but continued to hold public offices on and off for the next twenty years. When Stephen Watts Kearny led American troops into Santa Fe in 1846, Juan Bautista

[40] Pattie, *Narrative*, 38.

[41] Sibley, *Road to Santa Fe*, 114; testimony of James Baird in the case involving the embargo of the merchandise of Francisco Robidoux, December 9, 1825, MANM.

[42] Case concerning the embargo of merchandise of Francisco Robidoux, December 9, 1825, MANM; report of legislative committee to Narbona, January 11, 1826, MANM.

Vigil, as lieutenant governor of New Mexico, took the place of the fleeing Governor Manuel Armijo, and welcomed the conquerors with an impassioned speech.

Unlike François Robidoux, Sylvestre Pratte found Vigil to be a most obliging official and through him obtained from Governor Antonio Narbona a license to trap. Pratte dispatched at least three different trapping parties that winter. Twelve or thirteen men, he later reported, trapped on the headwaters of the Río Grande. Ceran St. Vrain led eighteen or twenty men to the area of Utah Lake, and still another group, whose destination is not clear, left in February and would not return to Taos until November. Pratte and François Robidoux themselves may have led a group into the mountains which returned in May, 1826.[43]

James Ohio Pattie and his father had considerably more difficulty than Pratte in obtaining a trapping license in the fall until a characteristically dramatic event intervened to help them. As Pattie tells it, Governor Narbona delayed answering their first request for a trapping license because he "did not know if he was allowed by law" to grant the license. Pattie's recollection seems quite plausible, for Narbona had just assumed office. When Pattie returned to see Narbona the following day, the governor had decided that issuing a license to trap beaver would be illegal, but an offer to pay him five per cent on any beaver caught, according to Pattie, kept the matter open for further consideration. While these negotiations were taking place, Pattie and his father, along with several of Pratte's men, effected a daring rescue of the daughter of a former New Mexico governor from Comanches. A license was forthcoming—or so the story goes.[44] It is just as likely, however, that this never occurred and that Pattie and his father trapped under the protection of Sylvestre S. Pratte's license. Theirs may have been one of the groups which Pratte outfitted that winter.

Regardless of the source of their license, James and Sylvester Pattie, along with two others who had accompanied them from

---

[43] Papers relating to the embargo of S. S. Pratte's furs, November 12, 1826, MANM.

[44] Pattie, *Narrative*, 40–46.

Missouri and three of Sylvestre Pratte's men, started south along the Río Grande in late November. Of these seven trappers, four remain nameless. Pattie refers to one member of the party as Allen. This might be José Manuel (Hiram?) Allen, a Canadian who was baptized later at Taos in 1828, when he was thirty-one years old, then became a Mexican citizen in 1830.[45] The Patties, "Allen," and their four companions were joined on the Río Grande by "seven hunters," and the enlarged group continued south. At a point four days' journey below Socorro, they struck out to the west for Santa Rita del Cobre (the Santa Rita copper mines), a place where Spaniards had been mining since the turn of the century. Here they hired two Mexican servants, probably as guides, and continued on to the Gila River. Beaver were plentiful; the traps yielded thirty beaver after the first night on the river. Their fortunes changed, however, when the seven who had joined the Patties on the Río Grande abandoned the party. The deserters trapped ahead on the Gila, leaving few beaver in their wake and forcing the Patties to travel north up the San Francisco River, a tributary of the Gila. Two weeks on the San Francisco yielded, according to Pattie, two hundred and fifty beaver. They returned to the Gila, cached their furs, and continued downstream hoping to find another beaver-laden tributary. The seven deserters, in the meantime, had been attacked by Indians and one of the party killed. The remaining six, aided by the forgiving Patties, eagerly returned to the copper mines. The Patties continued down the Gila to the San Pedro River, upon which their good fortune inspired them to bestow the name of "Beaver River." They were back at the Santa Rita mines by the end of April, 1826, and James Pattie set out for Santa Fe for supplies and horses to enable them to retrieve the beaver they had cached. By the time that Pattie and a party of fifteen, including four Americans, got back to the "Beaver River" where the main cache was located, the fur was

45 *Ibid.*, 46, 56; Chávez, "New Names," *El Palacio*, Vol. LXIV, Nos. 9–10 (September–October, 1957), 293; George C. Yount, *George C. Yount and His Chronicles of the West* (ed. by Charles L. Camp), 254, n. 18, suggests that this might be Hiram Allen, a former Ashley man. Perhaps Hiram and José Manuel were the same man.

gone. They recovered a "small quantity" buried at the San Francisco River, and returned to the copper mines in July, apparently poorer than when they had started.[46]

Despite their initial failure, Pattie and his father remained in New Mexico and continued to trap. So did many of the Frenchmen who came into the Southwest with the Robidoux brothers or Pratte. Men like Gervais Nolan, Jean Baptiste Trudeau, Anastasio Cariel, Jean Vaillant, Carlos Beaubien, Joseph Bissonette, and Antoine Leroux swore at a later date that they had first come to New Mexico in 1824.[47] Most of these Frenchmen settled quietly at Taos and elude mention in the documents of this period, but some of their number probably accompanied each of the expeditions from New Mexico that we are able to chronicle. When, in 1853, Antoine Leroux testified that he had "trapped the whole country, every river, every creek, and branch from the Gila to the head of the Grand River fork,"[48] his exaggeration was probably slight.

[46] Pattie, *Narrative*, 46–68.

[47] These men became citizens of New Mexico at a later date. In their applications for citizenship, they named the year in which they first entered New Mexico. These applications are cited in Chapter 9. Beaubien seems to indicate that he came to New Mexico in 1823, but a passport from William Clark for Beaubien and others to pass into Indian country by way of Council Bluffs is dated December 29, 1823, in Ritch Papers, No. 79.

[48] Statement of Antoine Leroux to Senator Thomas H. Benton, 1853, in Grant Foreman, "Antoine Leroux, New Mexico Guide," *New Mexico Historical Review*, Vol. XVI, No. 4 (October, 1941), 371. A recent biography is Forbes Parkhill, *The Blazed Trail of Antoine Leroux*.

VII OPPOSITION FORMS,

As a MARKET for merchandise, Santa Fe had been saturated by 1824, as many Missourians well knew. As early as January 25, 1825, the *Missouri Intelligencer* at Franklin lamented, "It appears that the prospect held out to future adventurers to that country, is very gloomy." On June 4, 1825, the *Intelligencer* published a letter written in El Paso in September, 1824, by a Missourian who announced, "This trade is done, as all will inform you." In the fall, a letter dated Santa Fe, August 25, 1825, appeared in the *Intelligencer* of November 4, reporting, "Every village is crowded with goods. . . . The little cash that was in the country has been expended."

Despite such pessimistic pronouncements, American adventurers continued to pour into Santa Fe. Some, such as George Yount, who arrived in 1826, hoped to become wealthy as "respectable" traders. But tight money in Santa Fe and an abundance of merchandise forced many out of the mercantile business and, like Yount, some were "induced to join a band of free trappers."[1]

Spring of 1825 saw the "commerce of the prairies" increase in both size and importance. Many of those who crossed the trail hoped to carry goods deep into Mexico, along the Chihuahua Trail. Others, clearly, came to trap and trade for furs—a business which

[1] Yount, *Yount and His Chronicles*, 25–27.

did not depend upon available currency. Josiah Gregg, who wrote
the classic account of the trade, records that the value of merchandise carried over the trail in 1825 almost doubled that of 1824.[2]
Returning to New Mexico with the annual caravans in 1825 were
such veteran trappers and traders as Ewing Young and William
Anderson, along with newcomers who would soon weave their
adventures into the fabric of western history—men like Mathew
Kinkead, Richard Campbell, Paul Baillio, Michel S. Cerré, William
Workman, Elisha Stanley, and Ira A. Emmons.[3]

The Santa Fe trade showed no signs of diminishing in 1826.
On April 14, 1826, the *Intelligencer* announced the arrival of mules,
furs, and specie from New Mexico and noted that almost one
hundred persons, "including all those lately returned," were pre-
paring to start for New Mexico. "Some of this party," the paper
reported, intend "to penetrate to some of the more remote provinces and to be absent for several years."

Clearly, the entrance of the Robidoux brothers and Bernard
Pratte and Company into the Santa Fe fur trade did not deter

[2] Gregg, *Commerce of the Prairies*, 332. See Chittenden, *American Fur Trade*,
II, 508, n. 14, for an indication of the size of these parties.
[3] Elisha Stanley's presence in the caravan is indicated in a letter of May 16,
1825, in the (Franklin) *Missouri Intelligencer*, June 4, 1825. Names of the other
traders appear in Mexican custom house records in Weber, *Extranjeros*, 17.

independent trappers and traders from also entering the field. To the contrary, the burgeoning Santa Fe trade, which offered a safe market for furs and a source of supplies, coupled with the attractions of Taos, continued to lure trappers, or would-be trappers, into northern Mexico.

Perhaps most indicative of the growing importance of the Santa Fe trade was the passage of Senator Thomas Hart Benton's bill providing for the survey and marking of the trail. The three commissioners appointed to this task hired the experienced Stephen Cooper, one of Benjamin Cooper's nephews, as a guide. The Walker brothers, Joseph Reddeford and Joel, were also along, as were such new arrivals to Taos as George West, Andrew Carson (half-brother to Kit), and William S. Williams, not yet celebrated as "Old Bill." The commissioners and their entourage left the Missouri settlements in late June, 1825, and worked their way to the Arkansas, finally reaching the Mexican border at the one hundredth meridian by mid-September. There they found that the Mexican government had not yet granted permission to continue the survey in its territory. While the other two commissioners returned to Missouri, George C. Sibley and twelve others pushed on to Taos to await instructions. Both in New Mexico and on route there, Sibley faithfully made entries in a diary which provides an unusual glimpse at the fur trade in New Mexico.

On the way west, Sibley followed the tracks of "Nat" Pryor for awhile—the same Pryor who had tasted mountain life as a member of the Glenn-Fowler party of 1821–22, and who was now returning to New Mexico with three companions for another try at trapping.[4] Just before entering Mexican territory, Sibley recorded meeting "a large Caravan of our People just from Sta Fee. . . . They had about 300 head of Horses, Mules, Asses, &c & some Beaver Skins." In St. Louis, these beaver skins weighed in at 2,044 pounds and, selling at $5.00 a pound, brought their owners $10,220.[5]

[4] Sibley, *Road to Santa Fe*, 21, 22, 30–37, 70. For a biography of Pryor, see Raymond W. Settle, "Nathaniel Miguel Pryor," in Hafen, *Mountain Men*, II, 277–88.

On October 19, as his group drew nearer to the Sangre de Cristos, George Sibley sent a message ahead to Paul Baillio at Taos, requesting a guide and mules to carry his supplies across the mountains. Five days later, Baillio showed up in person. The two had known each other since their days as Indian traders in the government factory system. George Sibley had operated the factory at Fort Osage from 1808 to 1821, and in 1820 Baillio had been assigned to a nearby factory as a subordinate to Sibley.[6] With the demise of the factories in 1822, Sibley, Baillio, and Lilburn Boggs had formed a partnership and, buying up the government supplies at Fort Osage, continued to trade there.[7] The partnership endured and was renewed, minus Boggs, in Taos in 1826.[8] Baillio had been involved in the Santa Fe trade as early as 1824, for William Clark mentions that Indians robbed Baillio in that year on his return from Santa Fe. He returned to Santa Fe again, however, in April of 1825 with the trader and trapper, Richard Campbell.[9] Soon after his arrival, Baillio entered into a partnership with Ceran St. Vrain —a partnership which still existed in 1828.[10]

Paul Baillio and Bill Williams also enjoyed a long-standing acquaintance. Both had Osage wives and, like Baillio, Williams had seen service in the United States factory system. In 1823, he and Baillio had opened a trading post on the Neosho River, but their partnership had failed to last out the year.[11]

Sibley's survey party had been in Taos a scant two weeks when

[5] Sibley, *Road to Santa Fe*, 85; (St. Louis) *Missouri Republican*, October 24, 1825.

[6] Sibley, *Road to Santa Fe*, 9; Thomas L. McKenney, Indian Trade Office (Washington, D.C.) to Paul Baillio at Chickasaw Bluffs, December 9, 1820, Department of the Interior, Office of Indian Affairs, copy in the "Fur Trade Envelope," Missouri Historical Society.

[7] G. C. Sibley, Fort Osage, to A. Leonard, May 18, 1827, in Santa Fe Trail Papers, Abiel Leonard Collection, Western Historical Manuscript Collection, State Historical Society of Missouri, Columbia, Missouri.

[8] Sibley, *Road to Santa Fe*, 149.

[9] Report of William Clark, Superintendent of Indian Affairs, to Lewis Cass, St. Louis, November 20, 1831, U.S. 22 Cong., 1 sess., *Sen. Doc. 90* (Ser. 213), 83; Weber, *Extranjeros*, 17.

[10] Dunham, "Ceran St. Vrain," in Hafen, *Mountain Men*, V, 299, and St. Vrain to Bernard Pratte, September 28, 1828, Chouteau Collection.

[11] Alpheus H. Favour, *Old Bill Williams, Mountain Man*, 63–64.

Williams, the party's interpreter, announced that he was going trapping. As Sibley remarked in his diary on November 14, "Wm. S. Williams having a desire to go Trapping, I consented to his doing So. . . . He started down the Rio del Norte." Although Williams planned to be gone until June, he returned to Taos in late February reporting "good Success." But he had already acquired one of the seemingly essential skills of the mountain man, which kept him from rejoining the survey party. Instead, as Sibley disapprovingly noted, Williams had "employed himself Gambling Since his Return from his Hunt."[12] Bill Williams's trapping operations in the years that followed are obscure, but he made the Southwest, and Taos in particular, his home. Albert Pike, who knew Williams in 1832, described him as the foremost "specimen of the genuine trapper." Williams, Pike said, was six-foot-one, "gaunt, and red-headed, with a hard, weather-beaten face, marked deeply with the small pox. He is all muscle and sinew, and the most indefatigable hunter and trapper in the world."[13]

Soon after Williams started down the Río Grande in the fall of 1825, another of Sibley's men decided to go trapping, but with less happy results. Joining a group under Ewing Young, youthful Benjamin Robinson "died of sickness before they got out of the settlements."[14] Ewing Young, whom we have seen among the vanguard of trappers in the Colorado Basin in the spring of 1824, had been on the trail almost constantly. In the spring of 1825, he was one of the first merchants to cross the Santa Fe Trail from St. Louis, arriving in April. He quickly sold his goods and, in May, started back to St. Louis with a herd of horses and mules, some of which Osage Indians reportedly robbed. Recrossing the trail in the fall, Young recruited a trapping party in Taos, Benjamin Robinson among them, and left for a brief hunt on November 27. He was back at Taos again on January 22, 1826, after what appears to have been a successful season.[15]

[12] Sibley, *Road to Santa Fe*, 132, 152, 155 (Williams may have started trapping on November 8, p. 114).
[13] Favour, *Old Bill Williams*, 75, 78, 88; Pike, *Prose Sketches*, 34-35.
[14] Sibley, *Road to Santa Fe*, 116, 132, 140.
[15] Holmes, *Ewing Young*, 21-24.

Sibley's men had ample time for trapping or for gambling, because they waited at Taos until June 14 before permission arrived from Mexico City for the survey of the Mexican portion of the trail to proceed.[16] The long wait was caused, in part, by Mexico's ambivalent attitude toward the growing Santa Fe trade. Officials at Mexico City had never welcomed commerce on the northern frontier, but in the confusion of the first years of Mexican independence the old restrictions of the Spanish colonial system were never enforced.[17] Beginning in 1824 the secretary of the treasury took measures to control the trade. In that year import duties were collected apparently for the first time at Santa Fe, and specific rules established for the issuance of *guías*, which Josiah Gregg defined as a "mercantile passport."[18] As foreigners continued to arrive in Mexico, the government took further steps to control their movements by issuing a circular on November 19, 1825, which required that every state and territory of the federation send a monthly statement of the number and whereabouts of all foreigners to the secretary of interior and foreign relations (secretario de relaciones interiores y exteriores).[19]

One of the more alarming reports of the growing importance of the Santa Fe trade reached Mexico City in 1825. Early that year the United States government published Augustus Storrs's description of the nature of the Santa Fe trade, including his report that considerable profits in bullion, mules, and furs were being taken back to Missouri.[20] The Mexican ambassador to Washington sent a copy of the document to his government almost immediately, and on March 28, 1825, the Mexican foreign office

[16] Sibley, *Road to Santa Fe*, 143.

[17] William R. Manning, *Early Diplomatic Relations Between the United States and Mexico*, 167.

[18] Weber, *Extranjeros*, 8; Circular, Secretaría de Hacienda, October 27, 1824, in Official Decrees and Circulars, Box 4 (1824), MANM.

[19] I have not been able to locate this circular, but find it mentioned in several documents: Governor Narbona to the legislature, December 29, 1825; Primer Secretario de Estado, Juan José Espinosa de los Monteros to Governor Narbona, March 1, 1826, both in MANM.

[20] Storrs, "Answers of Augustus Storrs to Certain Queries," in *Santa Fé Trail First Reports: 1825*, 1–45. A less satisfactory copy appears in Hulbert, *Turquoise Trail*, 77–100.

asked the governors of New Mexico and Chihuahua for their evaluation of Storrs's report. Antonio Narbona, who had just become governor of New Mexico, excused himself from making any comment, while the governor of Chihuahua expressed a view that was both sanguine and candid. Trade with the United States, he said, would help to civilize the New Mexicans, "giving them the ideas of culture which they need to improve the disgraceful condition that characterizes the remote country where they live, detached from other peoples of the Republic."[21] New Mexicans would not have put it quite so unkindly, but they too, since the arrival of William Becknell in 1821, had assumed that trade with Americans would benefit their territory.

Clearly, one aspect of the Santa Fe trade from which New Mexico officials had hoped to benefit was the nascent fur trade. Thus, governors Baca and Narbona had winked at the federal decree prohibiting foreigners from trapping and, during 1824 and 1825, had granted trapping licenses to William Becknell, Sylvestre Pratte, François Robidoux, and doubtless others as well. Even as they were doing this, however, national and local pressures were being exerted to enforce the law.

In January, 1826, Santiago Abreú, then serving as New Mexico's representative in Mexico City, penned a letter to the New Mexico deputation which urged the lawmakers to take action against foreigners. Abreú warned New Mexicans to be wary of Americans who "settle, buy land and even marry," without proper citizenship papers. He asked the deputation for a complete accounting of the activities of all non-Mexicans, "without ignoring the status of beaver trapping."[22] Abreú's worst fears must have been exceeded with the arrival at Mexico City of a report from Governor Narbona, dated September 18, 1825, that Americans had built a fort on the San Juan River, to the west of the New Mexico settlements. Although Narbona received immediate instructions to destroy the

[21] Governor José de Urquidi to the Minister of Foreign Relations, May 13, 1825, in Relaciones Exteriores, H[200(72:73)], L-E-55, Tomo I.

[22] Abreú to the New Mexico Deputation, January 18, 1826, Ritch Papers, No. 86.

"fort," there is no evidence that it existed.[23] Narbona had probably exaggerated the importance of a trapper's temporary encampment.

In New Mexico, in mid-April, 1826, the territorial deputation echoed Abreú's fears in a written complaint to Agustín Durán, the treasurer of the territory. Inspired, no doubt, by Abreú's letter, the deputation complained that "foreigners have continued to hunt beaver just as much as when they had the liberty to do so." The deputies urged that laws prohibiting foreign trapping be enforced. Agustín Durán forwarded this complaint to Governor Narbona on April 18, suggesting that the governor notify all alcaldes to be watchful for foreigners.[24]

Governor Narbona had apparently responded to the deputation's mood even before receiving its formal complaint. On April 12 he had warned the alcalde of San Miguel del Vado to be on the lookout for an American who was trying to return to his country with a large amount of beaver fur. Narbona told the alcalde that the American should surrender his license to trap and that this should be forwarded to Santa Fe. On April 14 the alcalde advised the governor that the American had been found on the eleventh of that month. Governor Narbona awaited the American's arrival in Santa Fe, but there is no further mention of this case in the documents.[25]

When some of their trappers returned from the mountains in May, François Robidoux and Sylvestre S. Pratte found themselves in the unhappy position of being among the first Americans to enter the hostile climate. On May 10, 1826, the alcalde of Taos informed Agustín Durán that, in compliance with orders, he had confiscated the beaver pelts of François Robidoux and Sylvestre S. Pratte. Robidoux had about 630 pounds (26 *arrobas*, 6 *libras*) of beaver fur, and Pratte had 1,885 pounds (75 *arrobas*, 10 *libras*). In his defense, Robidoux presented a license to the alcalde which had been issued

---

[23] Primer Secretario de Estado, Sección de Gobierno, to the governor of New Mexico, October 28, 1825, MANM.

[24] Durán's title was comisario sustituto. The duties of this office would seem to indicate that he was serving as treasurer. See Bloom, "New Mexico Under Mexican Administration," *Old Santa Fe*, Vol. I, No. 3 (January, 1914), 252. Durán to the Governor, April 18, 1826, MANM.

[25] Narbona to Durán, May 2, 1826, MANM.

to him in the name of Juan Bautista Vigil by Governor Baca, and Pratte produced a similar document from Governor Narbona. The alcalde suggested that Vigil's part in this matter be investigated and reported that the two owners of the embargoed fur were on their way to Santa Fe that day.[26]

When Pratte and Robidoux arrived in Santa Fe, they found that the deputation had revoked their permits to trap. Protesting to the governor, the two trappers argued with some justification that they had been treated unfairly and that some of their men had not yet returned and supposed themselves to be licensed. Apparently impressed by this argument, Narbona ordered Durán to return the furs of Robidoux and Pratte and extended protection to those who had departed on trapping expeditions before the licenses were revoked.[27]

Most of the trappers about whom Pratte and Robidoux professed concern had no apparent difficulty in getting their furs to market. Both St. Vrain's party from the Utah Lake area and a group of a dozen or so who had been on the headwaters of the Río Grande returned to New Mexico that summer without incident. A third group outfitted by Pratte was less fortunate. These men, who had trapped perhaps as far as the upper Colorado, returned to Taos on November 12. Notified of their arrival by the alcalde of Taos, José Antonio Martínez, Narbona ordered their furs confiscated "immediately" and the group's license sent to Santa Fe. If they had no license, Martínez was to send the entire group to Santa Fe.

Instead of complying with the governor's orders, Martínez wrote back on November 20 and asked to which furs the governor was referring, since in the previous May the governor had extended Pratte's now-rescinded license to include those trappers who had not yet returned. Narbona, who must have been in a rage, accused Martínez of insubordination and again ordered him to seize the furs. But, Martínez replied that he was still unable to carry out his orders. He explained that when he went to the house where the foreigners

[26] Agustín Durán to the Alcalde of Santa Fe, May 12, 1826, and borrador of Durán to unknown person, March 1, 1827, MANM.

[27] Borrador of Durán to unknown person, March 1, 1827, and Narbona to Durán, May 12, 1826, from copy made November 29, 1826, MANM.

kept the furs, he could not enter because the trappers who guarded the furs did not have the key. Martínez suggested that he should await the return of Pratte, who had the key, or if the governor desired, he would break into the house and take the furs. In addition he apologized for having questioned the governor in the first place. He had since discovered eight of Pratte's trappers and five of François Robidoux's guarding the furs, and he now realized that the governor had only given permission for three persons to continue trapping. Robidoux's men, he reported, had left their furs guarded in the "Indian County" (*naciones*) for want of animals to transport them back to Taos.

In the meantime, Pratte (with the key?) had hurried to Santa Fe to protest the attempted seizure on the grounds that his men had left in February before the license was rescinded. Beginning on November 30, hearings were held before the alcalde of Santa Fe, who questioned Pratte as to why he had maintained the previous spring that only three persons remained trapping when it now appeared that there were at least eight men. Pratte responded that he had never said *tres indivíduos* but merely *indivíduos*. Why, he asked, would he have said there were only three persons still trapping when he had several groups trapping? The alcalde was apparently convinced. On December 1 he ruled that since this group had left under the protection of a license, "it is very clear to see that Pratte's embargoed goods are free." But it was not clear to Governor Narbona. The next day he told Agustín Durán of his displeasure with the decision and refused to release the furs which, in the meantime, had been seized.

For his next gambit, Pratte obtained written declarations from five of Taos' most influential citizens, who testified that Pratte's men had left in February before his license was revoked. This, too, proved to be of no avail, for when Durán presented this evidence to Narbona in February, 1827, with the request that Pratte's furs be returned, the governor was still angered over what he referred to as the "malicious subterfuge" of Pratte, who had assured him that there were only three men still hunting. Narbona turned the case over to the central government for final judgment. The documents were apparently sent to Parral, where, as late as August, 1827, a decision had not yet been made.[28] Durán, who had sympathized with Pratte, remained highly critical of Narbona, urging him to return the furs and contending that Narbona had exceeded his authority by granting the license in the first place. The governor, Durán said, was now trying to correct his earlier error by upholding an unjust embargo.[29]

Some indication of the identity of the trappers who worked for Sylvestre Pratte and François Robidoux at this time is provided by Manuel Martínez in a remarkable report to Governor Narbona dated April, 1827. In March, 1827, according to Martínez, Robidoux had led a group from Taos to go "in the direction of the land of the Utes," to retrieve some "*entierros*," or buried items. Presumably, these were the cached furs which Robidoux's men had earlier reported leaving behind in "Indian Country." By explaining to the governor that Robidoux was going after "*entierros*," instead of furs, Alcalde Martínez revealed considerable discretion, if not candor. Traveling with Robidoux were men whose names Martínez rendered as follows: Dionicio Julián, Bautista Trudean, José Neuture, Manuel Gervais, Francisco Gervais, Antonio Blanchare, Antonio Leroux, Bautista Chalifon, Pablo Loise, Mauricio Ledue, Charles Chonteau, Jules Declovette, and a man named Metote.[30]

The majority of these Frenchmen probably made their homes in Taos. Antonio Blanchard ("Blanchare") had married there in July, 1826. "Metote" was apparently the fifty-eight-year-old "Francisco Mitote" who was to return to Taos in 1828 and marry María Josefa, a Flathead woman who had already presented him with four children during the eighteeen years they had been living together. In the fall of 1827, Metote would return to the Rockies with Sylvestre Pratte. Jules Declovette is evidently "Julio Decluet," a native of

[28] Papers pertaining to the seizure of S. S. Pratte's furs, November 12, 1826, MANM.

[29] Durán to Narbona, Santa Fe, February 16, 1827; Borrador from Durán to unknown person, March 1, 1827, MANM.

[30] Weber, *Extranjeros*, 38.

New Orleans, who received permission to marry at Taos in June, 1829.[31]

Jean Baptiste Chalifoux ("Chalifon") and his brother Pierre had trapped on the Gila in the fall of 1826, before joining Robidoux. Both settled in the valley of Taos for a while. "Pedro," whose life remains obscure, married in Taos in 1829. Jean Baptiste is better known since, among other things, he led a group of former trappers and Indians into California on a horse-thieving foray in 1837. In the 1840's he operated a trading post at Embudo. When George Frederick Ruxton passed through town in 1846, he stayed with Jean Baptiste Chalifoux, "an old Canadian trapper, who has taken to himself a Mexican wife and was ending his days as a quiet ranchero." In the 1850's, Chalifoux moved to the Arkansas Valley, finally building what was probably the first house at Trinidad, Colorado, in 1860.[32]

"Mauricio Ledue" is probably the same Maurice LeDuc who accompanied Peg-leg Smith on two earlier trapping expeditions. Two LeDucs, father and son, trapped in the West at this time. Maurice, the younger, lived until 1880 in southern Colorado and northern New Mexico, to become "old" Maurice, an irascible trapper and hunter almost to the end.[33] Jean Baptiste Trudeau, Antoine Leroux, and Denis Julien ("Dionicio Julián") probably also lived at Taos, for they continued to trap out of New Mexico in the next few years.

Like these trappers under François Robidoux, Sylvestre Pratte's men may also have cached some of their furs for in January, 1827, Pratte dispatched a group of trappers who, according to Manuel Martínez, were going "outside of the boundaries of the Mexican Federation." This group of twenty-two included Ceran St. Vrain,

31 Chávez, "New Names," *El Palacio*, Vol. LXIV, Nos. 9–12 (September–December, 1957), 297, 367, 303.
32 Strickland, "James Baird," in Hafen, *Mountain Men*, III, 34; Chávez, "New Names," *El Palacio*, Vol. LXIV, Nos. 9–10 (September–October, 1957), 300; Hafen and Hafen, *Old Spanish Trail*, 235; Charles Irving Jones, "William Kronig, New Mexico Pioneer, from His Memoirs of 1849–1860," *New Mexico Historical Review*, Vol. XIX, No. 3 (July, 1944), 199. A biography of J. B. Chalifoux by Janet Lecompte appears in Hafen, *Mountain Men*, VII, 57–74.
33 Janet Lecompte, "Maurice LeDuc," in Hafen, *Mountain Men*, VI, 227–40.

who was probably in charge; Luis Ambroise; Bautista Chauno; Juan (Jean) Vaillant; Manuel Lefaivre; (Charles) Beaubien; (Hugh?) Glas; S. Desporte; F. Braie; G. Olivier; Pled Riche; Sénecal; Duchaine; Vertefeville and son; Livernois; (François) Laforest; Lafargue; Brown; (Baptiste) St. Germain; Simon Clert; and Jurome.[34] Like Robidoux's trappers, many of these Frenchmen also resided in Taos. Manuel Lefevre, for example, had been married there only a month before they left, and Charles Beaubien would marry there in the fall.[35] Baptiste St. Germain, who may be the same St. Germain who was trading illegally with Indians in Iowa in 1818, had married at Taos in 1824 and continued to live there at least through 1841.[36]

Most of these men remain obscure, but as their stories unfold they will doubtless shed light on more than their own careers. The origin of the name of the Duchesne River in northwestern Utah, for example, has never been clear. Perhaps it is named for the "Duchaine" of Pratte's expedition of 1826–27.[37] If so it provides further evidence of the range that Pratte's trappers covered.

Perhaps the "Glas" whom Martínez named is the legendary Hugh Glass, remembered for his miraculous 1823 flight to civilization after being mauled by a grizzly. Indeed, Glass reportedly drifted into New Mexico about 1827. George Yount, a trapper who had known him then, remembered that at Taos a merchant named Provost hired Glass to lead a trapping party into Ute territory. Yount could well have meant Pratte, for Provost had been gone from New Mexico since 1824, and Yount did not reach New Mexico until 1826. On this expedition the ill-fated Glass was wounded in a skirmish with Snake Indians. Still, he managed another remarkable escape, according to Yount, in which "he travelled through the Wilderness *Seven Hundred Miles* with that arrow

---

[34] Weber, *Extranjeros*, 37.

[35] Chávez, "New Names," *El Palacio*, Vol. LXIV, Nos. 9–10 (September–October, 1957), 312, 296.

[36] Clarence Edward Carter (comp. and ed.), *The Territorial Papers of the United States*, XV, 381–82; Chávez, "New Names," *El Palacio*, Vol. LXIV, Nos. 11–12 (November–December, 1957), 374.

[37] I am obligated to Dale Morgan for calling this relationship to my attention. See Morgan, *Ashley*, 280, n. 160.

in his inflamed back." Glass spent several months mending at Taos and then set out for the Yellowstone River, which he is known to have reached by fall, 1828. Murdered by Arikaras in 1833, he never returned to Taos, although an impersonator continued to recite his adventures there, in the first person, as late as 1843.[38]

These expeditions of Pratte and François Robidoux, in the winter of 1826–27, are most noteworthy for the unusually complete roster that we have of their personnel. We know nothing more, unfortunately, of the activities of these men that season. Certainly, in the face of Governor Narbona's new hostility toward foreign trappers, Pratte and Robidoux took great care to keep their activities secret. Perhaps the foreigners had even made a "deal" with Manuel Martínez so that he would look the other way when they brought "*entierros*" into Taos. Clearly, foreign trappers would need either to circumvent New Mexico officials or to come to an understanding with them, for the opposition that surfaced in 1826 remained the official posture of the New Mexico government as still more pressure was put upon it to stop foreigners from trapping in northern Mexico.

[38] Yount, *Yount and His Chronicles*, 205–207. The chronology of events in Glass's life between 1823 and 1828 is unclear. See John Myers Myers, *Pirate, Pawnee, and Mountain Man: The Saga of Hugh Glass*, 189, 199–202, and Aubrey L. Haines, "Hugh Glass," in Hafen, *Mountain Men*, VI, 169–71.

VIII THE HUNT

THE GILA WAS NOT, as James Ohio Pattie suggested, "a river never before explored by white people," for Spaniards had long been familiar with it, as well as with most of its tributaries. In 1757 a Jesuit had even remarked that along the Gila there lived "beavers which gnaw and throw to the ground the alder-trees and cotton woods." When Pattie said white people, however, he clearly meant his fellow Americans,[1] and his hunt in the winter of 1825-26 may have represented the first American attempt to trap the Gila. The reports that Pattie and his companions brought back to Santa Fe and Taos in the spring of 1826 started a stampede to the area in the fall resembling the 1824 invasion of the Colorado Basin.[2]

In a roundabout way the Mexican government had received early warning of the Americans' intentions to trap the Gila in 1826. On January 25, 1826, Pablo Obregón, the Mexican minister in

---

[1] Pattie, *Narrative*, 46, 38; Father Barthólome Sáenz to Father Juan Antonio Balthasar, Cuchuta, March 6, 1757, in *Documentos para la historia de Mexico*, Series IV, Tomo I, 88–94.

[2] The movement of trappers into the Gila Basin in 1826 is a well-known episode in southwestern history, thanks to the pioneering article of Thomas Maitland Marshall, "St. Vrain's Expedition to the Gila in 1826," *SHQ*, Vol. XIX No. 3 (January, 1916), 251–60. Marshall based his article on documents which have since become inaccessible because of fire and loss. Fortunately, a typescript of an English translation of some of the documents, and transcripts of others, have been preserved among the Bolton Transcripts at the Bancroft Library, University of California, Berkeley.

ON THE GILA, 1826–1827

Washington, reported to his home government that Americans had continued to trap in northern Mexico, especially "in the unpopulated area from the boundries to New Mexico." Obregón advised his secretary of state that "no nation ought to tolerate that which is undertaken in its territory as commercial speculation, without its consent." Furthermore, Obregón had learned that three hundred men, who had recently left the United States for New Mexico, planned to trap for beaver on the Gila River. Perhaps Obregón had heard of the plans of the Robidoux brothers, or of Sylvestre Pratte, who led parties to New Mexico in the fall of 1825, for Pattie and some of Pratte's men were on the Gila in the spring of 1826. When Obregón's letter reached Mexico City, apparently in mid-April, 1826, a copy of it was transmitted to Antonio Narbona at Santa Fe. Obregón's letter, accompanied by instructions to Narbona to remain vigilant and to stop illegal trapping, probably arrived in New Mexico in the summer of 1826.[3] Since Narbona had been alerted to their coming, it is remarkable that at least four different groups of trappers invaded the Gila country in the fall of 1826, all carrying passports issued in late August, at Santa Fe, by Governor Narbona.

[3] Pablo Obregón to the Secretario de Estado, January 25, 1826, H/200(72:73)/1, L-E-55, Tomo I, Relaciones Exteriores.

That Narbona, who had been a major obstacle to Pratte and François Robidoux, should allow some ninety trappers (by his own count) to slip by him is puzzling. Even more puzzling, however, Narbona almost immediately reversed his action. On August 31 he penned notes to José Figueroa, comandante at Arizpe in northern Sonora, and to the governor of Sonora himself, warning them that foreigners were on their way to trap the Gila, San Francisco, and Colorado rivers, "thereby breaking our laws which do not allow them to maintain such business in our country." Narbona's explanation for why he let the trappers through his territory is not, in retrospect, convincing. He had only become suspicious of the trappers' intentions, he said, after noticing their lack of "business or other visible objects," and by the questions that the foreigners asked when requesting passports.[4] Yet, Narbona had, on the very day that he issued a passport for St. Vrain and Williams, written to one Francisco Pérez, asking him to aid the Americans who were going to Sonora to seek a license to trap beaver.[5] It seems clear that Narbona knew what the foreigners were up to when he issued passports to them.

Narbona's behavior cannot be easily explained. Perhaps the Americans had promised him they would not trap until they had received a license from the governor of Sonora and then did something to make Narbona suspect they would break their word. Or perhaps Narbona was playing a double game—accepting bribes from Americans for licenses, then reporting them to his superiors in order to cover himself. Or it may be that Narbona, a fifty-three-year-old colonel experienced at frontier warfare, recognized the futility of trying to stop the trappers and let them pass so that others could deal with them. A month after the Americans had left Santa Fe, Narbona explained his difficulties to the Mexican secretary of relations. Troops, Narbona said, were in short supply and

---

[4] Narbona to the Governor of Sonora, August 31, 1826, Gobernación, Comercio, No. 44, Archivo General de la Nación (AGN), Mexico, D. F. Bolton Transcripts, Bancroft Library. Figueroa to the Governor of New Mexico, October 6, 1826, MANM.

[5] Narbona to Pérez, August 29, 1826, in Tomo 42, Archivo del Gobierno del Estado de Sonora, Hermosillo, Mexico, Bolton Transcripts, Bancroft Library.

so poorly equipped that there were not even sufficient saddle horses to carry them. Thus, he could not send small companies to scout for Americans. Only, Narbona complained, through "miseries and sacrifices have I been able to maintain a small detachment of 10 men on the frontier of Taos." Even these men could not be spared for pursuing American trappers; they were too busy quieting American disturbances in the village and maintaining defense against Indians.[6]

It was, then, almost impossible for Narbona to keep track of the Americans who already possessed a great knowledge of the country. Twelve Americans, for example, showed up at Zuñi in October, 1826, apparently without passports. Those Americans already living in New Mexico, Narbona lamented, "lend protection to the latter arrivals in order to carry out their frauds, confident that it is not easy to recognize them because they are a wandering people, found scattered all over the state, especially on the frontiers of Taos."[7]

Whatever his reasons, Narbona's failure to stop the foreign trappers at Santa Fe had immediate repercussions in Chihuahua and Sonora. There, government officials quickly expressed alarm at the American invasion of the Gila. This concern was prompted in part by a letter of warning from a former United States citizen, James Baird.

Since we last saw him struggling across the Santa Fe Trail in the fall of 1822, in a futile attempt to beat an onrushing winter, James Baird had become a trusted citizen in the country where he had once suffered imprisonment. In 1824, after aiding the Mexicans in a battle against the Opatas in Northern Mexico, Baird applied for citizenship, claiming that he had lived in Mexico since 1812 and had received Catholic baptism in Durango. His request was granted, specific papers not being required because of his long residence. That eight years of this residence were spent as a prisoner was not mentioned. Along with his request for citizenship, Baird asked for "the exclusive privilege to establish there [in New Mexi-

[6] Narbona to the Minister of Foreign Relations, Santa Fe, September 30, 1826, Gobernación, Comercio, No. 44, AGN, Bolton Transcripts, Bancroft Library.
[7] Narbona to the Governor of Chihuahua, Santa Fe, February 14, 1827, Gobernación, Comercio, No. 44, AGN, Bolton Transcripts, Bancroft Library.

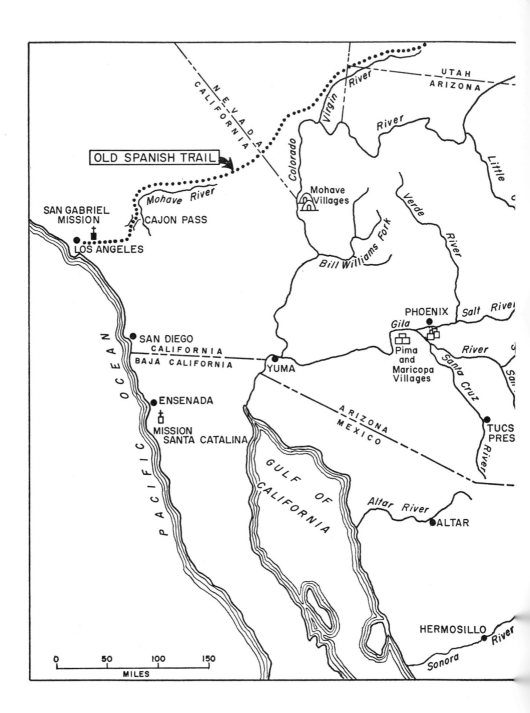

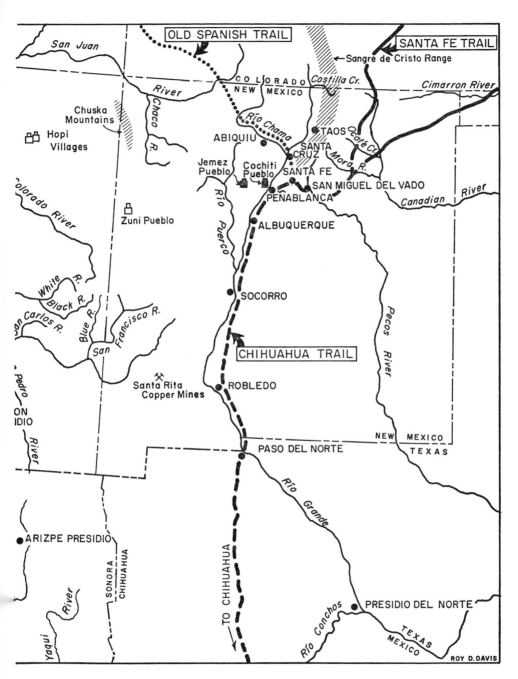

The area of fur trading activities southwest of Taos

co] a new distillery to make *aguardiente* of corn and wheat."[8] By the winter of 1824–25, as we have seen, he was already in the distillery business, making Taos lightning with Samuel Chambers, the future Peg-leg Smith, and a man named Stevens as his partners. Baird occasionally served as an interpreter for officials in Santa Fe and apparently found this occupation so lucrative that in August, 1826, he applied to Governor Narbona for a position as official interpreter. Narbona strongly recommended him and forwarded his application to the central government.[9]

There is no evidence that Baird trapped or traded in furs in New Mexico before the fall of 1826, but it would be surprising if he had not. By October, 1826, Baird had become alarmed at the large number of foreigners who were encroaching on his private trapping domain. In a vigorous protest to the president of the district of El Paso, a protest which was "not moved so much by personal interest as by the honor and general welfare of the nation to which I have heartily joined," Baird explained that over the last year and a half, small, illegal groups had taken over $100,000 worth of furs from New Mexico. This small-scale activity had not moved Baird to protest, but now he could no longer remain silent. Baird had learned that over a hundred "Anglo-Americans" planned to trap "in a body" in New Mexico and Sonora, along the Gila River. The Americans, Baird reported, were armed and arrogant: "They have openly said that in spite of the Mexicans, they will hunt beaver wherever they please." Baird, who had acted as an interpreter for Sylvestre Pratte in the fall of 1825, could speak with authority, for he knew many of the Americans. Baird asked that action be taken to enforce the law, so that *"we Mexicans* may peacefully profit."[10]

[8] Borrador, Ministro de Justicia y Negocios Eclesiásticos to the Governor of New Mexico, Mexico, October 5, 1825, in Justicia, Tomo 121, AGN.

[9] See borrador No. 74, Narbona to Ministerio de Hacienda, August 31, 1826, MANM. Baird's activities as an interpreter apparently dated from 1824, when he accompanied a Mexican delegation to Council Bluffs to treat with the Pawnees. See also the case involving the confiscation of the merchandise of François Robidoux, December 9, 1825, and Sibley, *Road to Santa Fe*, 153.

[10] The entire Baird statement is in Marshall, "St. Vrain's Expeditions," *SHQ*, Vol. XIX, No. 3 (January, 1916), 256–57, italics are mine.

Baird penned his protest on October 26. Eight days later he was dead. With a small party of hired men, Jean Baptiste Chalifoux and his brother Pierre, Luciano Grijalva, and possibly others (a "young man" was reportedly Baird's partner), Baird had set out for the Gila on a trapping expedition of his own. Shortly after leaving, he became too ill to ride on and returned to El Paso to die. A list of his possessions was drawn up in the presence of some Americans who happened to be in El Paso: John W. Rogers, W. Aitken, John G. Parrish, Edward Beavers, Paul Anderson, and Samuel McClure—all traders and perhaps occasional trappers. In the meantime, the brothers Chalifoux and Luciano Grijalva continued on to Tucson to trap.[11]

Baird's letter, though, which came to the attention of Chihuahua officials, was not written in vain. Alexander Ramírez, the President of the El Paso District, confirmed Baird's information. Ramírez had learned from "certain natives of Real del Cobre [the Santa Rita copper mine]" that Americans were trapping on the Río de San Francisco, a tributary of the Gila. His informants thought there were no less than seventy trappers and Ramírez reported:

> It is unquestionable that they entered the area through New Mexico. Up to the present date of this year they have not touched other parts of this state, but in former years they hunted along the entire river of this jurisdiction [the Río Grande] taking a number of beaver skins, and the former officials disturbed them not even to collect an exportation tax.[12]

The foreign trappers about whom Baird and Ramírez remonstrated were described tersely by Governor Narbona: "J. William

[11] Golley, "James Baird, Santa Fe Trader," *MHSB*, Vol. XV, No. 3 (April, 1959), 191; Strickland, "James Baird," *SHQ*, Vol. XIX, No. 3 (January, 1916), 34–35. Strickland's new information on Baird's last days was drawn from the "Documentos de la Ciudad de Juárez." In locating the Baird material in that archive, he seems to have mined its choicest fur trade item, for this writer's search has yielded nothing of comparable interest.

[12] Alexander Ramírez to Elías Bustamente at Chihuahua, El Paso, December 20, 1826, Gobernación, Comercio, No. 44, AGN, Bolton Transcripts, Bancroft Library.

and Sambrano is accredited with leading 20 and some odd men; Miguel Rubidu and Pratt 30 some odd; Juan Roles 18 and Joaquin Joven also 18."[13] The governor did not identify any of the personnel of these four parties, but among the merchants who received permits to travel to Sonora and Chihuahua in late August and early September of 1826 were such veteran traders as Eliseo Stanley, William Green, Paul Anderson, George West, Samuel McClure, James Purcell, and Francis Samuel. Later that fall Antoine Robidoux, Charles Beaubien, and Moses Carson received *guías*.[14] Perhaps some of them paused to trap on the Gila instead of pursuing their mercantile careers.

Three of the four groups identified by Narbona clearly reached the Gila, but almost nothing is known of the party of eighteen led by Juan Roles. It seems certain, however, that Juan Roles is John Rowland. A mysterious figure during these early years of trapping in New Mexico, Rowland had been on the Green River in the winter of 1824–25, and continued to trap and trade out of Taos until 1841. His activities on the Gila in 1826 remain shrouded with a secrecy that he and his men probably sought to achieve.[15]

Some details have come to light regarding the group led by J. Williams and Ceran St. Vrain, Narbona's "Sambrano." J. Williams, it has been hypothesized, might have been Isaac Williams, whose first introduction into the Southwest was with the Glenn-Fowler party in 1822. In another document, however, Narbona refers to him as S. W. Williams and in a third document calls him simply Julián—a name popularly used, instead of Guillermo, to mean William in New Mexico. Those who have suggested that S. W. Williams was really W. S. or William Sherley Williams are probably correct, for "Old Bill" Williams had arrived in New Mexico in the fall of 1825. He would still be in the employ of St. Vrain during the next trapping season, 1827–28, as well.[16]

---

[13] Narbona to the Governor of Sonora, August 31, 1826, Gobernación, Comercio, No. 44, AGN, Bolton Transcripts, Bancroft Library.

[14] Book of guías, Santa Fe, 1826–28, in Weber, *Extranjeros*, 31.

[15] Rowland acquired small fame as co-leader of the Rowland-Workman overland party to California in 1841. David J. Weber, "John Rowland," in Hafen, *Mountain Men*, IV, 275–81.

By late October, sixteen trappers under Williams and Ceran St. Vrain had arrived at a Maricopa village on the Gila near the presidio of Tucson. According to the Indians, they were armed, carried trapping equipment and trade goods, and three of their number spoke Spanish. The Americans spent four days at the village, giving gifts to the Indians and probably doing some trading. The Maricopas were troublesome, however, stealing blankets, mules, and a valise (*maleta*) from the trappers' "captain." Outnumbered, the Americans did not resist this thievery. They left when they heard that the Maricopas had sent a messenger to Tucson to inform the Mexicans of their presence. On October 28, when news of these trespassers reached Tucson, Comandante Ignacio Pacheco sent eight men in search of the trappers. On the Gila, Indians reported that the Americans had passed by three days previously en route to Apache country, the *apachería*. Unable to overtake the foreigners, the troops proceeded to the Maricopa village where they learned more details about the trappers and received the stolen *maleta*.[17]

When the troops returned to the presidio at Tucson, Comandante Pacheco ordered copies of the trappers' documents to be made and forwarded to Hermosillo. Among the documents was a passport from Governor Narbona to Seran Sambrano and S. W. Williams and thirty-five foreigners which allowed them to go to the state of Sonora for personal business. Another document was a note in a "foreign language" which the officials at Tucson laboriously copied as follows:

7bre [September] 14 the. 1826.
Recive of E. Bure one note on Wan. tope for forty Dollars one on Alexn. Branch for thirty five Dollars one an Boanch

---

[16] Joseph J. Hill, "Ewing Young, in the Fur Trade of the Far Southwest" *OHSQ*, Vol. XXIV, No. 1 (March, 1923), 8, identifies Williams as Isaac Williams. Cleland, *Reckless Breed*, 254, thinks he was "Old Bill." Favour, Williams' biographer, does not comment on the activities on the Gila. For Williams' association with St. Vrain in 1827–28, see the statement of the engagés of S. S. Pratte, September 1, 1829, Chouteau Collection.

[17] Ignacio Pacheco to the Governor of Sonora, Tucson, November 4, 1826, Tomo 42, Archivo del Gobierno del Estado de Sonora, Hermosillo, Mexico, transcript in the Bancroft Library.

and Slone [Stone] Due Eleben Dollars one on Louis Dolton forty Dollars one on ompt [account?] against Wan. Pepe Seven Dollars and fifty sents one acampt [against?] Alejr. Brauch Nine Dollars and fisty Cents which Spromise to mss. omty Eudeabante to Cllest of seren of posible [which I promise to make every endeavor to collect of Ceran if possible?].

John Rueland

This note, aparently a receipt from John Rowland to E. Bure is engrossing at the very least. Written on September 14, the transaction between Rowland and Bure probably took place after the trappers left the New Mexico settlements. Unfortunately, it cannot be said with certainty that those mentioned in the note were with St. Vrain and Williams. According to Narbona, all of the trappers held a "grand reunion . . . on their march" outside of Santa Fe on their way to the Gila. The note may have been written while the parties were united and then found its way into St. Vrain's hands. All we can conclude from this tantalizing transcription is that Alexander Branch, his inseparable companion Stone, Louis Dolton, E. Bure, and William Pope were probably among the trappers on the Gila. Peg-leg Smith also remembered that Stone and Alexander Branch were on the Gila that season. These men, apparently companions, are intriguing, for they are believed to have been in Thomas Fitzpatrick's party which made the effective discovery of South Pass in the winter of 1823–24.[18] Stone, whose first name was probably Solomon, remains an obscure and mysterious figure.[19] Alexander Branch and William Pope returned to New Mexico to participate in subsequent trapping ventures.[20] "Dolton,"

[18] James Clyman, *James Clyman, Frontiersman: The Adventures of a Trapper and Covered-Wagon Emigrant As Told in His Own Reminiscences and Diaries* (ed. by Charles L. Camp), 30.

[19] An S. Stone appeared on the list of persons owing money to the estate of S. S. Pratte, Chouteau Collection. This is probably the Solomon Stone who applied for Mexican citizenship in 1826. Antonio Narbona to the Ministro de Justicia y Negocios Eclesiásticos. November 30, 1826, in Archivo de Justicia, Vol. 121, AGN.

[20] A brief biography of William Pope, written without reference to his early appearance on the Gila, is Andrew F. Rolle, "William Pope," in Hafen, *Mountain Men*, II, 275–76. Alexander Branch is discussed herein in later chapters.

it seems likely, was actually Lewis Dutton, who was in and out of
New Mexico up to the time of the Civil War, when, accused of
being a Southern sympathizer, his property was confiscated. He is
probably the same Lewis Dutton who worked as a guide on the
1849 San Antonio-to-El Paso road survey conducted by Lieutenant
W. H. C. Whiting and who, at age forty-one, applied for a Mexican
passport on March 20, 1843. He may even be the Dutton who,
along with Hugh Glass, narrowly escaped death on the Missouri
at the hands of Arikaras in February, 1824.[21]

Further particulars concerning the Williams–St. Vrain party
remain unknown. It seems more than likely that this group was
financed by Sylvestre S. Pratte, however, for St. Vrain had been
in his employ in the previous season and would again be one of
Pratte's lieutenants in the winter of 1827–28.

The brief story of the third group which Narbona identified, the
one led by "Miguel Rubidu and Pratt," is known largely because
James Ohio Pattie was along. Miguel (Michel) Robidoux, young-
est of the Robidoux brothers, became the sole leader of this group
while Sylvestre Pratte remained at Santa Fe to fight the embargo
that Narbona had placed on his furs. Still, Pratte may have outfitted or owned a share in the party, too.

According to Pattie, Miguel Robidoux's party, composed almost
entirely of French trappers, traveled down the Río Grande and
over to the Santa Rita copper mines—probably in September, 1826.
There, James Pattie, lately returned from his own unsuccessful
sojourn on the Gila, joined Robidoux. Leaving Sylvester Pattie at
the mines, the trappers followed the Gila to the mouth of the Salt
River, at present-day Phoenix. There, as Pattie tells it, the care-
lessness of Miguel Robidoux enabled Papagos[22] to massacre the
entire party. Only Pattie, an unnamed Frenchman, and Robidoux

[21] Morgan, *Ashley*, 76; Yount, *Yount and His Chronicles*, 203, 271, n. 65;
J. Morgan Broadus, *The Legal Heritage of El Paso*, 80. Letter to this writer from
Bill McGaw, El Paso, October 3, 1968, with notes from his forthcoming book on
James Kirker. Archivo Historico, Legajo 476, 224, AGN.

[22] Although Pattie identifies their assailants as Papagos, two anthropologists
have suggested that they were Apaches or Yavapais. See Clifton B. Kroeber (ed.),
"The Route of James O. Pattie on the Colorado in 1826, A Reappraisal by A. L.
Kroeber," *Arizona and the West*, Vol. VI, No. 2 (Summer, 1964), 124, 125, 135.

escaped. These three soon joined a group of about thirty trappers operating nearby under Ewing Young, the "Joaquín Joven" of Narbona's description and leader of the fourth and final group that Narbona identified.[23] Previous to this encounter with Pattie and Robidoux, Young's men too had been beleaguered by Indians on the Gila.

In the summer of 1826, Ewing Young and William Wolfskill, trapping companions since 1822, had returned from St. Louis to Santa Fe, where Young hired some men to trap the Gila. Among them was Kentucky-born, Missouri-bred Milton Sublette, already a veteran trapper at age twenty-five.[24] Young became ill and had to remain at Santa Fe, so Wolfskill took his place as leader of the group. The party was soon augmented by Thomas Smith, his partner Maurice Le Duc, and perhaps three others. They may have numbered sixteen or possibly as few as eleven. Also along were Alexander Branch, S. Stone, Richard Campbell, and George C. Yount.[25]

Like Miguel Robidoux, Wolfskill also traveled to the Gila via the Santa Rita mines.[26] From there, the trappers followed the Gila to the mouth of the Salt where they encountered Indians—Apaches, according to Thomas Smith. At first an amicable discussion took place until, Smith later reported, an Apache "shot an arrow into an animal," which "was regarded as a declaration of hostilities."[27]

[23] Pattie never mentions Robidoux or Young by name, but it has long been accepted that his *Narrative*, 75–82, recounts the activities of Robidoux's party to the Salt River and then tells of Young's adventures, as demonstrated by Joseph J. Hill in "New Light on Pattie and the Southwestern Fur Trade," *Southwestern Historical Quarterly*, Vol. XXVI, No. 4 (April, 1923), 243–54. Hill's elaborate explanation of the conflict between Pattie's dates and those of Robidoux and Young, 253–54, is no longer necessary, now that we are able to correct Pattie's *Narrative*.

[24] Doyce B. Nunis, "Milton G. Sublette," in Hafen, *Mountain Men*, IV, 331–33.

[25] By comparing the similarities in the accounts of William Wolfskill, Peg-leg Smith, and George Yount, Joseph J. Hill and Charles Camp have demonstrated fairly conclusively that these three were working together under Ewing Young in the fall of 1826. The presence of Branch, Stone, Sublette, and Campbell is indicated in "Sketches from the Life of Peg-leg Smith," *HICM*, Vol. V, No. 7 (January, 1861), 320–21.

[26] Yount, *Yount and His Chronicles*, 27.

In the ensuing brawl, Milton Sublette was probably wounded in the leg and some of the pack mules died, but no trapper lost his life. Even though Alexander Branch reportedly killed two Indians with one shot, the trappers still found themselves outnumbered and were forced to return to the New Mexico settlements for more supplies and manpower. Some of the party remained "at the rancho of Señor Chaves" on the Río Grande, while five men hastened to Taos, soon returning with Ewing Young and sixteen more trappers. This time William Wolfskill remained in Taos while Young, with a group of some thirty strong, returned to the Gila where they "chastised" the Indians, added Pattie and Miguel Robidoux to their number, and resumed trapping.[28]

Young led his trappers all the way to the Colorado, the first Americans, so far as we know, to follow the Gila to its mouth. They ascended the Colorado to the Mohave villages, where their path intersected that of Jedediah Smith, who had traveled downstream from the summer rendezvous. Smith had crossed over to California on that trip, preceding the trappers from Taos into California by a year. When Jedediah Smith revisited the Mohave villages the following summer, 1827, he learned that "a party of Spaniards & Americans from the Province of Sonora," had arrived there shortly after he had left for California in November, 1826.[29] Certainly the Mohaves had reason to remember Young's trappers. According to Pattie, Indians had harassed them all along the way, but the Mohaves were the most troublesome. One night, for example, Mohaves shot sixteen arrows into Pattie's bed while he occupied it—none struck him. Such hostility required retribution, so the trappers pursued the group who had fired on them, killed many and hung their bodies in trees, "to dangle in terror to the rest." Yet the Mohaves' enmity toward the trappers may not have been un-

[27] "The Story of an Old Trapper," *San Francisco Evening Bulletin*, October 26, 1866; "Sketches from the Life of Peg-leg Smith," *HICM*, Vol. V, No. 7 (January, 1861), 320.

[28] The above is a composite account from "Sketches from the Life of Peg-leg Smith," *HICM*, Vol. V, No. 7 (January, 1861), 320, and Barrows, "The Story of an Old Pioneer," *Wilmington* (California) *Journal*, October 20, 1866, 290.

[29] Dale L. Morgan, *Jedediah Smith and the Opening of the West*, 238.

provoked. As one historian has suggested, some of Young's party were, themselves, "quite capable of stimulating hostility."[30]

After leaving the Mohaves, Young's route, according to Pattie, followed the north rim of the Grand Canyon, took a brief side trip up the San Juan River, and continued along the Grand River into the heart of the Rockies. At this point Pattie's *Narrative* becomes hopelessly tangled. Pattie, it would appear, finally returned to New Mexico from the north, following the Río Grande.[31]

Somewhere after leaving the Mohave villages, Young's party must have divided, although Pattie does not mention this. George Yount reports returning to Santa Fe via the pueblo of Zuñi, quite a different route from that described by Pattie.[32] Thomas Smith also mentions that the party divided on the Colorado, "two miles above the mouth of the Virgin," according to his account. Smith clearly broke with Ewing Young and was joined by Stone, Branch, and "Dutch George," whom Charles Camp has identified as George Yount.[33] Camp's identification may be in error, for the accounts of Peg-leg Smith and George Yount contain significant variations, indicating that they too might have returned in separate parties. Both Yount and Smith, for example, described a long period of starvation, but each recalled a different means of satisfying his hunger. Smith remembered eating his favorite dog, a popular story among trappers, and then feasting on deer, whereas Yount's group reportedly did not find relief until they had reached Zuñi. In a more serious discrepancy, Yount describes the confiscation of his furs by Mexican officials. Smith, on the other hand, tells that the furs of his group remained untouched. Smith had learned that Ewing Young's furs had been taken by Mexican officials, so he and

---

[30] Pattie, *Narrative*, 87. See also Yount, *Yount and His Chronicles*, 34–36; Jack D. Forbes, *Warriors of the Colorado: The Yumas of the Quechan Nation and their Neighbors*, 260.

[31] See William Goetzmann's admirable attempt to explain Pattie's wanderings in *Exploration and Empire*, 73–74, n. 1. Speculations on Pattie's route through Arizona appear in Kroeber, "The Route of James O. Pattie," *Arizona and the West*, Vol. VI, No. 2 (Summer, 1964), 119–36.

[32] Yount, *Yount and His Chronicles*, 36–39, 253, n. 11.

[33] "Sketches from the Life of Peg-leg Smith," *HICM*, Vol. V, No. 8 (February, 1861), 334; Yount, *Yount and His Chronicles*, 229.

his party cautiously entered the Mexican settlements only to be discovered by an alcalde who "drew a paper from his pocket," saying, "I have here an order from the Governor to seize all furs as contraband." With the aid of thirty dollars and other sundries, Smith managed to persuade the alcalde to ignore this order. The beaver safely hidden at Cienega, Smith made his way to Taos, where he met "his warm-hearted patron, Mr. Pratt." Then, as some imaginative reporter told the "genteel reader" of *Hutchings' Illustrated California Magazine* in 1860:

> In a few days the beaver was smuggled in [to Taos] "all right side up," and *such* a fandango came off as was never witnessed in those parts before, preceded by a scalp dance around the town. A long-haired scalp, taken by Smith, was carried on a pole, followed by the entire population, singing, dancing and yelling. Alas! for civilization in those halcyon days of the trapper, she could but "spread her wings and fly weeping away."[34]

Like Smith, many of those who trapped on the Gila in the fall and winter of 1826–27 got their furs to market without resistance from Mexican officials. Others, Ira A. Emmons, Ewing Young, George Yount, and James O. Pattie among them, were less fortunate. Emmons was the first of this group to run into trouble with authorities. Although he is an unfamiliar figure to historians, Emmons seems to have been a seasoned Santa Fe merchant. In the spring of 1825, George C. Sibley recommended that Emmons, who "has twice been to St. Fee and once commanded a party," be appointed captain and pilot of the United States government survey party.[35] Instead, Emmons became one of the leaders of the annual caravan to Santa Fe that summer and in autumn received a trade permit to travel to Sonora. Emmons then disappears from the record until the afternoon of April 23, 1827, when as one of five "Americanos," he showed up in Santa Fe, having "returned to the Territory from a distant land." Among his belongings New

[34] "Sketches from the Life of Peg-leg Smith," *HICM*, Vol. V, No. 8 (February, 1861), 336.
[35] Sibley, *Road to Santa Fe*, 29, 219; *Missouri Intelligencer*, June 4, 1825; Weber, *Extranjeros*, 24.

Mexico officials found 115 beaver pelts, trapped in the Gila River. These they promptly confiscated and ordered Emmons to appear before the alcalde of Santa Fe, Vicente Baca. In his defense, Emmons said he was trapping legally under a license issued by the governor to Manuel Sena of Santa Fe, and another license issued to Santiago Posel, of Sonora, by the "Alcalde of Sonora."

If Emmons' testimony is reliable, he had a fascinating patron, for Santiago Posel is almost certainly James Purcell, the carpenter who, as we have seen, had come to Santa Fe in 1805. Purcell had remained there even though Spanish officials regarded him with suspicion. Following Mexican independence, he continued to make New Mexico his home. In 1824 he returned briefly to Missouri where the *Intelligencer* reported, "We have conversed with Mr. James Purcel, for nineteen years a citizen of New Mexico." Purcell, like James Baird, had probably become a Mexican citizen on the basis of his long residence, and thereby obtained the trapping license to which Emmons referred. In early September, 1826, "Santiago Pursel" received a *guía* to go to Sonora and Chihuahua to trade. Probably at this time he and Emmons met. Purcell continued to occupy himself in the Santa Fe trade, but there is no further evidence of his direct involvement in the fur trade.[36]

Although Emmons claimed to have two licenses, he could produce neither because, he said, he had left them at the Santa Rita copper mines, where he claimed to be a resident.[37] When asked what right he had to hunt under a license granted to another person, Emmons replied that he was just an employee of the "company." One would suspect that Emmons and his American companions had purchased their licenses from Manuel Sena and James Purcell, but Sena, who was the armorer for the military garrison in Santa Fe, had a different story. He claimed that he gave the license to the foreigners as a favor since they had been denied a license by the

[36] *Missouri Intelligencer*, April 3, 1824. Purcell exhibited a great knowledge of the Navahos which the *Intelligencer* drew upon for a story. He was reported as being from Pennsylvania, contrary to Pike's assertion that he was a Kentuckian. Weber, *Extranjeros*, 31–33.

[37] Emmons said he was a resident "del cobre" and that he had left the license at the "cobre." This word, meaning copper, could mean little else in New Mexico at this time except the Santa Rita copper mines.

governor. Sena testified that he had no personal interest in the expedition, nor did he know that foreigners were not allowed to trap. Alcalde Baca found him innocent of any crime. Emmons was not as lucky as Sena, for on April 30, Governor Narbona ordered Baca to sell Emmons' furs.[38] Some of the furs and traps had been hidden at the copper mines, according to a note that the governor of New Mexico sent to El Paso, and these too may have been disposed of by government officials.[39]

The embargo of Emmons' furs proved but a rehearsal for a more spectacular episode involving Ewing Young. In early May, Young and his party returned from their hunt on the Gila and Colorado. Apparently aware of the New Mexican officials' new attitude toward foreign trappers, Young hid his thirteen packs (*cargas*) of pelts in the house of Luis María Cabeza de Baca at the village of Peña Blanca, on the Río Grande west of Santa Fe.

By May 16, however, news of Young's secret had reached the governor, for a Mexican who had accompanied Young, Ignacio Sandoval of Taos, informed on him. Narbona, immediately ordering Agustín Durán to seize the furs, sent a small military force to Peña Blanca, where Luis María Cabeza de Baca gave his life in a futile attempt to save Young's furs.[40] Young somehow avoided accompanying his confiscated furs to Santa Fe, and on May 21, Manuel Armijo, who had assumed Narbona's duties as political governor (*Jefe Político*) on the previous day, issued a circular for his arrest.[41] While the search for Young went on, Eliseo (Elisha) Stanley, a prominent and experienced American merchant, began petitioning Durán to locate a copy of the federal government's decree prohibiting trapping by foreigners. Durán forwarded Stan-

---

[38] Papers concerning the case of Ira A. Emmons (many of which are illegible), April 23, 1827, and Narbona to Baca, April 30, 1827, MANM.

[39] Letter of May 14, 1827, in Documentos de la Ciudad de Juárez, microfilm at Texas Western College, El Paso, Texas, Reel 3, 152.

[40] Durán to Narbona, May 16, 1827, MANM; Comandante Principal del Nuevo Mexico to Comandante General Simón Elías, June 6, 1827, MANM. A large portion of this document appears in translation in Cleland, *Reckless Breed*, 219.

[41] Narbona, who was political and military governor, now assumed the position of military governor (*Jefe Militar*) and was recalled to Sonora, where his services were more needed. Bloom, "New Mexico Under Mexican Administration," *Old Santa Fe*, Vol. I, No. 3 (January, 1913), 256. Governor's circular, May 21, 1827, MANM.

ley's request to the governor and five days later pressured the
governor for an answer, because Stanley's importunity was becoming a nuisance. The governor replied that he had searched the
archives and was unable to find the law; he would write to the
federal government for another copy. By May 31, Armijo had
found a copy which he sent to Durán, but which, unfortunately,
appears not to have been preserved.[42]

Young was apparently never brought to justice, nor did he
regain his furs. That summer, however, the affair grew even uglier.
On July 11, Young and two other Americans received permission to
clean the confiscated furs. While they, Agustín Durán, the alcalde
of Santa Fe, and perhaps other officials, were shaking the furs and
making an inventory of them, Milton Sublette seized a bundle of
pelts, threw it over his shoulder, and fled to the nearby house of
Cristóbal Torres. A number of Americans were staying there, all
of whom began to clean their guns and make other gestures that
New Mexico officials interpreted as hostile. By the time the house
could be searched, Sublette and the furs were gone. He did not
flee the territory, however, for that fall he accompanied a group
of trappers under Sylvestre S. Pratte into the Rockies.

Since Young had requested that the furs be cleaned, and since
he was among those who had taken arms in defense of Sublette,
Governor Armijo called Young to his office and suggested that
he be put in jail. Instead, the brash Young walked out in the midst
of the conversation. Outraged, Armijo ordered troops to pursue
Young. Only when they had surrounded the Torres house, where
Young was staying, did he surrender. Armijo then had Young
put into shackles and held incommunicado. Formal hearings followed, at which Young gave incredibly naïve answers to the
charges brought against him. When a fever struck him in jail, he
was released to two bondsmen and seems to have remained free,
probably because Mexican authorities could not prove that he
and Sublette had conspired. Ewing Young returned to his headquarters at Taos, and thereafter New Mexican officials viewed his

[42] Durán to Governor, May 22, 1827, and May 27, 1827, both in MANM.
Armijo's reply is in a marginal note on the latter letter. Governor to Durán, May
31, 1827, MANM.

activities with considerable suspicion and distrust. The remainder of Young's furs were damaged when a heavy rain leaked through the adobe building where they were stored. Selling for two pesos, or about three dollars apiece in Santa Fe, they still brought 2,328 pesos—over $3,500.[43]

Still, the affair did not come to a quiet conclusion. At Taos, on July 6, a group of Americans and Frenchmen gathered in the plaza and began to insult Felipe Sandoval, the father of Ignacio Sandoval, who had ordered his son to inform on Young when the trappers returned from the Gila. One of these foreigners threatened the elder Sandoval with a large knife, and a fight followed which the alcalde, Manuel Martínez, had great difficulty breaking up. One of the foreigners was drunk, and the fight degenerated into two Americans fighting each other over an unpaid debt, until men named Branch and "Sebet" [Sublette?] stepped in to stop it.[44]

In the meantime, news of Young's difficulties traveled to Mexico City. On July 15, while Young was still in jail, two of his associates in Santa Fe penned a letter to the American minister in Mexico City, Joel Poinsett. He, in turn, protested to the Mexican secretary of state, explaining that the governor of New Mexico "appears . . . to have committed an outrage," by arresting and imprisoning Young without sufficient cause, then holding him without a trial.[45] In retrospect, Armijo's conduct seems less "outrageous" than Young's.

The Taos trappers had performed well on the Gila, but many had little to show for their efforts. George Yount and James Ohio Pattie both record that their furs were also confiscated upon their return from the 1826 Gila expedition, but neither described a dramatic fight over the furs. Yount merely says he returned to Santa

[43] This account is based on papers concerning the arrest of Ewing Young, Archivo de la Secretaría de Relaciones Exteriores, Mexico, H [242.2(73:72)]-2, Legajo 12-12-12, and on Cleland, *Reckless Breed*, 220–24. Cleland had access to further materials from this archive which cannot now be located. These had been microfilmed by Ralph P. Bieber, of Washington University, St. Louis, who loaned them to Cleland.

[44] Manuel Martínez to Governor Armijo, Taos, July 17, 1827, MANM.

[45] Poinsett to the Secretary of State, Mexico, August 29, 1827, in Papers Relating to the arrest of Ewing Young, Relaciones Exteriores, H [242.2 (73:72)]-2, Legajo 12-12-12.

Fe to find a new governor, Armijo, who "refused to honor his passport." Perhaps he was with Ira Emmons. Penniless and unable to return to his family in Missouri, Yount remained in New Mexico for another trapping season.[46] Pattie's comments were unusually terse:

> The Governor, on the pretext that we had trapped without a license from him, robbed us of all our furs. We were excessively provoked and had it not been from a sense of duty to our beloved country, we would have redressed our wrongs, and retaken our furs with our own arms.[47]

If Young was with either Pattie or Yount, it is impossible to tell from these accounts. It seems likely that Young was not with Pattie, who re-entered New Mexico from a northerly route and would, therefore, have arrived at Taos, the northernmost settlement, first. Young, however, hid his furs to the west of Santa Fe at Peña Blanca. We have already seen that Young was not with Peg-leg Smith. Probably he was in the group that Yount described, but these various reminiscences are so bewildering that until further evidence is found this must remain speculative.[48]

American trappers did not soon forget the confiscation of Ewing Young's furs and took pains to avoid similar misfortune. Young's story must have been repeated on the trail and around the campfire for the next decade, and if some of the details were forgotten, few failed to recall how Milton Sublette had run off with his share of the furs. Although Sublette seems to have been with the famous Ashley-Henry expedition on the Missouri in 1822–23, he remained an obscure figure in the fur trade until this celebrated event. Thereafter, Sublette was a hero, remembered as the man who made the unpopular Governor Armijo " 'knock under' to one of those bold and daring spirits of the Rocky Mountains whom obstacles rather energize than subdue."[49]

[46] Yount, *Yount and His Chronicles*, 38–39.
[47] Pattie, *Narrative*, 93.
[48] If Young and Yount were traveling together, or if Yount and Smith were not in the same party, as I suspect, then "Dutch George" and George Yount are not the same person, as Camp has supposed.

Mexican attempts to apprehend foreign trappers in the spring of 1827 were probably not as successful as the foregoing summary implies. Accounts of the activities of those trappers who were caught would naturally constitute the bulk of the historical record, whereas successful evasions by other offenders would preclude their appearance in Mexican documents. Ironically, then, the adventures of men like Emmons and Young are remembered chiefly because of their failures, while trappers who roamed the Gila and its tributaries and escaped with their ill-gotten booty have been forgotten. In April, 1827, the Mexican government filed an official protest with the American minister in Mexico City, Joel Poinsett, who expressed regret and promised that future incidents would be prevented.[50] But, little could be done to stop the aggressive Taos trappers, and the fur trade in New Mexico continued much as it had before.

The activities of American trappers in northern Mexico had received considerable notoriety in 1826–27.[51] Curiously, however, it was Manuel Armijo, who is often pictured as an insensitive despot, who saw most clearly the long-range consequences of continued American incursions into his territory. In a letter to the Mexican foreign minister describing Ewing Young's conduct, Armijo sounded a passionate warning. "Every day," he said, "the foreigners are becoming more influential over the miserable inhabitants of the Territory." Someday, Armijo suggested, the New Mexicans might resist the Americans and "from this clash will result an evil of great consequence to all the Federation. And why? Because we have not put forth seasonable solutions in time to avoid the misfortune which threatens."[52]

49 Gregg, *Commerce of the Prairies*, 159; Nunis, "Milton Sublette," in Hafen, *Mountain Men*, IV, 331–39.

50 Marshall, "St. Vrain's Expedition," *SHQ*, Vol. XIX, No. 3 (January, 1916), 259–60; Ministro de Relaciones to Poinsett, Mexico, April 5, 1827, and Poinsett's reply, April 9, 1827, in Bolton Transcripts, Bancroft Library.

51 For a further example, see R. W. H. Hardy, *Travels in the Interior of Mexico in 1825, 1826, 1827, and 1829*, 459, who learned of the Americans while at Bavispe in northeastern Sonora.

52 Letter of July 31, 1827, in Relaciones Exteriores, Doc. H [242.2 (73:72)]-2, Legajo 12-12-12.

IX TRAPPERS' TRAILS

Having found their way to the Colorado River via the Gila River
to the south and the Spanish Trail to the north, the Taos trappers
were in a position to extend their trail blazing to its logical conclusion by opening new paths, farther west, to California. But the men
from Taos would not be the first trappers to reach the California
settlements by an overland route, for this honor belongs to Jedediah
Smith, who arrived there in the fall of 1826 after leaving the rendezvous on Bear River. Richard Campbell, who trailed Smith by
a year, is usually accorded credit for being the first of the Taos
trappers to reach California from a New Mexico base.

Although historian Robert Glass Cleland described Richard
Campbell as "one of the most important of the trapper merchants,"
he remains an obscure figure in the fur trade of the Southwest.[1]
Campbell had probably come to New Mexico as early as the spring
of 1824. He was certainly there by 1825, when he and Paul Baillio
checked into the Santa Fe custom house together.[2] In the fall of
1826, Campbell trapped on the Gila and Colorado rivers with
Peg-leg Smith, Alexander Branch, Stone, and others, probably as

[1] Cleland, *Reckless Breed*, 210; John E. Baur, "Richard Campbell," in Hafen,
Mountain Men, III, 69–70, is too brief.
[2] Goodwin, "John H. Fonda's Explorations," *SHQ*, Vol. XXIII, No. 1 (July,
1919), 45; Santa Fe custom house records, April 27, 1825, in Weber, *Extranjeros*,
17.

TO CALIFORNIA, 1827–1832

part of Ewing Young's party. The following season, doubtless using knowledge obtained from his 1826 expedition, Campbell reportedly led thirty-five men to San Diego, going by way of the Zuñi villages. He arrived in California in the fall of 1827 and apparently sold his furs to a Russian ship captain in San Francisco Bay.[3] In order to avoid New Mexico officials, Campbell may have planned to market his furs in California well before his departure. Santa Fe traders knew that foreign ships frequented California harbors; some Americans even feared British competition from the west. In 1826 rumor had it that the British were importing goods into California, then bringing them to Santa Fe "at less expense than goods can be brought from Missouri."[4]

Richard Campbell's route to California remains unclear. It is usually assumed that he went by way of the Gila, but this is not certain. Campbell later remembered taking a more northerly route which may have gone from Zuñi, northwest to the Hopi pueblos, and on to the Colorado at the Crossing of the Fathers, then heading

[3] "Sketches from the Life of Peg-leg Smith," *HICM*, Vol. V, No. 5 (January, 1861), 321; Alice B. Maloney, "The Richard Campbell Party of 1827," *California Historical Quarterly*, Vol. XVII, No. 4 (December, 1939), 347–50.

[4] Unsigned letter, Santa Fe, February 7, 1826, in the (St. Louis) *Missouri Republican*, April 20, 1826.

west well to the north of the Grand Canyon—a route such as the Mexican trader Antonio Armijo would take in 1829–30.[5]

By late February, 1828, Richard Campbell had returned to New Mexico. In September he married María Rosa Grijalva at Taos and five days later received a permit to travel to Sonora with David Waldo and Ceran St. Vrain. Campbell became a Mexican citizen in 1829 and, as we shall see, continued to trap. Before his death in New Mexico in 1860, he had enjoyed brief careers as a miner, sheriff, and probate judge.[6]

At about the time that Richard Campbell arrived in California, another party of trappers from Taos started in that direction. Led, it would appear, by James Ohio Pattie's father, Sylvester, this group included the chronicler George C. Yount and consisted of twenty-four men, including servants and campkeepers. Holding a *guía* dated September 22, 1827, which permitted Sylvester Pattie to travel to Chihuahua and Sonora to trade, they proceeded to the southwest, via the Santa Rita copper mines, to the Gila River to trap.[7] There they found, in Pattie's words, "but few beaver remaining, and those few were exceedingly shy." Pausing to trap on the San Pedro River ("Beaver River"), which still yielded beaver in "considerable number," the group continued down the Gila until they neared the Colorado. There the group split in two. According to Pattie, the majority of the men broke their contract with his father and refused to follow their planned route any farther. Yount, however, who was among those who left Pattie,

[5] Hafen and Hafen, *Old Spanish Trail*, 131, place Campbell on the Gila; Lieutenant James H. Simpson, *Navaho Expedition: Journal of a Military Reconnaissance to the Navaho Country Made in 1849 by Lieutenant James H. Simpson* (ed. and annot. by Frank McNitt), 160–61.

[6] Testimony of Richard Campbell, February 23, 1828, in papers pertaining to the embargo of beaver fur belonging to Vicente Guion and Felipe Thompson, February 22, 1828, MANM; Chávez, "New Names," *El Palacio*, Vol. LXIV, Nos. 9–10 (September–October, 1957), 299; Guía, September 30, 1828, custom house records, Santa Fe, Ritch Papers, No. 108; A. Wislizenus, *Memoir of a Tour to Northern Mexico*, 32; *Abert's New Mexico Report, 1846–47*, 52; Edward D. Tittman, "By Order of Richard Campbell," *New Mexico Historical Review*, Vol. III, No. 4 (October, 1928), 390–98.

[7] Weber, *Extranjeros*, 9, 32; Pattie, *Narrative*, 121; Yount, *Yount and His Chronicles*, 43.

says that at this point, eight of the party "became insubordinate and parted from the main body."[8] Whatever the reason for the division, the Patties remained on the Colorado while Yount and most of the men headed north.

Six men stayed behind with the Patties: Nathaniel M. Pryor, Richard Laughlin, Jesse Ferguson, William Pope, Isaac Slover, and Edmund Russell.[9] Soon losing their horses to Indians, Pattie and company loaded their beaver into hastily constructed canoes and descended the Colorado, hoping to find a Mexican settlement at the river's mouth. Being one of the first groups of white men to visit this little-known area, their hopes did not seem unrealistic, but their disappointment upon approaching the unpopulated head of the Gulf of California must have been great. Instead of locating a settlement, they found themselves in a desolate area with no sign of beaver, many signs of Indians, and no way to navigate back up the river. Pattie was moved to comment that the weather was "exceedingly warm." It was winter or he might have used stronger language. Caching their furs, they headed west on a near-killing trek across the sun-parched desert of northern Baja California, only to be imprisoned by Mexican officials when, weakened and help-less, they reached the Mission Santa Catalina to the east of Ensenada on the Baja peninsula on March 18. From there the trappers, now prisoners, were taken north to San Diego.[10] Pattie's success in making it through to the Pacific coast via the Gila River was a considerable achievement, for the route remained difficult and seldom traveled into the 1830's. That the trappers survived the crossing of northern Baja to reach Santa Catalina seems, on the surface, incredible. Yet, Indians from the Colorado delta visited

[8] Pattie, *Narrative*, 121, 124; Yount, *Yount and His Chronicles*, 45.

[9] A letter from Pattie's group, written in California and paraphrased in the St. Louis *Times* of July 7, 1829, identifies all eight men. Pryor, Ferguson, and Laughlin had been working at the Santa Rita copper mines before joining the party. See Stephen C. Foster, "A Sketch of Some of the Earliest Kentucky Pioneers of Los Angeles," *Historical Society of Southern California* (1887), 30; J. J. Warner, "Reminiscences of Early California, 1831 to 1846," *Annual Publications of the Historical Society of Southern California*, Vol. VIII (1907–1908), 183.

[10] Pattie's *Narrative*, 129–51.

the mountains near the mission regularly, and Pattie may have followed their trail.[11]

If we are to take Pattie's *Narrative* at face value, the trappers' arrival in California was the result of a number of unforeseen circumstances, such as the loss of their horses and their failure to find a Spanish settlement at the mouth of the Colorado. More likely, however, the trip to the coast was premeditated. Judge Stephen C. Foster, a friend of Nathaniel Pryor, tells us that Pattie's group "had heard there were American vessels trading on the coast, and they reasoned that . . . they could realize more by selling to American traders in California than they could by selling in Santa Fe."[12]

Foster's version seems credible and is substantiated by the testimony of Juan José García and Manuel Hurtado, two New Mexicans who accompanied Pattie's trappers as servants. They said they traveled with a company of trappers in the employ of "Sylvestre Prade," probably meaning Pattie rather than Pratte, who headed for the Rockies that autumn. In October, 1827, "Prade" journeyed down the Río Grande with the expressed intention of going to Sonora. When they "arrived at the place where the Gila River joins the Rio Grande [Río Grande del Colorado?]" the servants discovered that the real plan was to go to California. Not wishing to travel such a distance, the Mexican servants decided to return to their homes in Taos. Each received three beaver traps as payment since their employer "had no money or merchandise." The Mexican servants made the best use of this pay and trapped beaver on their way home.[13]

Pattie's *Narrative* describing his captivity in California takes on many of the qualities of a melodrama. His father died alone in his cell, while his son was forbidden to visit him. Governor José María Echeandía, the villain of the story, tore up Pattie's passport in a fit of rage. Pattie claimed that his "passport" permitted him to

[11] Warner, "Reminiscences," *HSSC*, Vol. VIII (1907–1908), 188–89; Peter Gerhard and Howard E. Gulick, *Lower California Guidebook*, 97.

[12] Foster, "Pioneers of Los Angeles," *HSSC*, (1887), 31.

[13] Testimony of Manuel Hurtado and Juan José García in papers pertaining to the case of H. Tomás Boggs and Ramón Vigil, May 5, 1828, MANM.

travel anywhere, but clearly the *guía* that Sylvester Pattie had received in New Mexico allowed him to go only to Sonora or Chihuahua to trade. Furthermore, it is doubtful that it was destroyed, for Pattie reproduces a reasonable translation of it in his *Narrative*.

As Pattie tells it, by serving as translator for the governor, he earned permission for his furs to be retrieved from the cache on the Colorado. Captain John Bradshaw of the ship *Franklin*, then in San Diego harbor, had expressed interest in purchasing the fur. Probably in November, 1828, the governor allowed six of Pattie's companions to go after the furs, but kept Pattie behind as a hostage. Four of these men returned, reporting that the furs had been spoiled by water, while two "concluded that rather than return to prison, they would run the risk of being killed by the Indians, or of being starved to death; and set forth on their perilous journey through the wilderness to New Mexico on foot."[14] The two escapees, Isaac Slover and William Pope, returned safely to Taos. Their flight may not have been as dramatic as Pattie implies—or even an escape at all—for Governor Echeandía had given Slover and Pope passports to return to New Mexico in November, 1828. Pattie and Nat Pryor did not receive their letters of security until the following February and April respectively. Pope's and Slover's memories of California could not have been totally unpleasant, for in 1837 they returned via the Old Spanish Trail to make California their home.[15]

The story of Pattie's release from prison on the promise that he would inoculate people against smallpox and his adventures in California have been recounted elsewhere and are well known.[16] The imprisonment of the eight trappers received some notice in the American press, and the United States chargé d'affaires at Mexico City was ordered, in January, 1830, to investigate their arrest, but with no significant result. After failing to obtain redress through a personal interview with Mexican president Vicente Guerrero

[14] Pattie, *Narrative*, 158, 163, 165–67, 174–80, 184; St. Louis *Times*, July 7, 1829.
[15] See Hafen and Hafen, *Old Spanish Trail*, 198–99, 224–25; Rolle, "William Pope," in Hafen, *Mountain Men*, II, 275–76.
[16] Hubert Howe Bancroft, *History of California*, III, 162–72. Cleland, *Reckless Breed*, 199–208

in June, 1830, Pattie returned to Kentucky by way of Veracruz and New Orleans. His later life remains shrouded in mystery.[17]

At least three of Pattie's companions, Nat Pryor, Jesse Ferguson, and Richard Laughlin, who switched from trapping beaver to hunting sea otter, remained in California.[18] Seven years later, in the fall of 1835, Ferguson returned to the Gila on a trapping expedition with three other men. They passed the site of their old cache, which he estimated had contained fifteen thousand to twenty thousand dollars in furs. Ferguson was no more successful on this trip, however, than he had been on the fateful trip with Pattie.[19]

While Pattie's contingent suffered imprisonment in California, George Yount and the trappers who had separated from Pattie on the Gila circled back toward New Mexico by traveling north on the Colorado. It was perhaps well that they did not return via the copper mines, for officials on the northern frontier of Sonora, at least by the summer of 1828, had learned of the capture of eight Americans in California and had been alerted to thirty foreigners who had come to the Gila via the copper mines. These men had no license or permission to trap and, if apprehended, were to be ordered to leave. If they resisted, they were to be imprisoned.[20] But the trappers were never found. Perhaps led by a transplanted Englishman, William Workman,[21] they trapped their way up the Colorado, avoiding the Mohaves, whom they suspected of treachery. Leaving the Colorado in the area of Spencer Canyon, they

[17] Articles, for example, appeared in the *Boston Commercial*, the St. Louis *Times*, July 7, 1829, and the (Little Rock) *Arkansas Gazette*, July 29, 1829. Robert Glass Cleland, "The Early Sentiment for the Annexation of California; An Account of the Growth of American Interest in California, 1835–1846," *Southwestern Historical Quarterly*, Vol. XVIII, No. 1 (July, 1914), 11; Cleland, *Reckless Breed*, 205–208. See also Ann W. Hafen, "James Ohio Pattie," in Hafen, *Mountain Men*, IV, 247–50.

[18] Foster, "Pioneers of Los Angeles," *HSSC* (1887), 35.

[19] Charles L. Camp (ed.), "The Journal of a 'Crazy Man,'" *California Historical Society Quarterly*, Vol. XV, Nos. 2, 3 (June and September, 1936), 109, 133, n. 15.

[20] José María Paciola to the First Alcalde of Altar, Concepción del Alamos, July 5, 1828, and Paciola to the Alcalde of Santa Cruz, July 17, 1828, in Alphonse Louis Pinart, "Colección de manuscritos relativos a la región septentrional de Mexico," Series II, Docs. 43 and 44, Bancroft Library.

[21] David J. Weber, "William Workman," in Hafen, *Mountain Men*, VII, 382–92.

returned to Taos by way of the Hopi villages, Zuñi and Laguna. Somewhere on the Jemez River they cached their furs before entering Taos, then later safely smuggled them in.[22]

The next Taos trappers to beat new trails to California were Peg-leg Smith and Ewing Young. If Smith's memory served him well, he may have reached California early in 1830, after trapping on the Virgin River in Utah. According to his own account, the hunt had gone so well that, although it was still early in the season, the trappers had enough fur "to make a cargo." Thus, they decided to send two men to Los Angeles to market the furs. Smith, of course, was chosen since the task "was considered to be extra hazardous." Perhaps Smith's recollection is correct for another source corroborates his presence in the Virgin River area in the fall of 1829.[23]

Considerably more is known of Ewing Young's trek to California, for in his employ was Kit Carson, whose reminiscences furnish us with the most complete record of the trip. This, Carson's debut as a mountain man, marks the beginning of a legend. Carson had first come to Taos in 1826 as a young boy of sixteen. He worked as a teamster and a cook before finally achieving the status of a trapper in 1829. Before his career ended, Carson would hunt buffalo, guide John Frémont and Stephen Kearny around the West, and serve as a soldier, Civil War officer, rancher, Indian agent, and Indian fighter.[24]

Ewing Young, according to one contemporary, had formed a partnership with William Wolfskill and Solomon Houck, a prominent Santa Fe merchant "who furnished pecuniary aid." Carson tells us that Indians defeated the first trapping party which Young had sent toward the Colorado in 1828, and that they "considered

---

[22] Yount, *Yount and His Chronicles*, 45–64. A man named Allen accompanied this group—perhaps the same Allen who was with Pattie in the previous season (José Manuel Allen?).

[23] Yount, *Yount and His Chronicles*, 69; "The Story of an Old Trapper," *San Francisco Evening Bulletin*, October 26, 1866.

[24] Numerous biographies of Carson exist, but his own unvarnished autobiography best captures the flavor of his life. This appears in Harvey L. Carter's *'Dear Old Kit': The Historical Christopher Carson*.

it prudent to return." Young then "raised a party of forty men, consisting of Americans, Canadians and Frenchmen," and took command himself, leaving from Taos in August, 1829.[25] Aside from Ewing Young, Carson identifies only James Lawrence and James Higgins (the latter shot the former near Los Angeles) as members of the party. Contemporary documents reveal that three Frenchmen from Taos, François Turcote, Jean Vaillant, and Anastasio Carier, were also along. François Turcote had been one of Sylvestre Pratte's employees on an expedition in 1827–28 and Vaillant, who was born in France and had come to New Mexico in 1824, had been with Pratte in the spring of 1827. Anastasio Carier, a Canadian, had married at Taos in 1824 and had lived there ever since.[26] These three deserted Young's party in California and tried to get passports to return to New Mexico. According to Young, "All the french that I have with me . . . were owing me Large Debts and wishing to not pay them Mutinied they had Concluded to all remain in this Country but the Americans were too strong for them and forced them out much against their wills."[27]

In order to circumvent Mexican authorities, with whom he had been unpopular since they had discovered his scandalous smuggling of contraband beaver in 1827, Young used a tactic that was probably common among the foreign trappers. As Kit Carson explained it, Young led his men north to throw officials off his track. Then, fifty miles above Taos he shifted his course to the southwest, skirting the New Mexico settlements and passing through the Pueblo of Zuñi, on his way to the Salt River.

On the Salt the trappers "routed" the Indians who had bothered Young's earlier party. They continued trapping through the awe-

[25] Warner, "Reminiscences," *HSSC*, Vol. VIII (1907–1908), 185; Carter, *'Dear Old Kit,'* 42–44.

[26] For Turcote, see the Estate of S. S. Pratte, 1828, Chouteau Collection. For Vaillant, see Report of Manuel Martínez, Taos, April 7, 1827, and papers concerning the naturalization of Juan José Vaillant, February 8, 1831, both in MANM. Carier is "Larié" in Chávez, "New Names," *El Palacio*, Vol. LXIV, Nos. 9–10 (September–October, 1957), 313.

[27] Young to John B. R. Cooper, October 10, 1830, in Mariano G. Vallejo, Documentos para la historia de California, Vol. XXX, 1830–32, 135, MS, Bancroft Library; Hill, "Ewing Young," *OHSQ*, Vol. XXIV, No. 1 (March, 1923), 23.

some canyons of the Salt until they reached the Verde River ("San Francisco River"). Again altering their course, they followed the meanderings of the Verde in a northwesterly direction until they reached its headwaters. There the party divided.[28]

Some of Young's men returned to Taos with their catch of furs. Obscure documents in the Mexican archives at Santa Fe mention a group of Americans returning from the Gila in Februray, 1830, going through Cochití on their way to Taos. They were suspected of trapping, but one witness said they were on foot and carrying no equipment. Perhaps they had cached their furs before reaching Cochití. Another document, perhaps referring to this same group, speaks of furs confiscated by the alcalde of Jemez.[29] Collateral documents have not yet appeared.

Meanwhile, Young led seventeen men west from the Verde. Although he pioneered a new route into California, it was a grueling one which he would avoid on later occasions. This route, and Young's subsequent adventures in California, have been well-described elsewhere.[30] It is sufficient to say that they arrived at San Gabriel Mission, probably early in 1830, then spent the remainder of the season trapping the San Joaquin Valley. There they encountered Peter Skene Ogden and some of his Hudson's Bay Company trappers. In late summer, Young sold his furs to the captain of a trading schooner whom they met at San José Mission. By September, Young was on the way back to New Mexico. He retraced his steps to the Colorado, then trapped down that river to the Gila, which he followed to the Santa Rita copper mines. Arriving there, probably in January, 1831, he left his furs hidden at the mines, which were then in the charge of Robert McKnight. Since the furs had been taken without a license, Young could not legally sell them in New Mexico. So Young and Carson traveled to Santa Fe where

[28] Carter, 'Dear Old Kit,' 44.
[29] Declaration of José Martín, Jemez, March 23, 1830 and José Ignacio Ortiz to the Governor, Santa Fe, March 20, 1830. MANM.
[30] See Hill, "Ewing Young," OHSQ, Vol. XXIV, No. 1 (March, 1923), 23–27, and Holmes, Young, 46–57. The accuracy of Carson's account is attested to by documents which Hill found in Bancroft's transcripts from California archives. See especially a letter of José Berryeza, July 15, 1830, in Departmental State Papers, II, 135–39, MS, Bancroft Library.

Young obtained "a license to trade with Indians on the Gila." Then he sent some men to bring in the beaver. As Carson later told it, "Everyone considered we had made a fine trade in so short a period." The fur, he said, was "disposed of to advantage at Santa Fe, some two thousand pounds in all."[31]

While Ewing Young found his way to California, his partner, William Wolfskill, kept shop in Taos. Among his customers were William Williams and Thomas Smith, both of whom bought liberal amounts of whisky at seventy-five cents a pint.[32] Some of Wolfskill's customers would soon accompany him to California. Perhaps learning from the trappers who returned from the San Francisco River that Young had pushed on to California, Wolfskill made plans to join his partner there. An important part of his preparation consisted of becoming a Mexican citizen and then obtaining a license to trap in Mexican territory. In early September, 1830, Governor Armijo granted Wolfskill's request to take twenty men on a beaver trapping expedition. By the end of the month they were on their way.

In Wolfskill's employ were many newcomers to the area: John Lewis, Francis "Ziba" Branch, John Rhea, Samuel Shields, David Keller, Love Hardesty, Martin Cooper, and Lewis Burton. Three New Mexicans were taken along, perhaps as cooks or campkeepers: Blas Griego, Manuel Mondragón, and José Archuleta. Traveling along with Wolfskill's contingent were George C. Yount and five veteran free trappers who may have been in his employ: Alexander Branch, whom we have seen on the Gila and the Colorado; Francisco Laforet and Baptiste St. Germain, both former trappers for Sylvestre Pratte; and Zachariah Ham and Bautista Guerra.[33]

Wolfskill's trek to California is best known for inaugurating the route that came to be called the Old Spanish Trail, connecting Los Angeles and Santa Fe. Wolfskill's party was the first to travel the

---

[31] Carter, 'Dear Old Kit,' 44–50. Jean Vaillant had returned to Taos by February 8 to apply for naturalization as a Mexican citizen (Vaillant's request of that date is in MANM).

[32] Wolfskill Ledger, 1830–31, photocopy in the Huntington Library, San Marino, California.

[33] Iris Higbie Wilson, *William Wolfskill, 1798–1866: Frontier Trapper to California Ranchero*, 61–66.

A Trapper and His Pony, from a drawing by Frederic Remington.

From Henry Inman, *The Old Santa Fé Trail*

Mexican Girls. American trappers admired New Mexican women and were fascinated by their "high skirts and loose blouses." One young observer even suggested that cigarette smoking "does enhance the charms of the Mexican *señoritas.*"

From George Wilkins Kendall, *Narrative of the Texan Santa Fe Expedition*

Don Fernando de Taos, view from the south, artist unknown. This small southwestern village rivaled St. Louis and Fort Vancouver as one of the most important markets for beaver in the Far West.

U.S. Signal Corps, National Archives

Pack Train to Santa Fe, from a drawing by Frederic Remington.

From Henry Inman, *The Old Santa Fé Trail*

A Beaver Hut. Beaver were the mainstay of the southwestern fur trade. Though sketched here by Charles Bodmer far north of the trapping grounds of the Taos traders, this scene graphically depicts the beaver in their natural state.

Courtesy of the Newberry Library

Camp Among the Wasatch Mountains.

Santa Fe, from the Great Missouri Trail.

Plaza of Albuquerque.
From W. W. H. Davis' *El Gringo*

Lieutenant J. W. Abert's Perspective of Bent's Fort, 1845.

Junction of the Gila and Colorado Rivers—looking up the Gila. In their search for furs the Taos trappers blazed trails to the Colorado Basin and the Gila River.

From John R. Bartlett, *Personal Narrative*
Courtesy California State Library

entire route. Following the northwesterly course pioneered by Domínguez and Escalante in 1776, they traveled well into central Utah before heading toward the southwest to reach the Sevier River and the route that Jedediah Smith had pioneered into California (via the Virgin River, the Mohave Villages, the Mohave River, Cajon Pass, and Los Angeles).[34]

As a trapping expedition, Wolfskill's venture was a failure. Upon arrival in California he decided that the season was too old to make a profitable hunt on the San Joaquin and allowed his party to disband. Wolfskill, Yount, Burton, Rhea, Cooper, Shields, Ziba Branch, and perhaps others decided to make California their home, and we shall hear no more of them as Taos trappers. Others, Francisco Laforet among them, returned to New Mexico to continue their careers in the mountains. Wolfskill and Yount each tried his hand at another aspect of the fur trade in California—sea otter hunting. Wolfskill's license from the governor of New Mexico permitted him to hunt *nutria*, a word which New Mexicans used to mean beaver, but which really meant otter. This enabled Wolfskill to hunt sea otter legally in California—an occupation which was ordinarily closed to nonresidents.[35]

While Wolfskill traveled toward California, Ewing Young had returned to New Mexico, and a rendezvous in California never took place. The fault, however, was entirely Young's, who was forced to leave California hurriedly. Young had originally planned to stay in California through the fall of 1830 in order to launch another trapping party. Then he would trade his furs for horses and mules and drive them back to New Mexico. His plans were interrupted, however, when some of his men became involved in a drunken brawl, forcing his precipitous departure. Back at Taos in the summer of 1831, Young planned an immediate return to California. However, he notified a prominent American ship captain on the coast that "owing to the bad situation I found my bisiness in here

---

[34] Hafen and Hafen, *Old Spanish Trail*, 139–53.

[35] Wilson, *William Wolfskill*, 78, 82–84; Weber, "Francisco Laforet," in Hafen, *Mountain Men*, VI, 213–18; John E. Baur, "Francis Ziba Branch," Hafen, *Mountain Men*, II, 55–60. A description of sea otter hunting during this period appears in Adele Ogden's *California Sea Otter Trade, 1784–1848*, 95–120.

on my arrival I have not been able to Return to California." When his affairs were settled, he hoped "to Come to that Cuntry To Settle my self."[36]

Young's desire to change his base of operations from New Mexico to California may have been motivated less by the mule and horse trade and the new beaver grounds of the West Coast, than by a strong desire to leave New Mexico. Officials in Santa Fe found him to be a perennial troublemaker. In July, 1829, Young, who assertedly had not paid sufficient duties on goods he brought over the trail that year, protested to the governor the injustice of his debt to the custom house and forwarded a number of documents to support his case.[37] In November, 1830, although in California, Young remained in legal difficulty in New Mexico. Governor José Antonio Chávez wrote to the alcalde of San Juan that proceedings against Young should await Young's return from trapping, but if Young was not back by the end of December, the alcalde should do what he thought necessary in view of the evidence. Young's difficulties are not illuminated by any other extant documents of those years, but in August, 1831, after Young had returned from California, the governor wrote to Luis Robidoux expressing surprise that the alcalde of Taos "has not complied with his obligations by immediately placing the foreigner, Joaquin Yon, who had committed the crime of which he is accused, in a secure prison and formed a suitable case [against him]." Governor Chávez thought "the crimes and impudence of the aforementioned foreigner, Yon, are already insufferable." The governor suggested to Robidoux that Young be arrested and brought to trial in Santa Fe since the witnesses against him lived there. In addition, Governor Chávez wished "the criminal" to be taken to the jail in Santa Fe because he thought it was a more secure place.[38] There is no record, however, of Young's having been brought to trial previous to his second and final departure for California.

[36] Young to J. B. Cooper, October 10, 1830, and Young to Cooper, Taos, August 24, 1831, in Vallejo, Documentos, Tomo XXX, 1830–32, 135, 241, Bancroft Library.
[37] Ewing Young to the Governor, July 9, 1829, MANM.
[38] Letters of November 6, 1830 and August 6, 1831, in governor's letterbook, October 21, 1830 to August 31, 1831, MANM.

Before Young could leave Taos for California, he had, as we have seen, to attend to some "business." In the summer of 1831, he formed a partnership with David Waldo and David Jackson; the latter would go to California in Young's place. According to plan, Jackson would lead a mule and horse buying expedition, and Young would follow later in the season with a trapping party.[39]

Young's new partner, David Jackson, along with Jedediah Smith and William Sublette, had bought out William Ashley in 1826 and by 1830 had succeeded to the point where they could sell out and retire from the mountains with a tidy profit. Looking for a place to invest their new-found wealth, Smith, Jackson, and Sublette had turned to the Santa Fe trade. When their caravan lumbered west in the spring of 1831, all three partners were along, but only two made it through to Santa Fe. Jedediah Smith, who had crossed and recrossed far more dangerous and remote trails, met his death at the hands of Comanches on the Santa Fe Trail—that most-traveled of highways in the Far West. Smith's own epic journeys into California had caused Mexican officials considerable concern, and news of his death was sent to Mexico City through Mexican agents in St. Louis and New Orleans. Smith was reported to have been renowned for his knowledge of the Colorado River and the internal states of Mexico, among other things.[40] But Smith never used New Mexico as a base for his explorations so his career is only peripheral to this study.

In Santa Fe, Jackson and Sublette dissolved their partnership. Sublette set up shop, trading his merchandise for fifty-five packs of beaver fur and eight hundred buffalo robes. By September 1, he was on his way home with another caravan. He was not "pleased with the country or the business" in New Mexico and would not return.[41]

David Jackson apparently liked what he saw of the Southwest,

---

[39] Warner, "Reminiscences," *HSSC*, Vol. VIII (1907–1908), 178; Job Francis Dye, *Recollections of a Pioneer, 1830–1852*, 18.

[40] John E. Sunder, *Bill Sublette: Mountain Man*, 83, 93–97; Morgan, *Jedediah Smith*, 329–30; Francisco Pizarro Martínez to Secretario de Estado, October 29, 1831, New Orleans, in Relaciones Exteriores, Doc. H/314(73:72)1; 2-15-3497.

[41] Sunder, *Bill Sublette*, 99–100.

for he formed a partnership with Ewing Young and David Waldo, the latter a prominent Santa Fe merchant and old friend. Jackson sold his merchandise for Mexican dollars, loaded these on mules, and on September 6, 1831, set out for California with his Negro slave and nine other men. Among these were one of Jedediah Smith's younger brothers, Peter, and J. J. Warner. According to the latter, they traveled south to the copper mines, followed the Gila west, and reached San Diego in early November.[42]

In October, Ewing Young (who in August had received a passport to go to Chihuahua) followed Jackson to California by a different route.[43] Thirty-six men reportedly comprised his party. Of these, we can identify twenty-nine by name: Pleasant Austin, Powell Weaver, James Wilkinson, James Basey, Hace, James Green, Cambridge Green, James Anderson, Isaac Williams, John Price, Job F. Dye, Sidney Cooper, Moses Carson, Benjamin Day, William Day, Isaac Sparks, Joseph Gale, Joseph Defit, John Higgins, Thomas Low, José Manuel Ortega, Manuel Leal, Julián Vargas, José Teforia, Santiago Cordero, José Manuel Servé, José and Mariano García, and Francisco Argüello. The first eleven of this list had just arrived in New Mexico that previous winter after an abortive attempt at trapping in the southern Rockies. Most of these eleven remained in California. The best account of Young's journey comes from one of these men, Job Francis Dye.[44]

Young waited until reaching Zuñi before picking up food supplies, perhaps, says Dye, to avoid calling attention to his activities. There Young's party paused for two days, stocking up on the "Pinole (roasted corn meal) and pinoche (sugar) and frijoles (beans) required on the route."[45] They continued to the Salt River,

[42] Warner, "Reminiscences," HSSC, Vol. VIII (1907–1908), 178–86; William Sublette to William Ashley, Walnut Creek, September 24, 1831, photostat in the Campbell Papers, Missouri Historical Society, St. Louis, Missouri.

[43] The passport of "Joaquin Jon" dated August 21, 1831, in book of passports, 1828–36, Santa Fe, Ritch Papers, No. 185.

[44] William Henry Ellison (ed.), The Life and Adventures of George Nidever, 1802–83, 20; Dye, Recollections, 18, 20; papers relating to the embargo of the furs of Ewing Young, July 12–July 25, 1832, MANM. A biography of Dye by Gloria Griffen Cline is in Hafen, Mountain Men, I, 259–71.

[45] Dye, Recollections, 18–19. Pinole was not an uncommon food for trappers

then followed that stream, setting traps as they went. On the Salt, James Anderson and Cambridge Green had a dispute over trapping rights, Green feeling that Anderson had placed his traps in an area which Green had claimed. Green complained to Young about this, and Young, according to Dye, replied, "What makes you let him do it—if I could not prevent him in any other way, I would shoot him." Young's remark, spoken in levity, was taken seriously by Green, who promptly dispatched the hapless Anderson.

Dye recalled that they also trapped for twelve days on the San Carlos River. This would have meant considerable backtracking and would have taken them well off their route. He probably meant the Verde, for Mexican trappers who were along described the route as following the Zuñi River to the Salt and the Verde, and then to the Gila.[46] When they reached the Colorado, thirteen men made the difficult crossing into California while the remainder trapped their way back to New Mexico. J. J. Warner heard that Young's beaver traps, "mostly new ones bought in New Mexico," were defective, allowing many beaver to escape. Dye does not mention this problem, however.[47]

As planned, Young and David Jackson rendezvoused in California. J. J. Warner, who was in Jackson's employ, tells that Jackson had gone as far north as San Francisco to search for mules, but neither he nor Young were as successful as they had hoped. Instead of the fifteen hundred or two thousand mules they had planned on they had only six hundred mules and one hundred horses. Jackson could get the animals back to New Mexico without Young's assistance. Young went as far as the Colorado River to help Jackson make the crossing, then returned to the coast.[48]

When Jackson returned to New Mexico, apparently in July, 1832, it was discovered that he had brought more than mules and

in the Southwest. See Camp, "Journal of a 'Crazy Man,'" *CHSQ*, Vol. XV, No. 2 (June, 1936), 105.

[46] Dye, *Recollections*, 23–24. See the testimony of David E. Jackson in papers regarding the embargo of the furs of Ewing Young, July 12–July 25, 1832, MANM.

[47] Dye, *Recollections*, 24–27; Warner, "Reminiscences," *HSSC*, Vol. VIII (1907–1908), 186.

[48] Warner, "Reminiscences," *HSCC*, Vol. VIII (1907–1908), 179.

horses. One of his party, José Manuel Ortega, told the second alcalde of Santa Fe that Jackson, four Americans, and two Mexicans were at the stopping place called "Contadero," on the Camino Real—apparently the road to El Paso—with six and one-half loads (*cargas*) of beaver fur. The furs, Ortega said, belonged to Ewing Young. Ortega had good reason for knowing this, for he also had been a member of Young's party and had returned to New Mexico with Jackson. Willing to testify to this were four other New Mexicans who had been trapping with Young: Manuel Leal, José Manuel Servé, and José and Mariano García, all of Taos. By fall, Manuel Leal would be on another trapping expedition with the Americans Albert Pike and Richard Campbell. Servé, it is interesting to note, was the son of Josef Charvet, who had guided Baptiste La Lande to New Mexico in 1805 and had remained.[49]

Agustín Durán, the *comisario*, ordered "Young's" furs confiscated and called upon David Jackson to explain where these furs had come from. Jackson said he did not know where the beaver had been trapped. He knew only that he had five hundred beaver skins which belonged to David Waldo. Jackson had been hired to bring them from California to New Mexico. The alcalde questioning Jackson, ignorant of the partnership between Jackson, Young, and Waldo, seemed certain that the furs belonged to Ewing Young, but Jackson expressed equal conviction that they belonged only to Waldo and that Young was merely the agent for Waldo. As proof, Jackson produced a license which the governor of New Mexico had given to Waldo. This may have been the trapping license that Governor Chávez had granted to Antoine Robidoux and David Waldo on September 19, 1831.[50] That Ewing Young's name did not appear on this is not strange, for he was not a citizen and therefore not entitled to a license. Furthermore, Chávez regarded him with contempt.

New Mexican officials remained suspicious, and rightly so, that

[49] Pike, *Prose Sketches*, 37–38; Chávez, "Addenda to New Mexico Families," *El Palacio*, Vol. LXIV, Nos. 5–6 (May–June, 1957), 186–87. Charvet has been discussed in Chapter 3.

[50] Waldo requested this in the name of himself and Robidoux. His request dated September 17 and Chávez's reply are in MANM.

the furs belonged to Ewing Young. On July 25, testimony was taken from one Francisco Alegro Argüello, who had also accompanied Young's party. He knew that Young was his employer, but knew nothing of David Waldo's interest in the expedition. The remaining documents in the Mexican archives of New Mexico are silent concerning the outcome of this case.[51] David E. Jackson's activities, both before and after this trip to California, remain obscure.

Ewing Young never returned to New Mexico. After helping David Jackson cross the Colorado River with his livestock and fur, Young and a few men—Moses Carson, Isaac Williams, Isaac J. Sparks, and J. J. Warner among them—returned to the coast, where they tried their hand at sea otter hunting. Sparks found this so profitable that he stayed in the business until 1849. After several dunkings in the Pacific, Young decided that terrestrial furs held greater appeal for him and led a party of fourteen to trap in the San Joaquin and Sacramento valleys in the autumn of 1832. On the Sacramento, Young encountered a group of Hudson's Bay Company trappers under Michel LaFramboise. Young continued north, getting as far as the Umpqua River. As J. J. Warner remembered, Young was on one continuous trapping expedition from the fall of 1832 to the summer of 1834. Before the hunt ended at Los Angeles, Young had even trapped again on the lower Gila.[52] This marked Young's finale in the Southwest. In 1834 he left California, persuaded to move to Oregon by the eccentric New England publicist Hall J. Kelley. Settling in the Willamette Valley, Young made Oregon his home until his premature death in 1841. During his last years he engaged in a wide range of economic activities, including lumber, cattle, banking, and wheat. He became one of the leaders of Oregon's American community and contributed significantly to loosening the control of the Hudson's Bay Company over the

[51] Papers relating to the embargo of the furs of Ewing Young, July 12–July 25, 1832, MANM.

[52] Warner, "Reminiscences," *HSSC*, Vol. VIII (1907–1908), 187–88. Some recollections of Isaac J. Sparks are in F. H. Day, "Sketches of the Early Settlers of California, Isaac J. Sparks," *The Hesperian*, Vol. II, No. 5 (July, 1859), 193–200. A biography is John E. Baur "Isaac Sparks," in Hafen, *Mountain Men*, II, 317–19.

territory. In twelve years of trapping, Ewing Young's search for beaver cut a wide swath across Mexico's far northern frontier. That he was, as his first biographer remarked, "one of the central figures" in the fur trade of the Far Southwest[53] can scarcely be denied. To Mexican officials, however, this prominent trapper and trader was a rogue and a scoundrel, and Taos would be none the poorer for his departure.

The opening of new trails to California had brought the Taos trappers into promising new beaver grounds with convenient access to Pacific ports where furs might be marketed. Yet, the extension of New Mexico–based trapping into California was short-lived. Partly this was the fault of the Hudson's Bay Company, whose efficient brigades once again formed stiff competition for the loosely organized independent trappers of the Southwest. The Britishers, who annually swept across northern California, probably made beaver scarce for the Americans.[54]

Yet, the opening of new routes from New Mexico to California started a flow of foreigners into California, many of whom remained there to serve as a "fifth column" in the critical years before the Mexican War. Thus, even before David Jackson returned to Santa Fe with mules in 1832, Archibald Stevenson and Juan Purcel (John Poisel?) had received in the fall of 1831 a passport to travel to California to trade mules.[55] In 1833 another group, which included trappers Cyrus Alexander, Lemuel Carpenter, William Chard, Joseph Paulding, Albert Toomes, and a Mr. Turk, entered California via the Gila route. In October, 1832, these men had taken out passports in Santa Fe to travel south to the "Internal States," which usually meant Chihuahua or Sonora. Instead, they took the liberty of moving on into California.[56]

[53] Hill, "Ewing Young," *OHSQ*, Vol. XXIV, No. 1 (March, 1923), 33.
[54] Lester Gordon Engelson, "Interests and Activities of the Hudson's Bay Company in California, 1820–1846" (M.A. thesis, University of California, Berkeley, 1939), 19.
[55] Passport of October 3, 1831, in book of passports, 1828–36, Santa Fe, in the Ritch Papers, No. 185; Janet Lecompte, "John Poisel" in Hafen, *Mountain Men*, VI, 353–58.

New trails across northern Mexico also gave rise to steady commerce between Los Angeles and Santa Fe. From the beginning of this trade in 1830, Mexican traders had slight interest in furs. Instead, the exchange of woven goods from New Mexico for California horses and mules became the mainstay of the trade. Yet, on occasion, woven goods were exchanged for furs. Jim Waters is even reputed to have taken abalone shells from the Pacific over the Spanish Trail to the Rockies, where he traded them for beaver fur and buffalo robes. The movement of trading caravans to California in the 1830's facilitated further settlement of Americans and their families in California. Many of these Americans were former trappers who had either seen California first hand or had heard of it from trappers. Thus, William Pope and Isaac Slover returned to California in 1837 with a trader's caravan. In 1841 William Workman and John Rowland led a large immigrant party to California, trapper and trader Benjamin Wilson among them.[57] In 1844 Louis Robidoux and Jean Jeantet, one of Sylvestre Pratte's former *engagés*, also settled permanently in California, having come with a train of Mexican traders. Neither returned to New Mexico and Robidoux became a prominent California rancher.[58]

Other American trappers, whose names have escaped the record, doubtless found their way into California by way of New Mexico. A ship captain at Monterey in 1836, for example, described a group of Tennessee trappers who had come to the Pacific via Santa Fe. Taking the *Peacock* up to San Francisco, the trappers had a good deal of trouble adjusting to the "closed atmosphere" of the ship. One of the trappers refused to go below deck to sleep: "He slept on deck," the captain recorded with a mixture of astonishment and

---

[56] Donald C. Cutter, and David J. Weber, "Cyrus Alexander," in Hafen, *Mountain Men*, V, 28.

[57] Hafen and Hafen, *Old Spanish Trail*, 154–89, 199–218.

[58] Ward Alan Minge, "Frontier Problems in New Mexico Preceding the Mexican War, 1840–1846" (Ph.D. dissertation, University of New Mexico, 1965), 247–52; Juan Estevan to Francis Cragin, April 24, 1908, and Cruz Jeantet to Cragin, May 6, 1908, Book XII, 48 and 73, Cragin Collection, Pioneers' Museum, Colorado Springs, Colorado, Weber, "Louis Robidoux," in Hafen, *Mountain Men*, VIII.

admiration, "using no other bedding than a blanket, and no other pillow than his arm."[59]

Many of the Taos trappers who settled in California enjoyed brief careers as sea otter hunters, but most of them eventually made their living from the soil. One contemporary reported that those who owned vineyards found that the steel springs of the beaver traps "had just the right shape to be forged into pruning knives," and used the iron from their traps for spurs and bridle bits, "thus fulfilling the words of the Scripture. 'They shall beat their swords into plough shares, and their spears into pruning hooks.' "[60] Certainly, the analogy is overdrawn, but the story is appropriate. As the era of the mountain men drew to a close, many would be content to take up the plow. The trails that the Campbells, Patties, Youngs, and Wolfskills opened to California would enable a later generation of American emigrants to do likewise.

[59] W. S. W. Ruschenberger, *A Voyage Around the World, 1835, 1836, 1837*, II, 412–13.
[60] Foster, "Pioneers of Los Angeles," *HSSC* (1887), 35.

X MEANWHILE,

WHILE SOME Taos trappers occupied themselves in the heady business of trail blazing, the fur trade in New Mexico continued apace in a quiet and unspectacular manner. Mexican officials remained vigilant against foreign trappers, but with limited success; the foreigners, wiser after the misfortunes of Pratte, François Robidoux, Young, Emmons, and others, exercised greater caution than before.

Authorities in New Mexico, despite their best intentions, remained hard pressed to stop Americans, for the military remained as undermanned and ineffective as it had been when Narbona complained about his failure to capture foreign trappers on the Gila in 1826. Thus, diversionary tactics such as Ewing Young had used in the fall of 1829—pretending to travel north into American territory and instead circling to the south—enjoyed an excellent chance of success. Also, furs could easily be cached near the New Mexico settlements, then smuggled into Taos or Santa Fe undetected. George Yount described how, on his return from the Gila and the Colorado in 1828, his party hid its catch on the Jemez River. Later, perhaps at night, the fur was taken to Taos and deposited in the distillery of Yount's "employer," who was "deeply engaged in smuggling." This may have been William Workman, who operated a still at Taos from perhaps as early as 1826 to 1841. As

156

BACK AT TAOS, 1827–1829

Yount remembered it, "an under ground passage, led to the grand subteranean cache, where goods, to an enormous amount, were being secretly deposited."[1]

José Agustín Escudero, a Chihuahua lawyer who passed through New Mexico in 1827 on his way to Missouri, described still another imaginative technique used by Americans bent on trapping. The Americans, he said, floated down the Río Grande on rafts, trapping as they went, then at El Paso they sold the lumber from the raft and spirited their furs out of the territory. The trappers, Escudero reported, "never presented their pelts to be registered; they transported them over unknown roads to the frontier."[2]

Trappers and traders not only bootlegged furs out of New Mexico but also profited by illegally importing trade goods without paying duty on them. Indeed, some felt justified in doing so, for they operated under a clear handicap when competing with other American fur traders who entered the Rockies to the north of the Mexican settlements and thus did not pay duty on their trade goods.[3]

Smuggling trade goods into New Mexico, or furs out, was not

[1] Yount, *Yount and His Chronicles* 64.
[2] Carroll and Haggard, *Three New Mexico Chronicles*, 105.
[3] Other aspects of this problem are discussed in Moorhead, *New Mexico's Royal Road*, 72–74.

difficult, even on the Santa Fe Trail. Neither Taos nor San Miguel del Vado, the two chief ports of entry on the trail, enjoyed the luxury of a customs house. Instead, Santa Fe remained the sole center for collection almost throughout the Mexican period. Government officials, such as Escudero, bemoaned the obvious—that the "custom house should have been on the New Mexican frontier from where the merchants and traders take back to the United States precious metals and a large number of rich peltries." Officials also worried over those Americans who lived in New Mexico, knew the language, the customs, and the terrain, and who helped to facilitate the passage of contraband through the territory.[4]

By 1829, at least, New Mexico officials began to take overt action to stop smuggling on the trail by ordering troops to intercept the American caravan at Taos and San Miguel del Vado.[5] This probably had little effect, however. The next year the *comisario*, or manager of the custom house, Agustín Durán, suggested that a fort and customs entry be built on the Canadian River, then called the Río Colorado, to control Indians and prevent American smuggling. Neither the fort nor the custom house was established, but Durán had decided that the Canadian River was the best place to intercept the incoming caravans and, perhaps from 1830 on, troops were sent there when the caravan was expected to arrive. Ceran St. Vrain, who was returning to Taos in the summer of 1830, reported that the caravan was met on the "Red River" by General José Antonio Vizcarra, some soldiers, and the custom house officer: "The object in coming out so fare to meet us was to prevent Smuggling and it had the desired effeck."[6] In 1831, Santiago Abreú was traveling with New Mexican troops on a similar mission when, on the Río de Ocaté (called Cache Creek by the Americans) near present-day Springer, he came upon some Americans digging a

[4] Carroll and Haggard, *Three New Mexico Chronicles*, 65–66; report of an official at Santa Fe (probably Governor Armijo), July 31, 1827, Ritch Papers, No. 96, in Weber, *Extranjeros*, 42.

[5] Agustín Durán to the Comandante General of New Mexico, August 4, 1829, MANM. The need for a custom house at these points is discussed in Barreiro, *Ojeada*, 65–66.

[6] St. Vrain to B. Pratte and Company, Taos, September 14, 1830, Chouteau Collection.

hollow in the side of the river bank in which to cache their goods. They probably intended to continue on to Taos, then return later with mules and take the merchandise in secretly. John Rowland demonstrated how this could be done when, in 1837, he loaded his mules with flour in Taos, then traveled to the Río Colorado— either the Canadian or the Red River to the north of Taos. There he met the caravan, exchanged his flour for merchandise, and returned secretly to Taos. He thus avoided paying both the export and the import duties.[7]

It was so well known that Americans commonly cached a portion of their goods before entering the settlements that in 1831 a Mexican agent as far away as St. Louis learned of the trick. Through him the Mexican foreign office would soon hear of it too. The agent (whose name the documents do not reveal) even knew the location of the American cache, identifying it as "the place called, in French, *des Oignons chauds*, or the hot onions."[8] Even this "precise" intelligence did not lead to the end of American smuggling. Goods continued to enter the territory illegally, and furs continued to be exported illegally for the remainder of the decade, and New Mexico was the poorer for it. As Agustín Durán lamented in 1831, New Mexico lost precious customs revenue and also witnessed the "extraction of beaver which the most energetic measures have not been able to contain . . . We have seen our rivers cleaned of the riches they contained."[9]

Foreign trappers did not rely on smuggling alone to "clean" New Mexico streams of beaver. A trapper might also pretend to have purchased from Indians or from native New Mexicans furs which he had actually trapped. Thus, the trapper could "legally" export the furs or could sell them to another merchant who would take them on to the St. Louis market. American merchants wel-

[7] Abreú to Agustín Durán, Santa Fe, July 5, 1831, MANM; Pike, *Prose Sketches*, 21; Weber, "John Rowland," in Hafen, *Mountain Men*, IV, 279.
[8] Francisco Pizarro Martínez to Secretario de Estado, New Orleans, October 29, 1831, in Relaciones Exteriores, Doc. No. H/314(73:72)1.
[9] Borrador of September 14, 1831, in book of borradores of the oficios which the Comisario Subalterno of New Mexico sent to the Director General de Rentas, 1831, MANM. Smuggling is discussed in Chapter 6 of Moorhead, *New Mexico's Royal Road*.

comed beaver fur since furs and mules could be exported from New Mexico duty-free, while they had to pay a tariff on exported specie.[10] American trappers could also operate "legally" by persuading a *Nuevo Mexicano* to apply for a license, which they would then buy from him. Sometimes, for additional safety, the Mexican license holder might even be taken along on the hunt.

That Americans, with their superior metal traps and knowledge of trapping techniques, succeeded at these ruses made many Mexicans painfully aware of their own failure to develop domestic trapping.[11] Although natives often accompanied foreign trappers, they usually appear to have gone along as servants rather than as apprentices, as governors Baca and Narbona had hoped. One of the few exceptions might have been José Achala, who in November, 1825, petitioned the governor for permission for himself and two others residents of San Miguel del Vado to trap, in order to alleviate their extreme poverty and hunger.[12] Perhaps Achala's interest in trapping was aroused by contact with Americans who frequented his village, which lay along the Santa Fe Trail. And perhaps Achala's efforts at trapping were duplicated by native New Mexicans in other towns, such as Taos and Abiquiu on the Chama, where American influence was strong. If so, the records are silent; it seems more likely that Achala did not trap at all, but sold his license to a foreigner.

A more certain exception was Domingo Lamelas, a young resident of the state of Chihuahua, who apparently learned the trapping business from James Baird.[13] After Baird's death in December, 1826, Lamelas may have continued on the trapping expedition that his deceased *dueño*, or employer, had instituted. Lamelas then drifted into Santa Fe, where in April, 1827, he applied for a license

[10] Barreiro, *Ojeada*, 108. Albert William Bork, *Nuevos aspectos del comercio entre Nuevo México y Misuri, 1822–1846*, 88.

[11] Barreiro, *Ojeada*, 110; José Agustín de Escudero to Ministro de Estado y del Despacho de Hacienda, José G. de la Cortina, April 1, 1839, in Bork, *Nuevos aspectos*, 124–28.

[12] José Achala to the Governor of New Mexico, November 10, 1825, MANM.

[13] Vicente Guion to the First Alcalde of Santa Fe, February 23, 1828, in papers relating to the seizure of beaver skins from Guion and Felipe Tomson, February 22, 1828.

to trap beaver with two other Mexican citizens on the "Colorado" River and the "Moro"—meaning, perhaps, the Canadian River, then called the Colorado, and the Mora, which flows into the Canadian to the east of present Las Vegas, New Mexico. Lamelas requested this license on the grounds that his parents and his sisters depended on him for their livelihood; trapping was the only trade he knew. Governor Narbona granted a license on the condition that Lamelas take no foreigners with him,[14] but this stipulation went unheeded. In September, 1827, Domingo Lamelas left Taos with another Mexican, José María Meras, but two Frenchmen, Simon Carat and Antoine Leroux ("Joaquín Leru"), also went along.[15] Juan Nepumuceno, a young servant, and another boy who served the two Frenchmen, accompanied them. According to Leroux's later testimony, they trapped under a contract to Sylvestre Pratte, with whose larger party they had apparently left Taos. Separating from Pratte, they trapped on the headwaters of the Río Grande and on the Conejos River, which empties into the Río Grande in the San Luis Valley. By February, 1828, they had returned to Taos with eight *tercios* of beaver fur, four belonging to the two Mexicans and four to the Frenchmen. Most of this was sold to American trader Vicente Guion.[16]

A *tercio* commonly meant half a load. It was not a rigid measure and its usage in New Mexico at that time seemed to be synonymous with "bundle." A small *tercio*, for example, contained fourteen or fifteen skins. Some of Lamelas' *tercios* contained twenty-four or twenty-five skins, and those confiscated later from Vicente Guion contained over thirty skins.[17] Since, at this time, a beaver pelt weighed between a pound and a half and a pound and three quar-

[14] Domingo Lamelas to the Governor, April 20, 1827, MANM, contains a marginal note by Narbona.

[15] Antoine Leroux' first name, which he occasionally used, was Joaquín; Parkhill, *The Blazed Trail of Antoine Leroux*, 24. Simon Carat may be the "Simon Clert" who was among Pratte's engagés in January of 1827.

[16] Hearings before Juan Estevan Pino, June 6, 1828, especially the testimony of Joaquin Leru; and papers relating to the seizure of beaver skins from Guion and Tomson, February 22, 1828, MANM.

[17] Testimony of Manuel Romero in the case of the embargo of the supplies of Pratte's trappers, May 24, 1828, and papers relating to the seizure of beaver skins from Guion and Tomson, February 22, 1828, MANM.

ters, a regular *tercio* of about thirty skins weighed about fifty pounds. This was the amount which George Yount remembered as the weight of a pack of furs and coincides with the size of William Ashley's packs of 1825, which averaged about thirty-one skins or fifty-two pounds. Packs prepared in "presses," however, were twice that weight so furs which reached the Missouri market by boat or wagon often arrived in packs of about one hundred pounds.[18] At New Mexico prices, in 1828, beaver fur brought $3.50 per pound, slightly more than the "mountain price" of $3.00, which remained constant between 1823 and 1833.[19]

Although few New Mexicans took up trapping after the coming of *norteamericanos*, many apparently continued the traditional fur trade with Utes, which had existed even before the famous trek of Domínguez and Escalante. One such group consisted of five residents of Abiquiu: José Ramón Martín, his brother Martín de Jesús, Tomás Chacón, Pedro León, and a young servant belonging to one Pedro Gallegos. In the summer of 1827, they traveled to Utah Lake, probably taking the Spanish Trail. In September they traded with Utes for beaver, then returned to Abiquiu, apparently by November. The traders brought back a modest return: the Martín brothers acquired thirty-one beaver pelts between them; Tomás Chacón got twenty-four; and Pedro León, eleven. Perhaps, in keeping with tradition, the traders also ransomed captive Indians from the Utes to bring back to New Mexico and sell as slaves. Mexican traders were still involved in this gruesome business in the 1850's, and Mormon officials caught and convicted Pedro León of leading a slave trading party into Utah Territory in 1851. By that time León must have been a man of considerable experience.[20]

Vicente Guion, who had purchased the furs from the Lamelas

18 Morgan, *Ashley*, 295, n. 239; Yount, *Yount and His Chronicles*, 71; Chittenden, *American Fur Trade*, I, 40; Account Book, No. 2, entry of August 16, shipment of furs to L. L. Waldo, Alvarez Papers, State Records Center, Santa Fe, New Mexico. See also Carl P. Russell, *Firearms, Traps, & Tools of the Mountain Men*, 156–58, for a discussion of how packs were made.

19 Morgan, *Jedediah Smith*, 230.

20 Papers relating to the seizure of beaver skins from Vicente Guion and Felipe Tomson, February 22, 1828, MANM; L. R. Bailey, *Indian Slave Trade in the Southwest*, 159–60.

party, also bought the majority of the pelts that these Mexican traders brought back to Abiquiu. Guion's entanglement with the law that season furnishes an unusual glimpse into the workings of the fur trade in New Mexico and testifies to the continuing watchfulness of New Mexico authorities toward the trade.

An American from an old St. Louis family, Guion had left Missouri in July, 1827, in a company which included such well-known fur traders as Paul Baillio, Thomas Boggs, Manuel Alvarez, and Luis Robidoux. This group reached Taos in November, and Guion lost no time in sending two agents to Abiquiu to buy furs. One was Juan Bautista Trudeau, a French-American who had been living in Taos, who had married there in July, 1826, and who would soon become a Mexican citizen. Trudeau had gone with François Robidoux in March, 1827, when he visited "Indian Country" in search of "*entierros.*"[21] The other agent is identified in the documents only as "Americanito," the little American. As Guion's agents, Trudeau and Americanito bought the furs that the Mexican traders had obtained from the Utes. Pedro León had already sold his furs to Mateo García, and Tomás Chacón had sold his to the alcalde of Abiquiu, and Trudeau bought the furs through these "middlemen."

Paul Baillio and Manuel Alvarez, both of whom had arrived in Taos in November with Guion, were also bidding in the Abiquiu market. Baillio had sent the son of Rafael Luna, the former custom house officer at Taos,[22] to Abiquiu with merchandise to trade for beaver skins or cash, but Luna apparently was unsuccessful. Manuel Alvarez, who went personally to Abiquiu in November, managed to buy twelve pelts from one Bernardino Baldés (Valdéz), who had purchased them originally from the "Nacion Comancha": one pelt from Pedro Gallegos, four "in the house of the Alcalde," and ten furs from two men "whose names he did not know."[23]

[21] Thomas J. Scharf, *History of Saint Louis City and County*, I, 171; Weber, *Extranjeros*, 36, 38, 43; Chávez, "New Names," *El Palacio*, Vol. LXIV, Nos. 11–12 (November–December, 1957), 377.

[22] Case of the embargoed merchandise of François Robidoux, December 9, 1825, MANM.

[23] Papers pertaining to the seizure of beaver skins from Guion and Tomson, February 22, 1828, MANM.

Some of the American merchants soon found that beaver obtained even through trade could be a risky investment. On the evening of February 21, 1828, the comandante of the Santa Fe presidio guard seized one *tercio* of fur from Missouri merchant Phillip Thompson, whose store was located in a room in the house of Cristóbal Torres, Ewing Young's old benefactor. That same evening five *tercios* of fur belonging to Vicente Guion were confiscated from a shed (*trasolera*) which belonged to the second alcalde of Santa Fe. Having been warned that the first alcalde knew where he was storing furs, Guion had boldly asked the second alcalde for the key to his shed, and stored his furs there. The second alcalde, according to Guion, did not know that he was keeping furs in the shed. In a hearing before Juan Estevan Pino, first alcalde of Santa Fe, Guion testified through his interpreter, Manuel Alvarez, that he had purchased the furs legally from Mexicans at Taos and Abiquiu, largely in exchange for merchandise. They, in turn, had obtained the furs from Utes and Kiowas. Guion conveniently forgot to mention that some of his beaver came from the American trappers Simon Carat and Antoine Leroux. When asked why he hid the furs if he had acquired them legally, he said that he had heard a rumor that a new law was in effect which prohibited this trade, so he hid his furs out of fear. At Guion's request, Pino received testimony from many of those who had sold furs to Guion. Their story checked with his, thereby ending suspicion that he had been trapping; his furs were probably returned. Guion continued to trade in New Mexico. In 1834, for example, "Vicente Guion et Companie" checked merchandise in at the custom house at Santa Fe.[24]

The task of determining ownership of the *tercio* of fur taken from Phillip Thompson's store aroused considerable controversy involving many of the New Mexico fur traders. At first, Agustín Durán thought that Richard Campbell, whose goods were also in Thompson's store, was the owner of the *tercio*. Campbell claimed

[24] Papers relating to the seizure of beaver fur from Guion and Tomson, February 22, 1828, MANM; manifiesto, July 26, 1834, in folio of manifiestos, Archivo de Hacienda, Legajo 176–3, AGN.

no knowledge of it, however, and he and Thompson testified that a foreigner called "Copos" had left it there. When the mysterious "Copos" was called before Pino to testify, he refused to say anything, even to give his name.[25] On February 24, however, John Pearson, another American merchant, claimed that he owned the furs. Pearson had just sold the *tercio* of fur to one Samuel D. Lucas, but Mexican authorities had seized it, he claimed, before he had had a chance to deliver it to Lucas. Pearson demanded that the *tercio* be returned to him or that Lucas be recompensed. Juan Estevan Pino then took the testimony from various people, Antoine Robidoux among them, to determine the origin of the furs. No one seemed to know from where they had come. Pearson testified that he had purchased them from Mexican citizens, but who these Mexicans were and where they had obtained them, he did not know. When queried, Pearson admitted to owning sixty more beaver skins which were at his home, but these too, he said, had come from Mexicans. Like Guion, Pearson was probably found innocent of trapping and his furs returned.[26]

While these proceedings were taking place, some of the trappers from whom Guion had obtained furs planned a second hunt. Apparently in March, 1828, Antoine Leroux and Simon Carat traveled to the Arkansas River and the "land of the caigua [Kiowa]," an area, Leroux later explained, which they thought was outside Mexican territory. Their party consisted of two Mexicans, Juan Nicolás and José María Meras, two Frenchmen called "Palla" and "Conta," and a boy, Rafael Córdova of Taos, who "was only serving as the keeper of animals for the two Frenchmen." On their return trip, they were met by François Guerin at the "paraje del costilla," perhaps on Costilla Creek, near the present-day Colorado border. Guerin had first come to New Mexico in 1825 in a short-lived partnership with Ceran St. Vrain. In 1827, he returned to New

[25] A Juan Manuel Copa or Copas, who had been in New Mexico at least as early as 1828 (Chávez, "New Names," *El Palacio*, Vol. LXIV, Nos. 9–10 [September–October, 1957], 302), lived in Taos and was a merchant. See the papers concerning his estate, February 18, 1836, Taos, MANM.

[26] Papers relating to the seizure of beaver fur from Vicente Guion and Felipe Tomson, February 22, 1828, MANM.

Mexico in the same company with Vicente Guion and the other fur merchants. At the *"paraje,"* Guerin reportedly purchased nineteen beaver skins, weighing twenty-five *libras*,[27] or about twenty-five pounds, from Carat and Leroux, and "some fur from some Mexicans."

When this party returned to Taos, the alcalde confiscated the remainder of its beaver skins: fourteen from Meras, seven from "Conta," and six from Leroux, a total of twenty-seven.[28] The alcalde then sent the trappers to Santa Fe, where depositions were taken by Alcalde Pino. Their testimony implicated Guerin, who was also brought before Pino. Guerin argued that he had not trapped but had legitimately purchased the furs. First he claimed that he had brought them into Taos at night. Then, when asked where they were being kept, Guerin changed his story. While traveling back to Taos, he said, the furs had fallen into a deep arroyo beneath the surface of the water and were lost. When asked to name a witness to this misfortune, Guerin said he could not for he had been traveling alone.

The hearing also revealed that Simon Carat and Antoine Leroux had earlier received a summons to appear before the alcalde of Abiquiu in March, probably as part of the investigation of Vicente Guion. They had not appeared at that time, however, because someone had told them that they would have to spend six months in jail. Instead, they had gone trapping again without a license, not knowing, they claimed, that trapping was forbidden to foreigners. Unimpressed, Pino concluded that Leroux and Carat had been trapping illegally in Mexican territory and ordered Agustín Durán to dispose of their furs. As a Mexican citizen, José María Meras may not have lost his beaver pelts.[29]

Guerin's supposedly waterlogged furs were found, for on June 16, Durán put 161½ *libras* of contraband beaver fur, which had

[27] A libra was represented in contemporary documents by a symbol which could mean either *tercios* or *libras* depending on whether the symbol clearly read two *t*'s or two *l*'s. Neither letter is clear, but usage indicates that the symbol stood for *libras*.

[28] Vicente Trujillo to Agustín Durán, Taos, June 1, 1828, MANM.

[29] Hearings before Juan Estevan Pino, Santa Fe, June 6, 1828, MANM.

belonged to Guerin, Carat, and Leroux, on public sale. This netted
363 pesos, or about $3.40 a pound. For Guerin it was a thoroughly
bad season. On the Red River, while returning to Missouri, Pawnees
robbed him of $490 worth of mules and beaver—or so he said.[30]
Perhaps he invented the story in an attempt to collect an indemnity
for the furs that Mexican officials had confiscated. Despite these
misfortunes, François Guerin remained a fur trader. Possibly he
had come to New Mexico in 1827 to work for Sylvestre Pratte, for
two years later he was a trusted employee of Bernard Pratte and
Company. In 1834, Guerin was still importing merchandise over
the road to Santa Fe.[31]

Spring of 1828 also found Thomas H. Boggs, alias José Tomás
Boggs, in trouble with New Mexico officials over furs he had
allegedly purchased. A prominent Santa Fe merchant, Boggs had
been suspected of trapping his way to California in the fall of 1826,
but Governor Armijo failed to apprehend him that season. After
a trip to Missouri, Boggs had returned to Taos in November, 1827,
in company with Guerin, Guion, Alvarez, and Luis Robidoux,
then had left immediately for Sonora, where he reportedly intended
to buy horses. On the way back from Sonora, in early 1828, Boggs
and Ramón Vigil bought some furs from three Mexican servants
who had traveled to the Gila with James Ohio Pattie's California-
bound party. Reaching Jemez on May 5, Boggs and Vigil had
some twenty-five beaver pelts confiscated by the alcalde. On May
16, depositions were taken by the alcalde of Taos and sent to Alcalde Juan Estevan Pino at Santa Fe. On June 7, Pino found Boggs
innocent of trapping and ordered his furs returned since he had
legally purchased them from Mexican citizens. Ramón Vigil, a
resident of Santa Cruz de la Cañada, also had his furs returned.
Perhaps, however, as one historian implies, Boggs really was trap-

[30] Agustín Durán, distribution of the revenue from contraband, June 16, 1828,
MANM. Report of William Clark to Lewis Cass, U.S. 22 Cong., 1 sess., *Sen. Doc.
90* (Ser. 213), 95.

[31] J. P. Cabanné to Pierre Chouteau, Jr., Near the Bluffs, December 7, 1829, and
Ceran St. Vrain to Pratte & Co., Taos, September 14, 1830, both in Chouteau
Collection. Manifiesto, July 29, 1834, in folio of manifiestos, Archivo de Hacienda,
Legajo 176-3, AGN.

ping and the whole story of the purchase was only a "good alibi."[32]

Following his own acquittal, Boggs acted as an interpreter for Simon Carat while he was being investigated for trapping. By fall of 1828, Boggs was in trouble again when his former cook, María Francisca Vargas, demanded that he keep his promise to marry her. William Workman successfully defended Boggs before the alcalde of Taos by arguing that the favors María Francisca had bestowed upon Boggs had not been exclusively his.[33]

The scrapes that Guion, Thompson, Guerin, Leroux, Carat, and Boggs had with the law all attest to the earnest efforts of New Mexico officials to prevent foreigners from trapping. Yet, while litigations proceeded in these cases, the largest expedition to work out of New Mexico during the 1827–28 season managed to trap into the Rockies and ship its fur to the Missouri before officials learned of it.

Sylvestre S. Pratte, backed by his father's powerful company, which had become the Western Department of John Jacob Astor's giant American Fur Company by 1827, seemed to have sufficient resources behind him to give him an edge over independent trappers who worked in the Southwest.[34] Yet somehow Pratte had been losing money ever since his arrival in New Mexico in the fall of 1825. Bad luck seemed to dog his every move, as when he outfitted Miguel Robidoux's party that was massacred on the Gila in the fall of 1826. Whimsical New Mexico officials first obligingly granted him a license, then hounded his trappers after Narbona had changed his mind about allowing foreigners to trap. By late 1826, Pratte's debts in New Mexico were mounting so rapidly that Pierre Chouteau, Jr., one of the partners in Bernard Pratte and Company,

[32] Cleland, *Reckless Breed*, 213. Papers pertaining to the case of Tomás Boggs and Ramón Vigil, May 5, 1828, MANM.

[33] Testimony of Simon Carat in hearing before Juan Estevan Pino, June 6, 1828, MANM; Vicente Trujillo to the Governor, Taos, September 16, 1828, MANM; Weber, "William Workman," *NMHR*, Vol. XLI, No. 2 (April, 1966), 157.

[34] Lavender, *Fist in the Wilderness*, 377. Grace Lee Nute, "The Papers of American Fur Company: A Brief Estimate of Their Significance," *American Historical Review*, Vol. XXXII, No. 3 (April, 1927), 522.

wrote to the elder Pratte of the "unfortunate business at Taos." The company must, he said, "terminate this business with the least possible loss." By 1827, Bernard Pratte's displeasure with his son's business conduct was so intense that he stopped paying drafts which Sylvestre had written on the company.[35] In an effort to recoup his losses, Sylvestre Pratte prepared to launch another expedition into the Rockies in the fall of 1827. This would lead to his final misfortune.

In August, 1827, with his boyhood friend Ceran St. Vrain as his clerk, Pratte led thirty-six men north from Abiquiu. The group included such prominent figures as Thomas L. Smith, Alexander Branch, William S. Williams, and Milton G. Sublette. Most of the other men were of French extraction: Joseph Junair, Joseph Bijouse (or Bissonette), Isidor Antaya, Pierre Laliberté, Jean Jeantet, Jean Chavelon, Jules Ducet, Baptiste Lafarque, P. Carpantuer, A. Alanard, L. Snecall, François Laforet, J. Leblond, F. Vertefeul and son, François Turcotte, F. Metote, B. Lusignant, T. Tourvill, B. Bissonette, and perhaps men named Manard, Bouchar, and Watkins. Antonio Romero, "Romero Spaniard" to the Frenchmen, was the only Mexican along.[36]

This was indeed an all-star cast, but not the least remarkable of Pratte's *engagés* was Joseph "Bijouse," or Bissonette *dit* Bijeau, who had guided Stephen Long's exploring party in 1820 and had displayed even then a surprising knowledge of the Rockies. Bissonette returned to New Mexico in 1824, apparently settling in Taos. He became a Mexican citizen in 1830 and was still living in New Mexico as late as 1837.[37]

Despite the high promise of Pratte's expedition, it would meet

---

35 Weber, "Sylvestre S. Pratte," in Hafen, *Mountain Men*, VI, 366.

36 Declaration of Pratte's trappers, September 1, 1829 [1828?], and a list of wages paid to Pratte's trappers, Chouteau Collection. Case of the embargo of the supplies of Pratte's trappers, May 24, 1828, MANM. In some cases I have supplied first names and corrected spellings. The eccentricities that remain are those of St. Vrain.

37 James, *James's Account*, XVI, in Thwaites, *Early Western Travels*, 58. See Bissonette, request for naturalization, February 12, 1830, MANM; Luttig, *Journal*, p. 149. Bissonette should not be confused with a onetime Frémont guide of the same name, whose biography, "Joseph Bissonette," by John Dishon McDermott appears in Hafen, *Mountain Men*, IV, 49–60.

frustration and failure. Trapping their way north into the Rockies on trails long familiar to Bissonette and the other experienced mountain men, Pratte's party (richer by some three hundred pelts), reached the tranquil meadows of North Park on the headwaters of the North Platte toward late September. In this place, about October 1, Sylvestre Pratte died following a brief illness.[38] Only ten days after Pratte's death, an Indian bullet struck Tom Smith in his fabled, but not yet "peg," leg. The story has been told and retold, but in the telling one must eventually turn to Smith's own reminiscence of the event, which seems as accurate as any other version. The Indian's bullet struck Smith

> a few inches above the ancle [sic] shattering both bones; he attempted to step for his rifle, leaning against a tree hard by; the bones stuck in the ground, and he sat down, calling upon his friends to cut it off! No one had the hardihood to undertake the operation; in fact, they were perfectly ignorant of what should be done. He then called upon Basil, the cook, for his butcher knife, who reluctantly, with tears in his eyes, handed him the knife, with which he severed the muscles at the fracture with his own hand; when Milton Soublette, compassionating his condition, took the knife from his hand and completed the operation by severing the tendon achilles, and bound it up with an old dirty shirt.

As the story goes, the wound was never cauterized, but Smith outlived many of his companions who felt certain he would not last out the night.[39]

Following the death of Sylvestre Pratte, the leaderless party turned to Ceran St. Vrain, who assumed responsibility for the men's wages if they continued with him. Almost a year later, St. Vrain would gain the courage to write to Sylvestre's father and, "with a trembling hand," tell the outcome of the expedition. After burying Pratte, St. Vrain said, he led the men to the Green River,

[38] Declaration of Pratte's trappers, September 1, 1829, Chouteau Collection.
[39] "Sketches from the Life of Peg-leg Smith," *HICM*, Vol. V, No. 9 (March, 1861), 420. Further analysis of this "event" is provided in Humphreys, "Thomas L. (Peg-leg) Smith," in Hafen, *Mountain Men*, IV, 324–25.

where they spent "the most rigurus winter I have yet Experience." In the spring, St. Vrain intended to take their furs back to Missouri by way of the Platte, thereby avoiding the New Mexico settlements and danger of having the furs confiscated. But, when they came across "a large Indian trace," St. Vrain changed plans and steered the group toward New Mexico, for they were short of ammunition. When the trappers had started out on this hunt, their forty pack animals had carried one thousand pounds of powder and 1,750 of lead! Perhaps some of this ammunition had been traded to friendly Indians for pelts.[40]

Returning to Abiquiu in mid-May, Ceran St. Vrain sold 1,636 pounds of beaver fur for $5,780.50, or a little more than $3.50 a pound. As Pratte's trappers claimed, this probably represented about 1,000 beaver skins. Perhaps St. Vrain sold these furs to Paul Baillio who was then his partner.[41]

Whoever purchased the furs from St. Vrain did a competent job of spiriting them out of New Mexico. About May 20, when some of St. Vrain's trappers were apprehended by the alcalde of Abiquiu, they had but eleven beaver skins in their possession.[42] These were confiscated along with some of their equipment. By May 24, St. Vrain was in Santa Fe attempting to justify the actions of his trappers. There he testified in hearings before Alcalde Juan Estevan Pino. When asked what license his men were using, St. Vrain said that he did not know what arrangements Pratte had made about that. St. Vrain explained that they had lost one hundred and fifty skins in the Río Grande, along with some guns and traps that they had cached in Ute country. For this reason they had returned with only eleven furs after nearly nine months of trapping. Understandably suspicious, Pino asked St. Vrain to give a day-by-day account of his activities. This, St. Vrain replied, was impossible; some days they had caught nothing, and other days

40 Ceran St. Vrain to Bernard Pratte, Taos, September 28, 1828, and declaration of Pratte's trappers, September 1, 1829, Chouteau Collection. Testimony of St. Vrain in the case of the seizure of the supplies of Pratte's trappers, May 24, 1828, MANM.
41 *Ibid.*
42 Agustín Durán to Juan Estevan Pino, May 27, 1828, MANM.

they had caught nine or ten beaver. He suggested that perhaps someone else had the rest of the furs, for only thirty trappers had returned to Abiquiu; three remained on the Green River, three remained on the San Miguel River, and one man's whereabouts was unknown. St. Vrain's eleven furs were never returned to him, but were kept at Abiquiu until late June, when the alcalde sent them to Santa Fe in response to Agustín Durán's request. These furs were probably sold at a public auction in Santa Fe, but their loss could not have disturbed St. Vrain greatly, for he had only to remember how many furs the Mexicans might have been able to seize. Juan Estevan Pino alerted the alcalde at Abiquiu that six of St. Vrain's men were still trapping, yet ordered that the thirty-two traps confiscated from St. Vrain be returned to him, "because I do not know the law or precedent regarding the seizure of such instruments."[43]

St. Vrain's experienced leadership and his good fortune in getting the furs to market did not prevent Pratte's last trapping venture from losing money. After paying off the hired men, "Expenses made for going to Biver" came to $6,915.41½, while the beaver pelts had sold for only $5,780.50. To make up the difference, St. Vrain sold some of Pratte's personal belongings—his horses, mules, rifle, pistol, traps, gloves, and some trade goods. A deficit of $522.66½ remained, which St. Vrain paid out of his pocket and asked Bernard Pratte to refund to Paul Baillio. Included in the inventory of Pratte's estate were notes from sixteen different persons, totaling $1,867.66½, all owed to Sylvestre Pratte.[44] The list of notes was forwarded to his bereaved father, but many of these debts may never have been collected. In January, 1831, Ceran St. Vrain wrote to B. Pratte and Company: "It is possible that I will be able to Collect, Some of the debts due to the estate of S. S. Pratte, as yet I have not Collected the first cent."[45]

Just as vexing to B. Pratte and Company were the debts that

[43] Case of the embargo of the supplies of Pratte's trappers, May 24, 1828, and José Francisco Vigil to Agustín Durán, June 29, 1828, MANM.

[44] Ceran St. Vrain to Bernard Pratte, September 28, 1828; inventory of Sylvestre Pratte's Estate, 1828, Chouteau Collection.

[45] St. Vrain to B. Pratte and Co., January 6, 1831, Chouteau Collection.

Sylvestre had charged to the company. Eventually, Sylvestre's creditors were paid off, but as one contemporary observed, "It is purely from parental feeling that Genl Pratte pays one cent on those drafts."[46]

Although St. Vrain, and perhaps others, continued to trap and trade in New Mexico with supplies furnished by B. Pratte and Company, the company's serious interest in the Southwest had come to an end with the death of young Pratte. No longer would it, or any other big concern, outfit large-scale expeditions into New Mexico. Perhaps the feeble resistance of the Mexican government and trapping conditions in the Southwest made the area unprofitable for heavy investors. Whatever the cause, New Mexico remained a haven for independent trappers and small-scale operators.

If Ceran St. Vrain failed to meet his expenses in the 1827–28 season, others apparently did not. Although extant records indicate that the Santa Fe fur merchants were dealing in small amounts, the aggregate of their trading was considerable. Beaver furs exported from New Mexico in the summer of 1828, with the Mexican government's knowledge, totaled some 1,200 pounds. At St. Louis prices, probably $4.50 per pound in 1828,[47] this would be worth over $5,000.00. Among those who declared their beaver were Ricardo Storrs with 566 pounds, Phillip Thompson with 221 pounds, James Barnes and James Holman with 400 pounds, and James Glenn and James Dempsey with 45 pounds. To meet the growing demand for buffalo robes, at least 186 of these were shipped east on the trail that summer.[48] The beaver which was legally shipped out of New Mexico, combined with that smuggled out by St. Vrain and perhaps others, represented a prosperous season.

While official records for the 1827–28 season are unusually complete, those of the next season are uncommonly sparse. No

[46] Moss [?] Prewitt to H. R. Gamble, Fayette, June 5, 1829, quoting a man named Glasgow, Hamilton Papers, Missouri Historical Society.

[47] Beaver sold at this price in 1827. Clyman, *Clyman*, 40.

[48] Foreigners granted passports for the exportation of merchandise, May 4–August 6, 1828, MANM. These documents are filed under January, 1829.

record remains of any party trapping out of New Mexico in the winter of 1828–29. The season was probably not that sluggish, however. More likely, historical sources, which are fragmentary at best, are completely lacking for this year. It is equally possible that the Americans had become more discreet, keeping their names out of Mexican court records. That trapping and trading continued seems clear, for when the caravan returned to Missouri in the fall of 1829, the *Missouri Intelligencer* of November 6, announced, "Few expeditions have been attended with greater success, since the commencement of this trade, than the present. Large quantities of beaver, mules, species, &c. have been brought in."

In the 1829–30 season, which saw Ewing Young lead a party to California, records remain of two other New Mexico–based operations. In the fall of 1829, George Yount claimed to have formed a partnership in Taos with a prominent trader, outfitted thirty men, and led them north to trap the Grand, Green, and White rivers. Beaver was apparently plentiful. In late autumn or early winter, they attempted to cross over the Sierra to California, but heavy snows forced them instead to spend a dreary and dangerous winter at Bear Lake. However, Peg-leg Smith, whom Yount remembered as being among the party, may have made it through to California. When spring melted the mountain snows, Yount's men trapped their way down Bear River and, somewhere in the area of Salt Lake, were met by a group of Rocky Mountain trappers who told Yount exciting stories of the abundance of game and gold (!) in California. Yount returned to New Mexico, caching, he said, eight thousand dollars worth of beaver on the Big Bend of the Río Grande on the way to Taos. The beaver was eventually brought in to Taos and sold. Yount, excited over the prospects of mule trading in California, headed west, as we have seen, with William Wolfskill. He would no longer trap out of New Mexico.[49]

On the Green River in the fall of 1829, George Yount later remembered, Ceran St. Vrain ("Savary") and a group of trappers were camped nearby. This seems unlikely, however, for in April, 1830, St. Vrain was back in St. Louis. On the nineteenth of that

[49] Yount, *Yount and His Chronicles*, 67, 71–73, 78–81.

month, he signed a note for $2,570.63 "for value received" from Bernard Pratte and Company, then headed west over the Santa Fe Trail. When he returned to Missouri again that fall, he aroused the envy of fellow traders by converting his investment of some $3,000 to $10,000.[50] Clearly, some of this profit was in beaver fur, for St. Vrain sent Andrew Carson, one of Kit's brothers, back to Missouri with "653 Skiens of Bever waing 961 lb." Bernard Pratte and Company found this worth $4.50 per pound and credited St. Vrain's account with $4,297.50. St. Vrain was not entirely pleased, however, for he complained in his inimitable writing style, "I arrived here two late to make collection the hunters as usale had Sold all there bever."[51]

St. Vrain's complaint indicates that there was considerably more trapping activity in New Mexico than the remaining sources disclose. After 1828, Mexican archives reveal few cases of foreigners' furs being confiscated. Old Bill Williams lost five beaver skins in 1830,[52] and David Jackson had his furs confiscated when he returned from California in 1832, but these are exceptional episodes. One reason seems plain. By 1829, many of the foreigners had found a new way, which did not necessitate smuggling or fraud to obtain Mexican beaver.

[50] *Ibid.*, 79 and 259, n. 26. Charles Camp identifies Savory as St. Vrain, but Yount's *Chronicle* is the only source that puts him on the Green during this season. St. Vrain's note, St. Louis, April 19, 1830, and Theodore Papin to P. M. Papin, St. Louis, February 24, 1831, Chouteau Collection.

[51] St. Vrain to Pratte and Company, Taos, September 14, 1830, and St. Vrain's Account in Book M of Bernard Pratte and Company, Chouteau Collection.

[52] Pablo Lucero to Governor José Antonio Chávez, June 29, 1830, MANM. Lucero speaks of foreigner Julián Julianes, meaning, there is little doubt, William Williams.

IF SOME MERCHANTS and trappers found that smuggling could be a profitable and only slightly risky operation, other of their cohorts began to find this an unnecessary exercise. Rather than evade the law, some foreign trappers found it easier and more to their advantage to operate legitimately by becoming Mexican citizens.

Foreigners who filed formal requests for citizenship in New Mexico before 1829 were rare, perhaps because one had to apply to the minister of justice in faraway Mexico City. One exception was James Baird, who in 1824 applied for and received Mexican citizenship which legalized his trapping attempts. In 1826, Solomon Stone, who might be the same S. Stone who had been a partner of Alexander Branch on several trapping expeditions, asked for citizenship papers, but nothing is known of the outcome of his case.[1] In 1825 and in 1826, Spanish-born Manuel Alvarez applied for Mexican citizenship three times, but there is no evidence that papers were ever granted.[2]

Although few American trappers or traders attempted to obtain

[1] Antonio Narbona to the Ministro de Justicia y Negocios Eclesiáticos, November 30, 1826, in Archivo de Justicia, Vol. 121, AGN.

[2] See Harold H. Dunham, "Manuel Alvarez," in Hafen, *Mountain Men*, I, 190, 194, 182, n. 4. The papers concerning Alvarez's petition for naturalization in Archivo de Justicia, Tomo 121, 117–18 and 257–59, AGN, do not indicate that citizenship was granted at this time.

NEW CITIZENS, 1829–1831

Mexican citizenship in the 1820's, as the decade wore on, the advantages of a change of allegiance must have become clear to many of them. For those who were slow to learn, Julian Wilson, a naturalized Mexican, and his English partner, Richard Exter, furnished an impressive example.

Julian Wilson had lived in Coahuila at least as early as 1822. He had come to the area as a merchant, then worked in the mines at Santa Rosa. In March, 1824, he had applied for naturalization papers which were issued that July.[3] In 1826, Wilson received an *empresario* grant from the state of Coahuila and Texas, consisting of a large piece of land to the east of New Mexico, with its northern boundary located some twenty leagues south of the Arkansas River. He soon sold half of his interest in the grant to English merchant Richard Exter, of Exter, Graves, and Company of Mexico,[4] and the partners hired Alexander Le Grand to survey their holdings. Le Grand, a Santa Fe trader who had been captain of the caravan of 1824, probably never finished the survey which he claimed to have made, but that did not discourage him from issuing a glowing

[3] Papers pertaining to the naturalization of Julian Wilson in Archivo de Justicia, Tomo 121, 75-82, AGN.

[4] Bancroft, *History of California*, III, 172, n. 47. Raymond Estep, "The LeGrand Survey of the High Plains: Fact or Fancy," *New Mexico Historical Review*, Vol. XXIX, No. 2 (April, 1954), 82-84.

and unrealistic appraisal of the grant. Among other things, he told Wilson and Exter their land offered outstanding opportunities in the Indian trade. He estimated that from "five to eight thousand Beaver Skins, and any number of Buffaloe Robes, may be purchased annually, and at a price to admit of a profit of at least 1,000 per cent." Le Grand reported that this estimate was based on his knowledge of the prices of beaver in Mexico City and of buffalo robes in Sonora.[5] He doubtless exaggerated the number of beaver in the area, but his report, along with others which may have reached Wilson and Exter, apparently excited their interest in furs.

On April 14, 1828, Wilson and Exter asked the Mexican government for the exclusive privilege of hunting sea otter, beaver, bear, and other kinds of animals in New Mexico and Alta California, within the area bounded by the United States, and excepting the Russian trading posts in California. They pointed out that citizens of Great Britain and the United States enjoyed a great advantage in being able to trap in Mexican territory, then "crossing the frontier with the fruits of their labor." The Mexican treasury was the chief loser. Exter and Wilson proposed that their own company be approved to check foreign trappers and the subsequent loss of national wealth. They planned to use Santa Fe and the port of San Francisco as their chief points of deposit and would, of course, pay a tax on their own furs.

On April 28, two weeks after Exter and Wilson drafted their request, the "ministro de relaciones" recommended that the chamber of deputies act favorably on it. That same day notice was sent to the national treasury and to the governors of New Mexico and Alta California, informing them that the president had granted provisional permission to Exter and Wilson to hunt the animals they desired.[6] Officials in Santa Fe may have asked for a clarification of the rights of Exter and Wilson, for in the fall these officials were again told that the permit was "not meant to be exclusive in any aspect or prejudicial to the local inhabitants." A similar assurance was sent to California.[7]

[5] Estep, "LeGrand Survey," *NMHR*, Vol. XXIX, No. 2 (April, 1954), 93.

[6] The documents concerning this case were published in the daily newspaper *El Sol*, Mexico City, July 31, 1828.

In Mexico, even then highly nationalistic, reaction to Exter and Wilson's plan was not entirely favorable. Two letters to the editor in the Mexico City daily, *El Sol*, protested the granting of the permit, arguing that natural wealth belonged to the nation and that those who most deserved to exploit this wealth were the residents of the immediate area.[8]

Nevertheless, Wilson and Exter pressed forward with their plans. In the fall of 1828 they placed an ad in a Missouri newspaper, and doubtless in others as well, which told the general public of their concession from the Mexican government. It then went on to give notice:

> To whom it may concern, that any person who shall infringe this privilege, by hunting on those lands without authority from the grantees, shall be liable to the penalties of the law and treated accordingly.
>
> Any person or company, who may wish to contract with the grantees to carry the privilege into effect, may know the terms on application at the office of the National Gazette, Philadelphia.[9]

This incredible ad may have been taken more as a challenge than as an admonition by seasoned frontiersmen—if they noticed it at all.

By spring of 1829 this ambitious project to monopolize the trapping grounds of California and New Mexico had dissolved. A representative of the company apparently never reached New Mexico, and in California, Governor José María Echeandía became angered at the "arrogant and haughty" manner of Wilson's and Exter's agent and refused to co-operate with him.[10] Thus the project died before it had gotten underway.

The boldness and audacity of Exter and Wilson's scheme was

---

[7] Borrador to the Secretaría de Estado, Santa Fe, September 30, 1828, MANM. For California see Ogden, *California Sea Otter Trade*, 103.

[8] *El Sol*, August 3 and August 11, 1828.

[9] (St. Louis) *Missouri Republican*, November 4, 1828.

[10] Ogden, *California Sea Otter Trade*, 102–103.

matched only by that of two other naturalized citizens, John Davis
Bradburn and Stephen Staples, who in the spring of 1828 acquired
exclusive rights to navigate the Río Grande by steamboat for fifteen
years. One Mexico City editor felt certain that the area drained by
the Río Grande, including New Mexico, "will in seven years export in gold, silver, corn, furs etc. to the amount of $6,000,000 at
least."[11] News of this plan also reached the American frontier and
served to show what imagination and citizenship papers could do
for an enterprising Yankee in Mexico.

On April 14, 1828, the same day that Wilson and Exter had
requested permission to hunt, the congress in Mexico City spelled
out for the first time specific conditions under which a foreigner
could become a citizen, thereby replacing a vague decree of 1823.
A foreigner now had to live in Mexico for two years, be a Roman
Catholic, be employed and well-behaved. Similar conditions had
been implicit before. Under the new law, the governor of the state
or territory in which the foreigner lived could issue citizenship
papers, although he was required to report all new citizens to the
president in December of each year.[12]

Despite these liberal terms and the convenience of obtaining
papers from the local governor, American trappers and traders did
not hasten to secure Mexican citizenship. Ewing Young, Richard
Campbell, and Julian Green are wrongly reputed to have applied
for naturalization papers in April, 1828.[13] As late as January, 1829,
when officials in Mexico City asked Governor José Antonio Chávez
why he had not obeyed the law and forwarded information about
persons who had become naturalized, Chávez answered that no one
had yet asked to become a citizen.[14]

11 Quoted in (Fayette) *Missouri Intelligencer*, August 29, 1828, from *Correo*,
Mexico City, May 2, 1828.

12 Manuel Dublán and José María Lozano, *Legislación Mexicana ó colección
completa de las disposiciones legislativas expedidas desde la Independencia de la
Republica*, II, 66–68; I, 648.

13 See Cleland, *Reckless Breed*, 225; Cleland misread John Pearson *et al.*,
Petition for Passports, April 26, 1828, Ritch Papers, No. 99.

14 Primera Secretaría de Estado, Departamento Interior to the Governor of
New Mexico, January 8, 1829, MANM; Chávez to Primera Secretaría de
Estado, Departmento Interior, borrador of February 28, 1829, MANM.

That foreigners were slow to change national allegiance was probably not due to any motives of patriotism. More likely, word of the new law had not yet circulated around Taos and Santa Fe. On February 22, 1829, however, two French-Canadians, Charles Beaubien and Gervais Nolan, expressed willingness to surrender their fidelity to the British Crown; on June 25, they became the first foreigners to be naturalized in New Mexico under the new law. By summer John Rowland and Antoine and Louis Robidoux had followed their example. The influential Robidoux brothers had asked for citizenship on July 16 and received papers the next day. Before the year had ended, Alexander Branch, Richard Campbell, José Tomás Boggs, Mathew Kinkead, Jean Jeantet, José Alejandro Marion, and José Francisco Brewer also became Mexican citizens.[15] With the possible exception of Marion and Brewer, all of these men were at one time associated with the fur trade in New Mexico and most of them used their new citizenship papers to continue that association in a legal capacity.

"Mateo" Kinkead, José Tomás Boggs, and "Carlos" Beaubien may have retired from careers as mountain men by 1829. Kinkead is remembered by historians as the "old mountaineer" who sheltered Kit Carson during his first winter in Santa Fe, but almost nothing is known of his fur trading activities.[16] Canadian-born Charles Beaubien, who would become one of Taos' most prominent citizens and one of three judges named to the first territorial court, seems to have been a trapper during only his first years in New Mexico. By the time he had become a citizen he contented himself with trading for furs, an activity that he continued into the 1840's.[17]

Jean Jeantet and Alexander Branch may have been more anxious than their compatriots to become citizens. In late December, 1829,

[15] Beaubien's request is in MANM, and Nolan's is preserved in the Ritch Papers; A. & L. Robidoux to Governor Chávez, July 16, 1829; list of those naturalized in New Mexico in 1829, Ritch Papers, Nos. 109, 111, 113.

[16] A biography of Kinkead by Janet Lecompte appears in Hafen, *Mountain Men*, II, 189–99.

[17] Lawrence R. Murphy, "Charles H. Beaubien," in Hafen, *Mountain Men*, VI, 23–35; Charles Bent to Manuel Alvarez, November 15, 1840 and Bent to Alvarez, Taos, February 6, 1841, in the Benjamin Read Collection, State Records Center, Santa Fe, New Mexico.

the first alcalde of Santa Fe, Juan Rafael Ortiz, had suspected that these two, along with José Manuel Allen and Stephen Louis Lee, had smuggled contraband beaver into New Mexico. They and three Mexicans, it was discovered, had been trapping on the headwaters of the Platte. Ortiz found them innocent of any crime, however, for he believed their story that they had not actually brought the furs into New Mexico, but had left them with companions who transported them to the Missouri River.[18] Branch and Jeantet may have decided to end this annoyance of being hauled before an alcalde by becoming citizens, as they did on December 31. Jeantet, who had been one of Pratte's *engagés* in 1827–28, finally drifted into California in 1844. Alexander Branch, who trapped on the Colorado in 1824, on the Gila in 1826, and in the southern Rockies with Pratte and St. Vrain in the 1827–28 season, continued to make Taos his home. Before his death in 1841, he was often seen on the Santa Fe and Chihuahua trails.[19]

Stephen Louis Lee and José Manuel Allen, who had been trapping with Jeantet and Branch in 1829, also became Mexican citizens soon after the episode with Alcalde Ortiz, on February 12, 1830.[20] Allen, a Canadian who had been best man at Lee's wedding, may be the same Allen who was with James Ohio Pattie on the Gila. His life, following his naturalization, remains obscure. Lee and Branch continued their association, and in 1838, if not earlier, the two formed a partnership. They were apparently in the retail business, importing merchandise over the Santa Fe Trail, and also dealt in furs. In early 1841, Lee tried to sell 382 pounds of beaver pelts to Charles Bent. No inexperienced trader, Charles Bent had the furs dried and beaten until they weighed 365 pounds when he bought them.[21]

Four of those who became Mexican citizens in 1829 took out

18 Statement of Juan Rafael Ortiz, first alcalde of Santa Fe, December 28, 1829, MANM.

19 See Janet Lecompte's "Alexander Branch," in Hafen, *Mountain Men*, IV, 61–67.

20 List of persons naturalized in New Mexico in 1829, 1830, and 1831, Ritch Papers, No. 113.

21 David J. Weber, "Stephen Louis Lee," in Hafen, *Mountain Men*, III, 181–88.

licenses to trap within the next year: John Rowland, Gervais Nolan, Antoine Robidoux, and Richard Campbell. In the fall of 1830, Rowland requested a license and would do so again the next two autumns. New Mexico officials, perhaps suspicious of Rowland after his illegal foray into the Gila in 1826, issued warnings along with his permits. In 1831, for example, he was exhorted "to care, very scrupulously, that no fraud is committed against the National Treasury, for in that case it will be necessary to bring to bear all of the weight of the law concerning this matter." In August, 1832, when Rowland again requested a license, this time to lead fourteen or more men on an expedition, Governor Santiago Abreú stipulated that at least two-thirds of his party should be Mexican citizens. Unfortunately, no record has been found of where Rowland trapped or who his companions were during these years.[22]

Gervais Nolan likewise led a trapping expedition in the winter of 1830–31. Nolan is one of those obscure Taos residents of French extraction whose activities are so baffling to historians. That he knew something of the fur trade there can be no doubt, for he was an employee of the well-known North West Company, in Canada, from 1816 to 1820. Although he arrived in New Mexico in 1824, he is not associated with a New Mexico–based trapping party until 1830. In the spring of 1831 he and some other Mexican citizens returned to Taos with about fifty pounds of beaver fur. Nolan purchased his companions' shares and sold the entire amount to "a foreigner of North America." An illiterate trapper, Nolan later used his citizenship to good advantage by obtaining a spectacular amount of Mexican land in the early 1840's.[23]

Like Rowland and Nolan, new citizens Antoine Robidoux and Richard Campbell asked for a license to trap in the fall of 1830. Campbell should be remembered as the first of the Taos trappers to find his way to California by an overland route. In their application to trap, Robidoux and Campbell professed concern with furthering Mexican commerce, as well as earning a living for themselves and their families. Thus, they had "already formed a company

[22] Weber, "John Rowland," in Hafen, *Mountain Men*, IV, 277–78.
[23] David J. Weber, "Gervais Nolan," in Hafen, *Mountain Men*, IV, 225–29.

of twenty-five persons, the majority of which are Mexicans, and the other part, naturalized citizens, and the smallest part, foreign hunters." Their license was granted.[24] Where Robidoux and Campbell trapped in 1830, or who constituted their party, remains unknown. Both, however, continued to trap from New Mexico. In the fall of 1832, with John Harris, Richard Campbell led a large trapping party down the Pecos River, intending to trap in Texas. Before heading east into the Staked Plains, however, most of the men, Campbell included, were scared off by Comanches and returned to Taos. It was just as well. Harris led the remainder across northern Texas to Oklahoma and Arkansas in a singularly unsuccessful hunt.[25]

More is known of Antoine Robidoux's trapping exploits in the 1830's than of Richard Campbell's. In September, 1831, David Waldo, who had become a Mexican citizen that June, asked for a license on behalf of himself and Robidoux. Their party would consist of twenty-five citizens, some naturalized, and five foreigners whom they were taking along because they were "very skillful" at trapping. Two days later a license was granted.[26] Waldo's license, as we have seen, was used by Ewing Young's party, which left that fall for California, and the license was then carried back to New Mexico by David Jackson, who produced it when Mexican officials confiscated his furs in the summer of 1832. Perhaps using the same license, Antoine Robidoux outfitted his own trapping party that season. Clearly Robidoux continued to trap and trade furs out of New Mexico. By the end of the 1830's he had constructed two trading posts to the northeast of Taos, but this takes us ahead of our story.

Antoine and Louis Robidoux provide outstanding examples of the power a naturalized citizen could achieve in the economic and political affairs of the primitive frontier province of New Mexico.

[24] Robidoux and Campbell to the Governor, Santa Fe, September 18, 1830, copy by Pablo Lucero, Taos, September 24, 1830, MANM.
[25] Pike, *Prose Sketches*, 33–43; David J. Weber, "John Harris," in Hafen, *Mountain Men*, VII, 155–59.
[26] Request of David Waldo, Santa Fe, September 17 and the response by Governor Chávez, September 19, 1831, MANM.

Each was elected first alcalde and *regidor*, or alderman, of Santa Fe on various occasions.[27] Antoine, in fact, was elected first alcalde in December, 1830, only a little over a year after he had become a citizen. His right to that office was challenged, it is interesting to note, on the grounds that he had only naturalization papers and not those of citizenship! In making this curious distinction, former Governor José Antonio Vizcarra received little support from other prominent New Mexicans. Governor Chávez felt that Robidoux was entitled to the office, but forwarded both sides of the argument to Mexico City for a final decision.[28] The outcome of the case is not clear. Antoine Robidoux also appears to have been one of the outstanding merchants of Santa Fe. He operated a store there which might have been well-provisioned, for it was robbed two years in succession. Antoine stocked his store with merchandise brought over the trail from Missouri and, like other merchants, sent goods to Chihuahua regularly. Louis Robidoux served a full one-year term as first alcalde of Santa Fe in 1839. Matt Field, a reporter for the New Orleans *Picayune* who visited Santa Fe that year, wrote that Louis Robidoux "shares the rule over the people almost equally with the Governor and the priests." Operating a grist mill and iron works in Santa Fe (where he might have manufactured traps), Robidoux seemed to personify American initiative and shrewdness.[29]

The year 1830 saw another handful of foreigners request naturalization papers: Abraham Ledoux, William Wolfskill, Gerónimo Lonté, Pedro Laliberté, Antoine Leroux, José Bissonette, Amablo

[27] In December, 1829, Antoine was elected ninth *regidor* of Santa Fe (Minutes of the Ayuntamiento meeting of December 20, 1829, MANM), and in 1833 he served as third alcalde of Santa Fe (sessions of January 1, March 30, and July 27, 1833, for example, in the Santa Fe Ayuntamiento Journal, 1829-36, MS, Coronado Room, Zimmerman Library, University of New Mexico). See also Weber, "Louis Robidoux," in Hafen, *Mountain Men*, VIII.

[28] Papers concerning the election of Antonio Robidoux in Archivo de Gobernación, Ramo I, No. 120, AGN. Some of the documents pertaining to this case are scattered throughout MANM.

[29] For robberies of Robidoux's store see the cases of December 4, 1829, and March 28, 1831, MANM. Antoine's name appears frequently in custom house records of the period. See also Weber, "Louis Robidoux," in Hafen, *Mountain Men*, VIII.

Pará, Antonio Blanchilla (Blanchard?), Jean Baptiste Trudeau, Luis Ambroise, Carlos Guará, Francisco Siote, Pierre Lesperance and Paul Anderson, as well as Stephen Louis Lee and José Manuel Allen, whom we have already mentioned. Some of these men— Allen, Laliberté, Leroux and Ambroise—frankly admitted that their occupation was that of a *cazador*, or hunter, which in New Mexico, when applied to foreigners, usualy meant trapper.[30] Almost all of this new crop of citizens had been involved in the fur trade and many would continue to be.

Little is known of Amablo Pará, a Canadian who claimed to have first come to Taos in 1822, and Carlos Guará, a Frenchman who had been at Taos since 1826. Gerónimo Lonté, a Canadian, remembered first arriving in New Mexico on October 26, 1825, the same day that James O. Pattie and Sylvestre Pratte first reached Taos,[31] and almost certainly came with them.

Among the other expatriates, Stephen Lee and José Manuel Allen have already been discussed in this chapter. Antonio Blanchard and Luis Ambroise were, respectively, in the employ of François Robidoux and Sylvestre Pratte in the spring of 1827.[32] Paul Anderson, as one of the partners in James Baird and Company, had been among the first mountain men to find his way into New Mexico after 1821. He continued to trade in northern Mexico, then shifted his headquarters to California in the early 1830's.[33]

The appearance of Joseph Bissonette and Abraham Ledoux on this list of new citizens of 1830 illustrates how little is known of the French trappers who lived in Taos. Abraham Ledoux and his brother Antoine (not to be confused with Antoine Leroux), had been on the Upper Missouri with Manuel Lisa in 1812. Both had

[30] List of persons naturalized between December 31, 1829 and December 31, 1830, Santa Fe, February 28, 1831, MANM.

[31] Papers concerning Pará's and Guará's requests for naturalization are in MANM, dated Taos, September 12, 1830. Guará was married at Taos in 1826 (Chávez, "New Names," *El Palacio*, Vol. LXIV, Nos. 9–10 [September–October, 1957], 310). Gerónimo Lonti, Petition for naturalization, Taos, March 3, 1830, Ritch Papers, No. 115.

[32] For an interesting note on Ambroise, see Morgan, *Ashley*, 279, n. 152.

[33] *Guías* of August 24, 1829, to Sonora and Chihuahua; *tornaguía* of April 15, 1831, to El Paso, MANM; Paul Anderson, Jr. to Abel Stearns, San Diego, March 5, 1834, Abel Stearns Papers, Huntington Library.

been living and trading among the Pawnees during the latter part of that decade and, when Stephen H. Long's expedition came along the Platte in 1820, Abraham Ledoux was hired as a hunter and farrier. After a Pawnee arrow almost took Abraham's life in 1824, the brothers drifted into New Mexico and there quietly lived out their days, Antoine finally becoming a Mexican citizen in 1841.[34] Joseph Bissonette, who also accompanied Long in 1820, later trapped with Pratte and St. Vrain in the winter of 1827–28. There is no other record, however, of either Bissonette or the Ledoux brothers trapping from New Mexico, but it would not be surprising if they continued in their old occupation.

If Bissonette and the Ledouxs laid their traps aside after becoming citizens of Mexico, others clearly did not. Soon after his request for naturalization was honored, William Wolfskill obtained a trapping license and, as we have seen, trapped his way to California, where he continued to profit from his new citizenship by hunting sea otter.[35] Pierre Lesperance and François Siote, two French-Canadians who had just received their naturalization papers late in the fall of 1830, almost immediately applied for and received permission to trap beaver. Siote had been living in Taos since 1826, if not before, and Lesperance may have been trapping in Mexican territory as early as 1815.[36] Jean Baptiste Trudeau ("Bautista Truido"), who was naturalized in September, 1830, had come to New Mexico in 1824, married in Taos in 1826, and had been trapping under François Robidoux in the spring of 1827. A resident of Arroyo Hondo near Taos, he used his new citizenship to trade with Indians in the southern Rockies. On a trading foray to the Arkansas in 1833 he met some Arikaras who were traveling to Santa Fe to make a treaty. According to Trudeau, they asked him to lead them to the governor and to obtain for them a sign of friendship. Trudeau, the governor

[34] Janet Lecompte, "Antoine and Abraham Ledoux," in Hafen, *Mountain Men*, III, 173–79; List of persons given naturalization papers by the governor of New Mexico, Santa Fe, November 27, 1841, MANM.

[35] Wilson, *Wolfskill*, 62, 64.

[36] Borrador of November 4, 1830, in governor's letterbook of October 21, 1830 to August 23, 1831, MANM; Chávez, "New Names," *El Palacio*, Vol. LXIV, Nos. 11–12 (November–December, 1957), 375; Janet Lecompte, "Pierre Lesperance," in Hafen, *Mountain Men*, VI, 241–46.

reported, spoke the language of the Arikaras (Pawnee) perfectly and wanted the job of official interpreter.[37]

Because he later achieved fame as an overland guide, Antoine Leroux remains one of the better-known Taos trappers. We have already encountered his name among those whom François Robidoux sent to lift a cache in Ute country in the spring of 1827. The following year, apparently in the employ of Sylvestre Pratte, he trapped in the San Luis Valley. In 1832, the names of Leroux and another new citizen, Pierre Laliberté, appear on a list of persons to whom the American Fur Company owed drafts which their representative in the mountains, William Henry Vanderburgh, had drawn upon them. Leroux was owed $1,600.00 and Laliberté, $789.42, perhaps for furs which they sold to Vanderburgh. It is difficult to connect Leroux with any specific trapping parties out of Taos in the 1830's, but he continued to make it his home and, it seems clear from his subsequent reminiscences, continued to trap in the Southwest. In 1835 he inscribed his name on a cliffside to the south of Ouray, Utah. How he got there, or who he was with, is not known.[38]

Among those who became naturalized in 1831 were three trappers who had been in California and back again: William Pope, one of the men who was imprisoned with Pattie in San Diego; and François Turcotte and Jean Vaillant, both of whom had attempted to desert from Ewing Young's first California expedition. Vaillant claimed to be from France; Turcotte, from Canada. Further trapping or fur trading exploits of these men have not yet come to light. Two others who became citizens in 1831, David Waldo and Ceran St. Vrain, certainly continued to deal in furs. St. Vrain, a veteran

---

[37] Trudeau to Governor Sarracino, Santa Fe, November 11, 1833, and borrador of November 30 in governor's letterbook, April 12, 1833 through November 30, 1833, MANM; Trudeau's request for naturalization, September 12, 1830, MANM; Chávez, "New Names," *El Palacio*, Vol. LXIV, Nos. 11–12 (November–December, 1957), 377.

[38] K. McKenzie to P. Chouteau, Jr., Fort Union, September 14, 1832, Chouteau Collection; Parkhill, *Antoine Leroux*, 71–73; Leroux's petition for naturalization, Taos, February 12, 1830, Ritch Papers, No. 114; photograph by George E. Stewart of Roosevelt, Utah, copy provided me by O. D. Marston of Berkeley, California.

trapper at age twenty-eight, had just formed a partnership with Charles Bent which would soon result in the construction of Bent's Fort on the Arkansas and launch St. Vrain's career as one of New Mexico's most outstanding citizens. Kit Carson later reminisced, "All mountaineers look to him as their best friend and treat him with the greatest of respect."[39]

Trapping parties led by naturalized citizens, there is no reason to doubt, continued to be licensed in New Mexico, although there is but scant record of them in Mexican archives. In July, 1831, for example, the governor gave the alcalde of Abiquiu permission to grant a trapping license to an unnamed "foreigner," but nothing else is known of this.[40] New Mexican officials apparently did not discriminate against naturalized citizens by forcing only them to procure trapping licenses. Native New Mexicans, such as José Antonio Miera y Pacheco of Abiquiu, also needed licenses in order to trap. Other examples could be cited.[41]

After 1831, as trappers began to rely on intermontane trading posts as markets for beaver, and as the fur trade itself slowly slid into decline, there was slight advantage in becoming a Mexican citizen in order to trap legally. Yet, some mountain men continued to do so. By 1833, for example, Francisco Laforet, who had trapped with Sylvestre Pratte in the southern Rockies and with William Wolfskill on the way to California, had become naturalized. In that year Laforet incurred a debt to Mexican citizen David Waldo, part of which represented the rental of three traps "for the spring and autumn hunt," and the purchase of some powder. In the fall of 1835 he paid off twenty-one pesos of this debt by presenting Waldo with seven *libras* of beaver worth three pesos per *libra*.[42]

Although many of the foreigners who became citizens in New

---

[39] List of persons naturalized from January 1, 1831, to November 30, 1831, Santa Fe, MANM; Carter, 'Dear Old Kit,' 79.

[40] Borrador of July 18, 1831, in governor's letterbook, October 21, 1830 through August 23, 1831, MANM.

[41] Borrador of September 6, 1830, in book of decrees issued by the governor since January 7, 1830, MANM. Perhaps Miera was a descendant of the map maker of the Domínguez–Escalante party, Bernardo Miera y Pacheco.

[42] David J. Weber, "Francisco Laforet," in Hafen, *Mountain Men*, VI, 213-15.

Mexico profited personally from their new status, the consequences of allowing a community of foreign-born citizens to develop in New Mexico were more profound and far-reaching than most contemporaries supposed. Many naturalized Mexicans remained Americans at heart. By the 1840's they began to grow more concerned about the administration of justice and the protection of their property rights as they settled into careers more sedentary than trapping, and as a few acquired vast tracts of land. Some of the new citizens self-righteously began to wonder why should "a land abounding in many of nature's favors, be occupied by men who appear to be incapable of either moral or political advancement?"; others openly wished for the "occupation of this country by the Anglo Saxon race."[43] When President James K. Polk, Stephen Watts Kearny, and the Army of the West brought this hope to fruition, few of the former mountain men were surprised. In July, 1846, even before the Army of the West had reached the New Mexico settlements, Thomas (Broken Hand) Fitzpatrick, who was stationed at Bent's Fort on the Arkansas, had received reports from Santa Fe predicting that New Mexicans would not resist; there would be "no fighting." He went on to add, "It has always been my opinion that there would not be a blow struck at Santafee whatever may be the case elsewhere."[44]

To what extent the presence of American traders and trappers in New Mexico for the past quarter century facilitated the Americans' initially "bloodless conquest" of the area may never be determined. Their contribution, however, as a cultural advance guard for American manifest destiny should not be overlooked.[45]

[43] Editorial in the (St. Louis) *Daily Missouri Republican*, December 24, 1841, which probably reflected the opinion of many of the foreign residents of New Mexico.
[44] Thomas Fitzpatrick to A. W. Sublette, Fort William, July 31, 1846, Sublette Papers, Missouri Historical Society.
[45] The theme of foreign dissatisfaction with Mexican government and the role of the foreign traders in facilitating the conquest, runs through Chapters two and three of Howard Roberts Lamar, *The Far Southwest, 1846–1912: A Territorial History*.

XII MARKET FOR

THE FOREIGNERS who became Mexican citizens in 1829–31, did so in the midst of the period many consider the golden era of beaver trapping—the years between 1828 and 1833. It was then that the Rockies were being thoroughly exploited by American trappers and that competition for the remaining beaver streams grew increasingly ruthless.[1] The Taos trappers, their attention momentarily diverted by the virgin streams of the Gila area and by the promise of California, had returned to the Rockies by 1827. In the fall of that year, Sylvestre Pratte and others trapped there again in force. From then on, the trappers from Taos seem to have dominated the fur trade of the southern Rockies; by the early 1830's, they were marketing a significant per cent of the fur wealth of the Rockies.

Since 1825, when William Ashley inaugurated the rendezvous system, he and his successor companies—Smith, Jackson, and Sublette, and the Rocky Mountain Fur Company—had attempted to make the Rockies their private preserve. Although their operations extended well beyond the forty-second parallel, which separated Mexico from the United States and the Oregon Territory, only occasionally, as when the Mexican government learned of the 1827

---

[1] James L. Clayton, "The Growth and Significance of the American Fur Trade, 1790–1890," *Minnesota History*, Vol. XL, No. 4 (Winter, 1966), 214.

THE MOUNTAINS, 1831–1833

rendezvous on Bear Lake, did it protest the presence of these intrepid intruders on its nebulous far northern frontier.

The report of the rendezvous reached Mexico City indirectly through Governor Antonio Armijo, who had heard it from José María Sandoval of Taos, who heard it from a Ute chief at the Great Salt Lake. As Armijo explained it, one hundred Americans had gathered under command of an American general at a lake four days north of Salt Lake and had built a fort there. Then, after a few months, on August 1, 1827, the Americans had left the fort with one hundred mules and horses laden with beaver skins. Twenty-five of the Americans, Armijo had learned, headed for California. When the Mexican secretary of state received this report, in April, 1828, he protested to the American minister in Mexico City, Joel Poinsett, who apologized for his countrymen by explaining that they simply went about their hunting "without being aware that they are committing a trespass," for they did not know where the boundary was. Actually, relying on the 1821 map by John Melish which showed the forty-second parallel passing through the Salt Lake, Poinsett did not know where the boundary was either. He seems to have been reflecting the best knowledge of the day. Even Governor José María Echeandía of California, reported to the Mexican foreign minister in June, 1829, that the line ran through Salt Lake. In fact, it ran through Bear Lake to the north of Salt Lake. In an attempt to show good faith, Poinsett asked for a copy of the "laws and regulations . . . respecting the pursuit of Game within the Mexican Territories by Foreigners," so that he might publicize them in the United States. A copy of such laws could not be located in the national archives, however, and apparently no reply was sent to Poinsett's request.[2]

Mexico, then, offered no effective resistance to Ashley and his successors, or to others who worked in the Rockies below the forty-second parallel. Only when foreign trappers ventured too close to California settlements or smuggled beaver into New Mexico did officials become seriously agitated. In the absence of real opposition from Mexico, the Taos trappers offered the only challenge to the operations of large Missouri-based companies that dominated the Rockies. William Ashley recognized this challenge as early as 1827. While negotiating with Bernard Pratte and Company to help him supply Smith, Jackson, and Sublette in the mountains, Ashley stated as one condition that "Messrs. B. Pratte & Co will not suffer any person trading for them at Taus or other place . . . to interfere with the business of the proposed concern."[3]

As the decade drew to a close, John Jacob Astor's American Fur Company began to compete with Smith, Jackson, and Sublette for a share of the beaver from the Rocky Mountains. The partnership that Astor formed with B. Pratte and Company in late 1826 had only served as the opening wedge for his entrance into the mountains. Soon after, Astor acquired the Columbia Fur Company and his own cautious attempts to enter the Rockies got underway. Astor's strategy was to buy out his competitors and to monopolize the marketing of beaver in order to control prices.[4] By 1829, if not

<hr/>

[2] Correspondence concerning this is in Relaciones Exteriores, H[200 (72:73)]1, L-E-1076(1), Tomo XXI. The exchange between Poinsett and the Mexican minister is in U.S. 25 Cong., 2 sess., *House Doc. 351* (Ser. 332), 228–30, as indicated in Morgan, *Jedediah Smith*, 229. See also Carlos Bosch García, *Historia de las relaciones entre México y los Estados Unidos, 1819–1848*, 143–44, which puts this incident in a broader context.

[3] Ashley to Pierre Chouteau, Jr., Lancaster, Pennsylvania, February 2, 1827, in Morgan, *Ashley*, 160.

before, Astor recognized that the furs coming out of the mountains through Santa Fe and Taos threatened his attempted monopoly. He told Pierre Chouteau, Jr., in December, 1829, "If you were not to buy the Santafee Beaver, it would nevertheless find its way here [to New York], and might fall into other hands than ours which could not fail to be injurious." Although Astor recognized that the beaver from New Mexico "is generally not so good as Ashleys," he urged Pierre Chouteau to buy it nevertheless, because "the article is very high it will answer very well," and it would keep others from getting it. Chouteau was to buy "at a moderate price," of course. By late December, however, the market had become glutted by a large shipment of Hudson's Bay Company furs. When Astor learned that Ashley had outbid Chouteau for the Santa Fe beaver, he told Chouteau that it was just as well—"Ashley will find [it] is a hard bargain."[5] Astor would continue to bid on the beaver from Santa Fe for the next few seasons, for, as we shall see, some of the fur from free trappers operating in the mountains found its way south, instead of being sold at the rendezvous.

Since Étienne Provost had shown up at the first rendezvous, demonstrating that Taos was within reach from the central Rockies, mountain men had found their way to New Mexico almost instinctively. As early as the spring of 1825, a small group of Ashley's men under the leadership of James Clyman were trapping the upper Green River when Indians attacked. Reaching high ground in safety, Jim Beckwourth allegedly asked Clyman if that would be the place to make a stand. " 'No,' said he, 'we will proceed on to New Mexico.' " Beckwourth later remembered (for what the memory of this notorious liar is worth), "I was astonished at his answer, well knowing—though but slightly skilled in geography—that New Mexico must be many hundred miles farther south."[6] Indeed, it was several hundred miles away, but what was closer?

[4] Lavender, *Fist in the Wilderness*, 392.
[5] Astor to Chouteau, New York, December 3, November 17, and December 23, 1829, Chouteau Collection.
[6] T. D. Bonner, *The Life and Adventures of James P. Beckwourth* (ed. by Bernard DeVoto), 37–38; Clyman, *Clyman*, 37–38.

For trappers in trouble, New Mexico might be the only place to go. This was illustrated in 1830 by a group that has come to be known as the Bean-Sinclair party.[7] This group was made up of citizens of Arkansas and environs who had responded to an advertisement in the *Arkansas Gazette* at Little Rock, in which John Rogers of Fort Smith promised "a prospect of great profit" to anyone who signed up for a trapping expedition to the Rocky Mountains. Rogers had planned to leave for the mountains in September, 1829, with one hundred men, but concerned about the shortage of game in the winter and the difficulty of foraging pack animals, he "reluctantly" postponed departure until the following April 15. Again in spring of 1830 his advertisement appeared, running from February 19 to April 15. This time, the announced plans were more ambitious. Rogers claimed to have already signed up one hundred men and promised to outfit a total of two hundred to three hundred. The prospective trapper needed to bring along only two horses and a gun.[8] Yet, when Rogers' party finally got underway, apparently in May, it numbered only forty-two men. Included were George Nidever and Job F. Dye, both of whom left reminiscences of the experience.

Trappers being as democratic as any Americans of the period, Rogers allowed them to elect their own leader; in this way the inexperienced Colonel Robert Bean was chosen captain. Sometime in May they started out, following the North Fork of the Canadian toward the west, although some made a lengthy detour via Texas when their first encounter with Comanches resulted in an outbreak of "Comanche fever."[9] Colonel Bean, himself shaken, nevertheless led his men to the Arkansas, which they followed into the Rockies while Arapahos and Pawnees dogged their tracks.

Nothing seemed to go right. The men soon lost confidence in

[7] LeRoy R. Hafen, "The Bean-Sinclair Party of Rocky Mountain Trappers, 1830–32," *Colorado Magazine*, Vol. XXXI, No. 3 (July, 1954), 161–71.

[8] (Little Rock) *Arkansas Gazette*, July 29, September 2, 1829, and February 9, 1830. All quotes from the *Gazette* are from Dale L. Morgan's transcriptions of items from western newspapers, filed at the Huntington Library as "The Mormons and the Far West."

[9] Dye, *Recollections*, 5.

Bean when he suffered an acute case of "fever" and fled during a skirmish with Indians. Then, in November, Indians killed George Nidever's brother, Mark. By that time they had taken few beaver —only forty or fifty skins—and were apparently in danger of starving to death at their winter quarters. So, the trappers abandoned camp and started for New Mexico. At the Arkansas they threw their traps into a "deep water hole" for safe keeping, then journeyed on, reaching Taos by mid-December.[10]

At Taos they received a mixed reception. Soon after their arrival the alcalde received a directive from the governor to order the trappers to leave the country. One of the party, a Dr. James S. Craig, explained, "It was impossible for us to obey the order, without subjecting our company to the risk of perishing in the mountains." About Christmas time Craig and Colonel Bean journeyed to Santa Fe to see the governor and ask him to rescind his order. Craig hoped for success and said "We have been fortunate as to enlist several of the most influential men in the country in our favor."[11] But, even this did not help. They were ordered to leave the settlements within ten days. As Dye remembered it, "The order was not respected by the people and we refused to obey it, so we remained all winter unmolested." Actually, the trappers came closer to losing their freedom than Dye suspected. By the end of January troops had been readied to march on Taos and arrest the thirty-six foreigners, but the "abundance of snow" made the road impassable. By mid-February the troops were still unable to get through.[12]

That winter, George Nidever, Isaac Graham, and Alexander Sinclair tried to return to the Arkansas to retrieve their traps, but snow and Arapaho Indians forced them back to New Mexico. Nidever regretted being unable to bring in the traps, "as they were

[10] Dye, *Recollections*, 13; Dr. James S. Craig, letter, Santa Fe, January, 2, 1831, in the *Arkansas Gazette*, June 8, 1831; Ellison, *Nidever*, 6–17, 19; José Antonio Vizcarra to the Governor, Santa Fe, December 21, 1830, MANM.

[11] James S. Craig, letter, Santa Fe, January 2, 1831, in the *Arkansas Gazette*, June 8, 1831.

[12] Dye, *Recollections*, 17. Letters of January 31 and February 14, 1831, in book of correspondence to the Comandante General, January 15 through December 29, 1831, MANM.

very dear at San Fernando." Indeed, they cost about eight dollars apiece at Taos, which was one dollar less than Ashley intended to charge for traps at the 1827 rendezvous. When spring came, fourteen or fifteen men who remained from Bean's original group, now led by Alexander Sinclair,[13] trapped on a tributary of the North Platte. They returned to Taos with two packs of beaver containing sixty skins each and probably weighing close to one hundred pounds apiece. They smuggled the furs into Taos at night in order, as Nidever recalled, to avoid paying "a heavy duty on all beaver skins bro't into New Mexico." The fur commanded four dollars a pound at Taos, according to Nidever, but there is no reason to trust his memory in these economic matters, for he also reported that this price equaled about ten dollars a skin. That would have been very heavy beaver.[14]

In September, 1831, while others of their original group started for California with William Wolfskill, some fifteen of the trappers from Arkansas, again under Alexander Sinclair, returned to the mountains. Sinclair's contingent took along "3 or 4 Mexicans, who had been hired by different members of our company," and, interestingly, "kept company with a band of trappers composed of French and Mexicans, about a doz. in all." They traveled north to the Arkansas, which they followed to its headwaters. Here, according to Nidever, "the Mexican and French trappers left us, going South, down the Platte, while we crossed over to the Green River."[15]

The French and Mexican party seems to have traveled in a different direction than Nidever remembered, for December found them on the Little Snake River in northwestern Colorado. This group, according to a Mexican account, was led by John Harris ("Juan Jares") and had left New Mexico with "Alejandro Siclaid" and his men. After the group divided, Harris led his contingent over the Rockies into the Green River basin, to the "Río de los Sozones." *Sozone*, or *Shoshone*, being the tribal name for Snakes in New

[13] A biographical sketch by LeRoy R. Hafen, "Alexander Sinclair," appears in Hafen, *Mountain Men*, IV, 297–303.
[14] Morgan, *Ashley*, 159; Ellison, *Nidever*, 21–22.
[15] *Ibid.*, 22–23.

Mexico, doubtless referred to today's Little Snake River, then known simply as Snake River.[16]

There, on December 20, an ugly incident occurred. According to one witness, Frenchman Isidore Antaya (who had been one of Pratte's and St. Vrain's *engagés* in 1827–28), a fight between a Mexican, Rafael López, and a Frenchman, Alarid Blanco, came to a sudden end when José Santos "Susamo" stabbed López a fatal blow in the back. The knife blade broke, but the resourceful Susamo used the remaining portion to wound still another Mexican before the fighting ceased. Not all of the hazards of a trapping expedition resulted from bad weather or hostile Indians. Susamo, a foreigner, had apparently killed a man in the previous year and was generally regarded as a troublemaker. After the brutal murder of López, Harris' men seem to have lost their taste for trapping. On Christmas Day they broke camp and a month later, on January 25, 1832, reached Taos. The amount of furs gathered on this interrupted hunt is not known.[17]

Meanwhile, the Sinclair-Nidever group trapped in the area of the Green and may be the party that pre-empted an area that Warren Ferris and some American Fur Company *engagés* intended to trap. Traveling south through Cache Valley, Ferris' party learned "that a certain district where we intended to make our hunt, had already been trapped by a party from Toas [*sic*], last fall."[18] Sinclair's men later achieved small fame as participants in the well-known battle of Pierre's Hole, but Sinclair lost his life in that confrontation. Nidever and some of the trappers remained in the mountains for another year, and then joined a group of Captain Benjamin Bonneville's men under Joseph Reddeford Walk-

---

[16] Dale Morgan kindly called this to my attention. For contemporary references to the Little Snake as the "Snake," see the 1831 Smith-Frémont-Gibbs map, the Ferris map of 1836, and Wilkes' map of 1841 in Wheat, *Mapping the Transmississippi West*, II.

[17] These activities are described in José María Martínez to Governor José Antonio Chávez, Taos, January 31, 1832, MANM. A "José Santos Supaume" had asked for permission to marry at Taos in July of 1831, at which time he was listed as a foreigner and a vagrant (Chávez, "New Names," *El Palacio*, Vol. LXIV, Nos. 11–12 [November–December, 1957], 376).

[18] Ferris, *Life in the Rocky Mountains*, 138.

er, and soon found themselves in California. There Nidever remained and, among other things, hunted sea otter.[19]

Further details of Sinclair's party need not concern us, for none of the men returned to Taos to market their furs. That circumstances had forced the Arkansas trappers to winter in Taos, and outfit from there for two subsequent trapping expeditions, further reveals the importance of New Mexico to trappers working in the Rockies.

In 1831 the Rocky Mountain Fur Company, lineal descendant of William Ashley's company, also used New Mexico as its supply base. This occurred quite accidentally when Thomas Fitzpatrick, one of five partners in the newly organized company, arrived at the Missouri settlements too late to pick up supplies for that season's rendezvous. On his way to St. Louis, Fitzpatrick sought out the former partners, Jedediah Smith, David Jackson, and William Sublette, who, as it turned out, were on their way to Santa Fe with a trading caravan. They were probably Fitzpatrick's only convenient source of credit and supplies, and they persuaded him to join them, pick up his outfit in New Mexico, then proceed to the rendezvous. But the caravan did not lumber into Santa Fe until July 4, about the time that Fitzpatrick should have been back in the mountains. At Taos, Fitzpatrick took on supplies and additional trappers—Kit Carson among them—and then headed north along the Front Range of the Rockies. By the time he reached the North Platte, the rendezvous had already broken up.[20] Fitzpatrick's bad experience, it has been suggested, helped to prevent the growth of a system in which New Mexico would have furnished supplies to northern operators[21]—an impractical scheme at best, because of

[19] A biography of Nidever is Margaret E. Beckman and William H. Ellison, "George Nidever," in Hafen *Mountain Men*, I, 337–54; Hafen, "Bean-Sinclair Party," *Colorado Magazine*, Vol. XXXI, No. 3 (July, 1954), Ellison, *Nidever*, 23–24.

[20] This episode is discussed in Morgan, *Jedediah Smith*, 322–28; Sunder, *Bill Sublette*, 95; and LeRoy R. Hafen and W. J. Ghent, *Broken Hand: The Life of Thomas Fitzpatrick, Chief of the Mountain Men*, 81–87.

[21] J. W. Smurr in Phillips, *Fur Trade*, II, 524; Hafen and Ghent, *Broken Hand*, 88–89.

the increased cost of a double haul of merchandise from Missouri to Santa Fe, then to the mountains.

Before he left Taos, Fitzpatrick signed a note promising to pay Jackson, Sublette, and the estate of the recently murdered Smith for the merchandise. They designated New Mexico as the site for repayment, and Jackson and Sublette appointed the resident trader and Mexican citizen, David Waldo, as their "true and lawful agent and Attorney in the province of New Mexico." Waldo was authorized to collect payment from the Rocky Mountain Fur Company to Jackson and Sublette "in good clean, well handled mountain fur, at the rate of four dollars and twenty-five cents per pound to be delivered as near this place as the danger from seizure by Mexican Authorities will allow." A safe place was thought to be "within 60 miles of Toas." The note was due on December 1, 1831, but as late as March, 1833, Jackson and Sublette had still not collected.[22]

The Bean-Sinclair party and Thomas Fitzpatrick had used Taos as a supply base only because of emergency situations. This was not the case with Captain John Gantt, who seems to have had a clear idea of New Mexico's strategic location and planned to take advantage of it even before he left for the mountains in the spring of 1831. Before Gantt started west, J. P. Cabanné at Council Bluffs had heard that "he appears to wish to go by way of Taos, according to the word of one of the men." Cabanné's informant was probably correct, for Gantt's permit to travel through Indian country was written entirely in Spanish. There is also evidence that, prior to his departure, Gantt planned to build a trading post on the Arkansas, at the edge of Mexican territory.[23]

Among the many who sported the title of "captain" in the American West, John Gantt was one of the few who had earned it. From

[22] Letter appointing Waldo as agent, Taos, August 23, 1831; D. E. Jackson receipt to William Sublette, March 20, 1832; statement of D. E. Jackson, March 29, 1833, all in Sublette Papers.

[23] Cabanné to Pierre Chouteau, Jr., January 12, 1831, Chouteau Collection, quotation from the translated typescript accompanying the document; William Clark, permit for sixty-one persons to pass through Indian country, St. Louis, May 5, 1831, Ritch Papers, No. 125; Dale L. Morgan and Carl I. Wheat, *Jedediah Smith and His Maps of the American West*, 42.

1823 to 1829 he had served as a captain in the United States Army before being dismissed in the latter year for tampering with pay checks.[24] In the spring of 1831, with Jefferson Blackwell as his partner, Gantt started west with sixty-one men. Following the Platte, they finally reached the Laramie River—after a journey so difficult that they had to eat some of their horses. Gantt divided his men into three parties to trap. By late December, only two of the groups had returned to the appointed rendezvous on the Laramie. Since one of these had lost all of its horses, Gantt and five others took the autumn's catch of beaver and started toward Taos for more supplies and animals.[25]

Gantt's third contingent, which never returned to winter camp, had also run short of horses. Far up the Laramie, its leader, A. K. Stephens, who had once been to Santa Fe, decided that it would be more prudent to continue south to New Mexico for supplies rather than to return to the rendezvous site. A very severe mountain winter and a formidable sign of Indians had caused them to make this decision.[26] They were probably wise in doing so. That same winter two Mexican servants of a man named "Fellen" were frozen to death on their horses while trying to take supplies from Taos into the mountains to a group of American Fur Company trappers. "Fellen" may be the "O'Felon" whom George Nidever met on the Platte River in the spring of 1832. "O'Felon" was taking liquor, blankets, and other items to the rendezvous at Pierre's Hole. Perhaps he had come from Taos, for some Mexicans accompanied him, as well as a man who might have been John Harris.[27]

Meanwhile, John Gantt, who had left winter camp on the Snake on Christmas Day, managed to make it through to Taos, arriving on January 29, 1832. There Gantt traded beaver pelts for mules and supplies, then wrote a letter to the new governor, Santiago

[24] Harvey L. Carter, "John Gantt," in Hafen, *Mountain Men*, V, 101–102.

[25] Janet Lecompte, "Gantt's Fort and Bent's Picket Post," *Colorado Magazine*, Vol. XLI, No. 2 (Spring, 1964), 111–13.

[26] Zenas Leonard, *The Adventures of Zenas Leonard, Fur Trader* (ed. by John C. Ewers), 1–26, recounts Gantt's trip from the Missouri to the mountains and the subsequent adventures of A. K. Stephens, with whom Leonard traveled.

[27] Ferris, *Life in the Rocky Mountains*, 206; Ellison, *Nidever*, 24; "William O. Fallon," in Morgan, *Ashley*, 296–300.

Abreú, telling of his plans to construct a fort at the junction of the Purgatoire and the Arkansas rivers. As Gantt envisioned it, "The subsistence of the fort would always be taken care of in the valley of Taos." Gantt expressed concern about the Comanches; he asked the governor for advice regarding the construction of the fort, and for a copy of the laws regulating Indian trade in Mexican territory. Adding nine New Mexicans to his party, he returned to the Snake with his supplies.[28]

In the spring, Gantt and some of his men trapped "on the sources of the Arkansas and tributaries of the Green," according to one contemporary.[29] Gantt then led some of his trappers into North Park, where Kit Carson and four others who had gone into the mountains with Tom Fitzpatrick in the summer of 1831 found him trapping. Carson had been trapping on the Bear and Green rivers that spring before seeking out Captain "Gaunt." With Carson in his retinue, Gantt worked his way back to the Arkansas, left his men there to trap, and continued on to Taos again to market the group's furs.[30] He may have tried to smuggle these furs into Taos, for his activities there that autumn involved some dealing in contraband. In fact, the first alcalde of Taos, José María Martínez, lost his job as a result of condoning foreigners' smuggling, or so it would appear. Martínez denied that any smuggling had occurred, but officials in Santa Fe were unhappy that Ceran St. Vrain's mules, which were being used to haul cargo between Taos and some point to the north, remained at the house of the first alcalde's brother for twelve days. There was some talk of Mexican officials going north to investigate the fort that the Americans were reported to be building, but this seems not to have been done.[31]

John Gantt's trip to Taos, according to Kit Carson, required two

---

[28] José María Martínez to Governor José Antonio Chávez, Taos, February 1, 1832, MANM; Gantt to Governor Santiago Abreú, Taos, February 20, 1832, in Ritch Papers, No. 129. This letter is translated in Lecompte, "Gantt's Fort," *Colorado Magazine*, Vol. XLI, No. 2 (Spring, 1964), 113-14.

[29] Ferris, *Life in the Rocky Mountains*, 150.

[30] Carter, *'Dear Old Kit,'* 52.

[31] A letter from José María Martínez to Governor Santiago Abreú, Taos, December 24, 1832, MANM, which leaves much unsaid, is the only source I have uncovered which discusses this activity.

months. When Gantt returned to the Arkansas, he and his men continued to trap "until the rivers began to freeze, and then went into winter quarters."[32] "Quarters" were located on the Arkansas, perhaps at the mouth of the Purgatoire, and consisted of at least two buildings, probably surrounded by a picket stockade. In the spring, when Gantt headed back to the Rockies, he left his furs cached near this "fort." These, however, were not destined for the New Mexico market. Two of his men deserted on the South Fork of the Platte, retrieved the furs, and made off with them down the Arkansas with Kit Carson in futile pursuit.

Gantt continued to trap and trade until 1835, using his fort on the Arkansas to outfit trappers and to capture the Indian trade of the area. Since his post seems to have depended upon Taos, it served to extend and complement the influence of that village. Once forts such as Gantt's became fashionable, however, Taos would also surrender some of its importance as a fur depot. At least to 1833, Taos remained the most important market for furs taken in the southern Rockies.

Just how important Taos was as a market for the furs of the Rockies cannot be said with precision. Too many small groups trapped north from New Mexico of whom nothing is known. Some of these were led by naturalized Mexicans such as Antoine Robidoux, Richard Campbell, Gervais Nolan, Pierre Lesperance, and others whose operations, we have seen, remain hazy. Perhaps representative of these small-scale, independent trapping parties was a group led by Peg-leg Smith in 1832. Albert Pike, who probably met Smith in that year, said that, despite his peg-leg, Smith still "stumped about after beaver nearly as well as the best of his trappers." With Smith in 1832 were Aaron B. Lewis, a man named Alexander (probably Cyrus Alexander, who acquired some prominence as an early California pioneer), and two others whose names are not known. In the spring of 1832 this party trapped in the mountains between the Gunnison and the Colorado rivers. Reaching the Colorado, they journeyed upstream to "Smith's Fork," probably

[32] Carter, 'Dear Old Kit,' 52–53.

today's Eagle River, then crossed over to the Arkansas and the Río Grande on their way back to New Mexico. In one narrow canyon in the area of the Gunnison, beaver were abundant; Lewis found eight beaver in his traps one morning. Their return to Santa Fe, while circuitous, was made in safety, for the intrepid Smith scared off a band of Utes, and the men survived a starving time by eating some dogs that they purchased from another band of Utes.[33]

Mexican trappers and traders probably also continued to make forays into the mountains, bring their furs back to the settlements, and sell them to the Americans. Jacob Leese, one of the men who had been with the Bean-Sinclair party, found his "taste for hunting life . . . satisfied," and went to work trading furs for Ceran St. Vrain in Taos. In the spring and fall, St. Vrain sent Leese to Abiquiu, a town which Mexican fur traders traditionally frequented. Leese apparently traded for St. Vrain until the fall of 1833, when he moved to California.[34]

Like many Americans, some Mexican trappers found that trapping could be a dangerous business. In the spring of 1832, one group of eleven Mexicans was trapping three days' journey to the northeast of Taos, on "el Rito de la uña del gato," (today's Uña del Gato Creek near the Colorado border), where five of their number were killed by Indians.[35]

Occasional setbacks notwithstanding, trading and trapping by Americans and Mexicans between 1831 and 1833 resulted in the shipping of a substantial amount of beaver fur to the East over the Santa Fe Trail. One fur trader in St. Louis, William Gordon, estimated that the total amount of furs brought back from the Rockies in the fall of 1831 amounted to one hundred and fifty thousand dollars. Of this, fifty thousand dollars' worth, or one third, came from "two companies of American citizens fitting

33 Pike, *Prose Sketches*, 29–32, 281–82.

34 F. H. Day, "Sketches of the Early Settlers of California, Jacob P. Leese," *The Hesperian*, Vol. II, No. 4 (June, 1859), 147–48. A biography of Leese is Gloria Griffen Cline, "Jacob Primer Leese," in Hafen, *Mountain Men*, III, 189–96.

35 José María Martínez to Governor Santiago Abreú, Taos, April 21, 1832, MANM.

out from Santa Fee."[36] Some of these furs may have come from
Ewing Young's party, which had just returned from California
that spring, but most of it probably came from the Rocky Mountains. William Sublette, who purchased a large amount of that
season's catch in New Mexico, claimed that "our furr is generly
of an Excelent quality taken in the mountains but not so well
handled." Sublette wrote drafts on William Ashley's account for
some $17,500 to purchase beaver in the Santa Fe market. Among
the recipients were Ewing Young ($2,484.82), John L. Langham
($2,000.00), William or David Waldo ($3,377.71), Strother
Rennick ($2,825.00), and Robert Isaacs ($2,260.00). Antoine
Robidoux received $3,806.50 from Sublette's own account. These
payments to prominent Santa Fe traders and trappers represented
Sublette's purchases of furs. He returned home with 55 to 60 packs
of beaver and 200 buffalo robes. The furs carried by this caravan
alone must have valued something close to Gordon's $50,000
estimate. Sublette reported that beaver fur sold for $4.00 to $4.25
per pound in Santa Fe and that buffalo robes sold at $2.00 each.[37]
At St. Louis prices this beaver would bring at least $5.00 a pound.
If sold directly in an Eastern market, the beaver furs would fetch
$6.00 a pound. This, or $5.99, to be precise, was the average price
paid for beaver in Philadelphia between 1828 and 1833.[38]

The returns from New Mexico for 1832 were equally impressive. One observer in St. Louis, Nathaniel Wyeth, learned that
90 packs of beaver had been brought in from Santa Fe.[39] This
estimate may have been too modest, for on November 10, 1832,

[36] William Gordon to Lewis Cass, October 3, 1831, in U. S. 22 Cong., 1 sess.,
Sen. Doc. 90 (Ser. 213), 29. This is not the same William Gordon who lived in
Taos for a time and became a California pioneer.

[37] William Sublette to William Ashley, Walnut Creek Near the Arkansas,
September 24, 1831, Campbell Papers, Missouri Historical Society. Account of
Jackson and Sublette with William Sublette, October 12, 1831, through October
25, 1832, in Sublette Papers. See also, Morgan, *Ashley*, 201.

[38] Clayton, "Growth and Significance of the American Fur Trade," *Minnesota
History*, Vol. XL, No. 4 (Winter, 1966) 214.

[39] Nathaniel Wyeth to J. Baker & Son, November 17, 1833, in F. G. Young
(ed.), *The Correspondence and Journals of Captain Nathaniel J. Wyeth, 1831–6*,
84.

the *Missouri Intelligencer* reported that Charles Bent and Company returned from Santa Fe in the fall of 1832 with 13,182 pounds of beaver. Even if these were large packs (Wyeth's packs each weighed 100 pounds), Bent would have brought back at least 131 packs of beaver. Bent's furs, the *Intelligencer* said, represented the results of two years of trading and also included 355 buffalo robes. Even at Wyeth's cautious estimate, the beaver that came from New Mexico constituted one third of the total catch from the Rockies in 1832. The only larger single source of furs from the mountains in that year was the annual rendezvous itself, which netted 168 packs of beaver.[40]

Nathaniel Wyeth estimated that the Santa Fe traders would bring sixty packs of beaver out of New Mexico in 1833, or about one fourth of the total trapped and traded in the Rockies. This was an admitted estimate, however. Other sources are silent on the returns from 1833, the *Missouri Intelligencer* reporting only that "a large quantity of furs," returned with the caravan.[41]

Unknown for a time to the Taos trappers, the early 1830's, which saw them garner an important share of the furs from the mountains, also saw the price of beaver drop in the markets of the world. One reason was noted by John Jacob Astor, when he wrote to Pierre Chouteau, Jr., from Paris in the summer of 1832, "I very much fear Beaver will not sell well very soon unless very fine, it appears that they make hats of silk in place of beaver." In New York that autumn, William Astor advised Chouteau not to buy any beaver, for the market had fallen:

> I recommend you to let the owners of that coming from Santa Fe, as well as Sublette and Co do what they please with this years supply. . . . A loss must be sustained by the holders of Beaver, and we shall suffer sufficiently ourselves without

[40] J. W. Smurr in Phillips, *Fur Trade*, II, 523; (Columbia) *Missouri Intelligencer*, September 29, 1832.

[41] Wyeth to Baker, November 17, 1833, and (Columbia) *Missouri Intelligencer*, November 9, 1833.

interfering to save either of these parties—I repeat that I would not touch a pound of either parcel.[42]

The situation failed to improve during that winter. In January, William Astor gloomily announced, "This is our very dullest business season." The price of Rocky Mountain beaver sold in New York had dropped to $4.00 a pound and Santa Fe beaver remained unsold on the market. If a buyer could be found, Astor supposed that it could be bought for $3.75 per pound.[43]

The following season the price of beaver remained low, and William Astor again advised Chouteau not to buy any of the Santa Fe or Rocky Mountain beaver, "at any price." "We had better allow the owners, or speculators in Santa Fé, and Rocky Mountain, to try their luck in our market [on the East Coast], than to become the purchasers ourselves." The New Mexico traders managed to sell their beaver in the East that season, but Astor reported that, along with William Sublette's fur from the rendezvous, it "appears to have been sold cheap."[44]

Thus, although the Taos trappers had been strong competitors for the beaver pelts of the Rockies, and a significant amount of that fur found its way to New Mexico markets, profits were no longer as great as before. But mountain men did not immediately disappear from the scene, nor did the decline in the price of beaver fur result in the decline of the fur trade. Buffalo robes rose in importance, and their volume and value increased in succeeding decades.[45] The drop in the price of beaver would, however, bring about a change in the very nature of the fur trade throughout the Far West.

[42] J. J. Astor to Chouteau, Paris, August, 1832, and W. B. Astor to Chouteau, New York, October 12, 1832, Chouteau Collection.
[43] W. B. Astor to Chouteau, New York, January 14, 1833, Chouteau Collection.
[44] W. B. Astor to Chouteau, New York, July 31, 1833; October 28, 1833; December 14, 1833, Chouteau Collection.
[45] Clayton, "Growth and Significance of the American Fur Trade," *Minnesota History*, Vol. XL, No. 4 (Winter, 1966), 212.

XIII YEARS OF DECLINE,

As BEAVER FUR fell from favor in the early 1830's, it was quickly eclipsed by the woolly hide of the American bison, which, for at least three decades after 1832, became the most sought-after animal in the Far West.[1] Unlike beaver pelts, which few Indians trapped, buffalo robes were readily available through trade with Indians so that the fur trade could be carried out at strategically located fixed trading posts. Thus, the gradual demise of the Taos trappers accompanied the slow decline in beaver trapping which took place in the 1830's, and the stationary trading post came to dominate the fur trade in the Far West.

The 1830's saw the construction of a number of trading posts on the high plains to the north of New Mexico, inside United States territory. John Gantt built the first of these in the winter of 1831–32, as we have already seen, and continued to trade on the Arkansas until 1835. In May, 1834, he changed locations, moving near a rival trader, William Bent. Gantt's new post, called Fort Cass, was located six miles below the mouth of Fountain Creek and was constructed of adobe (sun-dried mud bricks) by Guadalupe Avila and Domínguez Madrid, who had been brought up from Taos. By August, 1835, however, John Gantt had also

[1] Clayton, "Growth and Significance of the American Fur Trade," *Minnesota History*, Vol. XL, No. 4 (Winter, 1966), 213.

1834–1846

abandoned Fort Cass, having succumbed to competition from a more popular establishment downriver, Bent's Fort.[2] Built in late 1832 or early 1833 by veteran trapper Ceran St. Vrain and Charles Bent, a former Missouri River fur trader who had shifted his field of operation to the Southwest in 1829, Bent's Fort sat astride the mountain branch of the Santa Fe Trail on the north side of the Arkansas near the mouth of the "Picket Wire," as the Americans would call the Purgatoire.[3] Bent's Fort dominated the area. After 1835, forts Vásquez, Jackson, and Lupton would rise on the South Platte, but none successfully challenged Bent's and St. Vrain's supremacy, partly because Bent and St. Vrain countered by building Fort St. Vrain on the South Platte in 1837 and by buying out the owners of Fort Jackson in 1838.[4]

Taos was able to supply some manpower for the construction

[2] Lecompte, "Gantt's Fort," *Colorado Magazine*, Vol. XLI, No. 2 (Spring, 1964), 115–25.

[3] LeRoy R. Hafen, "When Was Bent's Fort Built?", *Colorado Magazine*, Vol. XXXI, No. 2 (April, 1954), 105–19. A biography of Charles Bent by Harold H. Dunham appears in Hafen, *Mountain Men*, II, 27–48. See the discussion regarding St. Vrain and the alcalde of Taos in the previous chapter.

[4] The founding and operation of these forts has been described by LeRoy R. Hafen: "The Early Fur Trade Posts on the South Platte," *Mississippi Valley Historical Review*, Vol. XII, No. 3 (December, 1925), 334–41, and in articles which appeared in *Colorado Magazine* in 1928, 1929, and 1952.

and operation of these new forts (all were built of adobe, a popular material among fort builders), and a north-south commerce developed in which Mexican flour and whisky were sold and bartered as far as the North Platte.[5] To some extent this augmented the New Mexico fur trade, but many of the pelts and buffalo robes that might have been marketed in Taos or Santa Fe now found their way directly into the United States via the Platte, or the Santa Fe Trail from Bent's Fort.

Bent's Fort was Taos' strongest competitor for the furs of the southern Rockies. Statistics illustrative of the fur trade at this trading post are scarce, but the few we have reveal a lively trade in buffalo robes and beaver furs. In 1839, for example, the partners shipped 600 packs of buffalo robes and 10 packs of beaver back to Missouri. The following year their wagons carried 15,000 robes and, in 1841, 895 beaver skins weighing 1,338 pounds.[6] In May, 1842, 283 packs of robes and only 30 packs of beaver reached St. Louis from Charles Bent. Meanwhile, however, writing from Taos in April, 1842, Bent reported that 435 more packs of beaver were en route and acknowledged that he had still more furs which he could not send to market for want of transportation. The trade in beaver skins was far from dead.[7]

Much of the beaver which Bent and St. Vrain marketed probably came from trade with Indians and from trappers working out of the fort, for some of the mountain men who had earlier operated out of Taos now relied on the new forts to obtain supplies and to market beaver. Old Bill Williams, for example, spent the winter of 1842–43 in Taos, but when spring came he went to Bent's Fort to obtain a trapping outfit, agreeing to repay his debt in "good merchantable beaver" at that place.[8] Some of the beaver pelts sold in the United States by Bent and St. Vrain, however, came from

[5] This topic, and some of the sources concerning it, is discussed in Phillips, *Fur Trade*, II, 531–33.

[6] Dunham, "Charles Bent," in Hafen, *Mountain Men*, II, 42. Account Book EE, 246, Chouteau Collection, reference through the kindness of Janet Lecompte.

[7] (St. Louis) *Daily Missouri Republican*, May 19, 1842. John B. Sarpy to Pierre Chouteau, Jr., September 17, 1842, Chouteau Collection, reference through the kindness of Janet Lecompte.

[8] Favour, *Old Bill Williams*, 148–49.

the Taos traders. Stephen Lee, for example, sold Charles Bent nearly four hundred pounds of beaver in 1841, and Bent bought an unspecified amount of beaver fur from Manuel Alvarez in 1840.[9] Thus, Bent's Fort may have complemented the fur trade from New Mexico as well as rivaled it.

While Bent, St. Vrain, and other builders of forts on the high plains siphoned off many of the furs that would ordinarily have found their way to Taos, Antoine Robidoux's mountain forts served to extend the New Mexico fur trade. Antoine and Louis Robidoux had become Mexican citizens in 1829 and remained influential politician-merchants in Santa Fe for the next decade. Sometime in the 1830's Antoine built two trading posts to the northwest of Taos. He probably built Fort Uinta (also called Fort Robidoux) in the winter of 1837–38. Located near the forks of the Uinta and Whiterocks rivers, near present-day Whiterocks, Utah, the post occupied a site in an area that Robidoux and other Taos trappers knew well. In 1831, for example, Denis Julien, a trapper who had been in the employ of François Robidoux in 1827, inscribed his name on a rock near the Uinta.[10] Along a route that trappers would take to Fort Robidoux (in the Willow Creek drainage, south of Ouray, Utah), carvings on a cliffside reveal the names of Juan Valdes, "B. Chalifou" (who must be Jean Baptiste Chalifoux), an F.R.B., and a name that looks like "Acosta." All were carved in May, 1835.[11] In the winter of 1833–34, Kit Carson remembered meeting a "Mr. Robidoux" who had twenty men trapping and trading on the Uinta. Since Antoine seems to have been in Santa Fe that winter, this Robidoux might have been one of his brothers—perhaps Louis—assuming that Carson remembered the season correctly.[12]

[9] Weber, "Stephen Louis Lee," in Hafen, *Mountain Men*, III, 184. Charles Bent to Manuel Alvarez, Taos, November 15, 1840, Benjamin Read Collection, State Records Center, Santa Fe.
[10] Albert B. Reagan, "Forts Robidoux and Kit Carson in Northeastern Utah," *New Mexico Historical Review*, Vol. X, No. 2 (April, 1935), 122.
[11] Photograph by George E. Stewart of Roosevelt, Utah, copy courtesy of O. D. Marston, Berkeley, California.
[12] Carter, *'Dear Old Kit,'* 58–59. On December 6, 1833, Antoine's signature appears as one of the members of the commission in charge of the formation of

About the time that Antoine Robidoux built Fort Uinta, he also constructed Fort Uncompahgre on the Gunnison River near the mouth of the Uncompahgre. Perhaps, in point of time, this was the second of the two posts, built as a way station to the Uinta.[13] Or, it may be that Fort Uncompahgre was built first to offset the influence which Bent's Fort and the South Platte forts were gaining on the Indian trade. In that case, Fort Uinta might have been built later to counter the establishment of Fort Davy Crockett, built in Brown's Hole on the Green in northwestern Colorado about 1837. Still, the years in which Robidoux's temporary trading sites became permanent posts cannot yet be ascertained. The earliest known description of either fort comes from a sixty-six-year-old Methodist minister, Joseph Williams, who visited Fort Uinta in July, 1842. Scandalized by the trappers' keeping of Indian women, their drinking and swearing, and unfavorably disposed toward Roman Catholics anyway, Williams found Robidoux and his trappers "as wicked men, I think, as ever lived." Furthermore, "Some of these people at the Fort are fat and dirty, idle and greasy."[14]

Another visitor to Fort Uinta in 1842 was more interested in Robidoux's trading activities than with the morals of his men. Trapper Rufus B. Sage described the chief business of the post as outfitting "trapping parties frequenting the Big Beaver, Green, Grand, and the Colorado rivers." He noted that "a small business" was carried on with Snakes and Utes who lived near the post and who traded pelts and skins with Robidoux in exchange for guns and ammunition, among other things. "The trade," Sage said, "is quite profitable. The articles procured so cheaply, when taken to Santa Fe and the neighboring towns, find a ready cash market." Both of Robidoux's forts depended heavily on New Mexico for supplies and used New Mexico as a market for beaver on occasion.

---

election districts, Santa Fe, MANM. On February 19, 1834, Antoine purchased a mine in Santa Fe. See the certificate of sale of that date, cited in Twitchell, *Spanish Archives*, I, 215.

13 Wallace, *Antoine Robidoux*, 14, 53, n. 31; Hafen and Hafen, *Old Spanish Trail*, 102.

14 Joseph Williams, *Narrative of a Tour From the State of Indiana to the Oregon Territory in the Years 1841–1842*, 80–81.

Perhaps Louis Robidoux served as the Santa Fe agent for his brother. On at least one occasion in the spring of 1841, Louis journeyed from Santa Fe to Fort Uinta.[15]

Trappers who used the services of Robidoux's forts, then, were spared the long trip to Taos. After 1839, when the annual mountain rendezvous was no longer held, Robidoux's location became particularly strategic. A party which had been trapping as far away as the Gila, for example, arrived at Fort Uinta in the fall of 1842, "bringing with them a rich quantity of beaver," according to Rufus Sage. That same fall a group of trappers left from Fort Uinta for the headwaters of the Columbia River.[16] Kit Carson, who had formerly trapped out of Taos, furnishes another example. In the spring of 1840, after trapping high on the Missouri and the Snake, Carson took his furs to Fort Uinta. Again in the spring of 1841, after hunting on the Grand River, wintering in Brown's Hole on the Green, and trapping in North Park, Carson and five others returned to Fort Uinta to sell their furs. They remained there for the summer. By then, according to Carson, "beaver was getting very scarce." With Old Bill Williams and three others, Carson journeyed to the Arkansas and took brief employment as a hunter at Bent's Fort. Like many mountain men who had made Taos their home, Carson failed to find life at a fur trading post a suitable substitute for civilization. After a brief visit to the United States and a journey to South Pass with Frémont, Carson returned to Taos and married.[17]

It is probably more than coincidence that by 1839, soon after Fort Uinta was established, the traditionally friendly relations between Utes and New Mexicans had begun to deteriorate. By 1844 the situation became critical. On September 5 of that year, a delegation of 6 Ute chiefs and 108 warriors entered Santa Fe, demand-

[15] Hafen and Hafen, *Rufus B. Sage*, II, 97–98. Alvarez Ledger, 1840–42, entries of August, 1840, and August, 1841, 14 and 101; photo of inscription in Willow Creek drainage, May, 1841, by George E. Stewart, Roosevelt, Utah.

[16] Hafen and Hafen, *Rufus B. Sage*, II, 126, 133.

[17] Carter, *'Dear Old Kit,'* 78–84. I have followed Carter's chronology for 1840–41, although Dale Morgan has suggested that Carson retired to Bent's Fort in the fall of 1840 instead of 1841. See the exchange between Morgan and Carter in *Montana Magazine*, summer and autumn issues, 1968.

ing presents as compensation for some of their number who had been killed, according to one version of the story, by "a trapping party of Spaniards under PORTELANCE," a Frenchman. The chiefs visited Governor Mariano Martínez, who tried to placate them with presents. Displeased with his gifts, they attacked the governor, whose guards took the lives of eight Indians before the fighting ended.[18] As Antoine Robidoux later told it, the enraged Utes returned to their own country and spent some of their fury on Mexicans who were working at his Fort Uncompahgre ("the Tampagarha Fort"). At least three Mexicans were killed. One American who was there, however, "was spared and sent to let Mr. Robidous know (who was 120 miles distant [probably at Fort Uinta]), that the peltries were unharmed." Robidoux maintained that Utes were not hostile to Americans,[19] but another contemporary reported that an American had been killed at the fort, as were five or six Mexicans. News of the attack on Fort Uncompahgre demoralized Robidoux's employees at the Uinta Fort. Some of them stole weapons and supplies and fled the post.[20]

Following the hostilities at his fort, Robidoux suddenly left New Mexico and the mountains, returning to Missouri. His biographer, William S. Wallace, sees the low price of furs, danger from Indians, and general financial losses as contributing to Robidoux's departure. His final action, Wallace suggests, was precipitated by the attack on the fort which was "the last straw for Antoine." Despite some setbacks, however, Robidoux's trading post seemed to be doing well;[21] it is difficult to explain why he would leave his home and

[18] (St. Louis) *Daily Missouri Republican*, October 31, 1844. The best account of these troubles with the Utes, especially the war of 1844, is Minge's doctoral dissertation, "Frontier Problems" (University of New Mexico, 1965), 65–70, 256–81.

[19] (Fayette) *Missouri Democrat*, September 17, 1845, quoting the *St. Joseph Gazette*, which seems to have obtained Robidoux's story from his own lips. This article is copied in Dale Morgan's collection, "The Mormons in the Far West," copy in the Huntington Library.

[20] A. W. Sublette to William L. Sublette, Taos, October 20, 1844, Sublette Papers, Missouri Historical Society. Janet Lecompte's forthcoming *Fort Pueblo* contains an outstanding account of these events.

[21] Wallace, *Antoine Robidoux*, 31; Solomon P. Sublette to William L. Sublette, October 31, 1842, Sublette Papers.

store in Santa Fe. Yet, his brother Louis also quit New Mexico about this time, moving to California in late 1843. Deteriorating commercial conditions may have prompted their departures, but they may also have been motivated by self-defense. Mexican officials in Santa Fe suspected that the Utes had been obtaining arms and ammunition from one of Robidoux's forts and were satisfied that the results of an investigation, which they ordered, showed this to be the case.[22] Antoine could not have felt very comfortable walking the streets of Santa Fe as a known gunrunner.

Although many of the furs gathered in the southern and central Rockies in the late 1830's and early 1840's found their way to forts operated by Robidoux, Bent and St. Vrain, and others, mountain men and Mexican traders still brought furs to New Mexico settlements. Taos continued to garner a significant share of the coarser furs—buffalo, deer, bear, and elk skins—that had been dominant in the Spanish period. Buffalo hunts took place twice annually, in June and October, but the latter month was most important for the skins were then "very woolly and valuable." In 1832 it was estimated that New Mexicans killed ten to twelve thousand buffalo each year, although the amount probably decreased in subsequent years as Americans became more active in this business. In addition to the skins from these animals, buffalo robes were brought in by *comancheros*, the Mexican traders who ventured onto the plains to barter with the Comanches.[23] Most of the buffalo robes gathered by native New Mexicans found their way down the Chihuahua Trail to the interior states of Mexico, where, along with such things as piñon, sheep, and serapes, they were exchanged for manu-

[22] Borrador of January 27, 1845, to Prefect Juan Andrés Archuleta, in the book of borradores sent by the Secretaría de Gobierno Superior of New Mexico to various persons, 1844, and the entry of February 15, 1845, in the book of borradores from the Governor of New Mexico to the Ministro de Relaciones Exteriores y Gobernación, 1844, both in MANM.

[23] Barriero, *Ojeada*, 101–102; Gregg, *Commerce of the Prairies*, 63, 67, 371; Bloom, "New Mexico Under Mexican Administration," *Old Santa Fe*, Vol. II, No. 2 (October, 1914), 164; Pike, *Prose Sketches*, 37, 40–43.

factured items. A few deer and elk skins, and an occasional bear skin, also entered the trade to the south.[24]

By New Mexico standards, furs and hides brought good prices in the south. In 1840, for example, a sheep on the hoof or a *fanega* (about a bushel and one half) of laboriously gathered piñon nuts was valued at one peso. A good buffalo robe, on the other hand, brought two pesos and seems to have been equal in value to the best serape.[25]

Although there is little documentary evidence of it, this trade in coarser furs may have attracted some of the American merchants who annually brought manufactured goods down the Chihuahua Trail. In 1834, Samuel Parkman, a former employee of Jedediah Smith, wrote from Guanajuato to Peter Smith at Santa Fe, "Choice Buffalo robes and Bear Skins and dark colored Beaver Skins and Otter Skins would I think sell well [here]. . . . Let skins be only choice ones for this market as you already know." Parkman repeated this advice to Smith the following year.[26] Most Americans, however, probably preferred to send their buffalo robes to the United States market, where they would bring a higher price. Thus the Taos distiller, Simeon Turley, wrote to his brother Jesse in Missouri, "I expect to send to the lower country this fall with robes and blankets as I had no chance to send in the robes [to Missouri]."[27]

Although coarser furs seem to have formed the mainstay of the New Mexico trade by the mid-1830's, some beaver fur also found its way into Taos and Santa Fe. In 1834, despite the low price of beaver for the last two seasons, the annual caravan rolled back to Missouri with $15,000 worth of beaver pelts, according to one newspaper account. That the caravan also carried fifty packs of buffalo robes was symptomatic of the changing times.[28] This,

---

[24] Documentation illustrating this trade is numerous. See, for example, Minge's dissertation, "Frontier Problems" (University of New Mexico, 1965), 247–50, and the report of Governor Antonio Narbona, April 8, 1827, in Carroll and Haggard, *Three New Mexico Chronicles*, 90.

[25] See the *guías* granted between August 10 and August 28, 1840, MANM.

[26] Samuel Parkman to Peter Smith at Santa Fe, Guanajuato, October 20, 1834 and December 1, 1835, Peter Smith Papers, Bancroft Library.

[27] Simeon Turley to Jesse B. Turley, Taos, April 18, 1841, Turley Papers, Missouri Historical Society.

however, may have been one of the last big shipments of beaver from New Mexico. Perhaps more typical cargoes of the period (if a merchant had any beaver at all), were those of David Waldo, who took 1,000 beaver skins and 1,000 buffalo robes in 1836, and John R. White, with 200 buffalo robes and 2 packages (*bultos*) of beaver, in 1837.[29] An examination of the business papers of Manuel Alvarez reveals only an occasional dabbling in furs in the 1830's. In 1839, an exceptional year for Alvarez, he shipped 383 pounds of beaver back to St. Louis. It was almost not worth the trouble. A merchant in Taos or Santa Fe paid an average of $3.00 a pound for beaver from 1834 to 1840, and Alvarez was able to sell his furs in St. Louis for only $3.25 per pound. Freight cost ten cents a pound and L. L. Waldo took a five per cent commission for the sale, which did not leave a great deal of profit for Alvarez,[30] unless he obtained the furs for $3.00 worth of trade goods rather than $3.00 in cash. At least the wagons did not return empty.

Some of the beaver fur that was marketed in Santa Fe and Taos in the mid-1830's may have been acquired through trade with Indians, but much was also obtained through trapping. Despite the falling price of beaver, some of the Taos trappers continued to practice their trade. The activities of these men remain as shadowy as ever.

By the mid-1830's, beaver in the overtrapped streams near the Mexican settlements may have had a chance to replenish their numbers while trappers had worked more distant waters. In 1838, for example, four Frenchmen, apparently outfitted by Charles Beaubien, were trapping near Mora, on the eastern slope of the Sangre de Cristos. Even this close to the Mexican settlements, however, trapping could be a risky business. All four were killed by

---

[28] (St. Louis) *Missouri Republican*, October 24, 1834.

[29] David Waldo request for and granting of a *guía*, Santa Fe, July 24, 1836, MANM; John R. White, request for a *guía*, Santa Fe, May 11, 1837, Ritch Papers, No. 158.

[30] Account of Damasio López with Alvarez, October 6, 1834, in Alvarez Ledger, No. 1; entry of July 28, 1840, Alvarez to Waldo, in Ledger Book No. 2, 144; page from the account of Manuel Alvarez with L. L. Waldo, October 17, 1839, Alvarez Business Papers, State Records Center, Santa Fe; Gregg, *Commerce of the Prairies*, 214.

Indians.[31] More common in the 1830's, however, was trapping in the once nearly exhausted Gila area, which could also be very dangerous.

After the large-scale hunt on the Gila in the 1826–27 season, there is little record of trapping parties working in that area, except for those who used it as a road to travel to California. If the beaver supply had diminished, as James Ohio Pattie seemed to think, the danger from Indians had not. This was discovered in 1830 by four Americans: Joshua Griffith, a veteran trapper who had been on the Upper Missouri with Ashley and Henry in 1822;[32] Robert Isaacs, who had just come to New Mexico with the caravan that year;[33] Joshua Reynolds; and William Bent, brother of Charles. With four horses, nine mules, "Lolo, a cur of no mean prowess," and a Mexican servant named Leone, the four Americans left Santa Fe on August 25, 1830, according to an account by Robert Isaacs. They headed for "a small tributary of the Pacific," which Isaacs called the "Yancha" but which seems to have been the Yaqui River.

Isaacs does not record the route that the men took to the "Yancha," but once there they found no sign of beaver. So, they "crossed its stream and bore northerly, arriving at Santa Pedro, a small river," which they followed to the Gila. When they tried to travel west on the Gila, "Humoes [Yumas?], Popponays [Papagos?], and Mauricopas," scared the trappers off, and they retraced their tracks up the Gila. Passing by the mouth of the San Pedro, they continued up the Gila until the "Beaver sign . . . was abundant. The banks of the river were literally smooth from the small trees and timber which had been slid down them, for the construction of their dams." In this rich area they made camp and set their traps, but

[31] Francis Cragin copied this information from a notebook of one Gaspar Luciano Gallegos, at Mora, March 12, 1908, who was presumably a contemporary to the event. Notebook XIII, 15, Cragin Papers, Pioneers' Museum, Colorado Springs, Colorado.

[32] For Griffith's presence on the Upper Missouri see Morgan, *Ashley*, 71–72 and n. 216. Griffith had come to New Mexico at least as early as the spring of 1829. That summer, Solomon Houck, an American merchant, authorized him to bring one Juan Beltrán, who had robbed Houck of one thousand pesos, from the Santa Rita copper mines to justice in El Paso. See also papers pertaining to the robbery of Houck, El Paso, July 13, 1829, MANM.

[33] Bork, *Nuevos Aspectos*, 117.

during the first night, Indians stole a number of their horses and most of their traps. The next day found the trappers defending themselves from "a numerous body" of attacking Indians. Victorious, the Americans made a judicious retreat to the "nearest Spanish settlement," perhaps the copper mines. As the story was retold in later years, the Indians came to number between 150 to 200 "warriors," and "the battle went on with scarcely any intermission for two days." The trappers may have enjoyed some success that season, however, for at Santa Fe in the summer of 1831, William Sublette paid Robert Isaacs $2,260.00, which probably represented payment for beaver fur.[34]

Following the difficulties of Robert Isaacs and company, Americans making their headquarters at the Santa Rita copper mines apparently continued to trap in the rugged country near the headwaters of the Gila. Operating without publicity of any sort, these trappers failed to attract the attention of Mexican officials until 1834, when increased Apache depredations on settlements in Sonora and Chihuahua caused officials to take notice of American activities in Apache country.

The most colorful, and perhaps most important of those who operated on the Gila in the early 1830's was the soon-to-be celebrated scalp hunter, James Kirker. An experienced fur trader, Kirker was with William Ashley on the Upper Missouri between 1822 and 1823. Soon after 1824, it is said, Kirker drifted into New Mexico; a Santa Fe custom house notation refers to a "Kinker" who arrived there in the fall of 1825. Following his arrival Kirker trapped in New Mexico, being among those whose furs Governor Antonio Narbona confiscated in 1827. Then, according to a contemporary account, he "repaired to the copper mines of Mr. Robert McKnight [at Santa Rita], where he remained for a period of eight years, trapping the Rio Gila every winter."[35]

34 "Perils of a Mountain Hunt," (Columbia) *Missouri Intelligencer*, October 6, 1832; Waldo, "Recollections," *MHSGP*, Vol. V, Nos. 4–6 (April–June, 1938), 65; Morgan, *Ashley*, 201.

35 "Captain Don Santiago Kirker, The Indian Fighter, His Warring Against the Apaches From 1836 to 1847," *Santa Fe Republican*, November 20, 1847, re-

In 1835, as Kirker remembered it, Governor Alberto Pérez had given him a license to trap and trade with Apaches for one year. With eighteen men working for him, Kirker was "highly successful." Before the year was out, however, officials in Mexico City ordered Governor Pérez to arrest Kirker and to confiscate his property, "alledging that the Governor possessed no authority to grant such a license to an alien and a heretic." With an eight hundred-dollar price on his head, Kirker reportedly fled to Bent's Fort until Pérez was killed in an uprising in 1836 and Manuel Armijo assumed the governorship. Armijo then "invited Captain Kirker to return to the province."[36]

In telling his story, however, Kirker had forgotten that part of his stock of trade goods consisted of arms and ammunition. Residents of Chihuahua had long suspected that Americans had contributed to Apache strength by furnishing them with arms. A Chihuahua newspaper made this specific charge in the fall of 1834.[37] By early 1835, the Apache menace had become so serious that Chihuahua officials issued a printed circular restricting trade with the Apaches and prohibiting the sale of arms, ammunition, and alcohol to them. In particular, it specified that "the foreigners who, under the pretext of hunting beaver, enter the lands of the Apache Indians," be subject to all of the trading restrictions that affected Mexicans. Foreigners caught trading arms, powder, or lead would be executed. A prime candidate for execution was James Kirker. In April, 1836, the comandante general of Chihuahua, José Joaquín Calvo, notified New Mexico officials that Kirker was trapping without a license and trading gunpowder with the Indians. Calvo claimed that Kirker's trapping was only a front for his trade in armaments.[38]

---

printed from the St. Louis *Saturday Evening Post*; Morgan, *Ashley*, 23; Weber, *Extranjeros*, 26. A biography of Kirker by William Cochran McGaw appears in Hafen, *Mountain Men*, V, 125–43.

[36] "Captain Don Santiago Kirker," *Santa Fe Republican*, November 20, 1847.

[37] *El Fanal* de Chihuahua, October 21, 1834.

[38] Circular from the Palacio del Gobierno del Estado, Chihuahua, February 25, 1835, in the Documentos de la Ciudad de Juárez, Reel 35, 143; José Joaquín Calvo to the Comandante General of New Mexico, April 13 and April 19, 1836, MANM.

Kirker and his men were not the only Americans trapping and trading on the Gila at this time. In the fall of 1836, officials in El Paso and New Mexico learned of three more Americans who were on the way to the Gila to trade in munitions.[39] Coincidentally, or perhaps not, that same season Benjamin D. Wilson was leading a group of six men to the Gila. Wilson, who would become a well-known California pioneer, had first come to New Mexico in 1833, spending at least one season trapping the Gila with Kirker before outfitting his own party. Wilson later recalled that until 1836 the Apaches had befriended the Americans, even though these Indians were at war with the Mexicans. That the Americans' deadly trade goods promoted this friendship, Wilson does not say. The friend-ship of the Apaches, according to Wilson, was profitable to the Americans, for the Mexican government "would not give permis-sion to the Americans to trade or trap in their territory, we were there as interlopers, and smugglers." Thus, Americans operated in the Gila area almost under the protection of Apaches until the season of 1836–37, a time which represents a turning point in American-Apache relations. In the spring of 1837, John Johnson treacherously betrayed his former friend, the Apache Chief Juan José, reportedly killing him with his own hands. As a result, no trapper on the Gila was safe. Wilson barely escaped from the area with his life and remembered that a group of twenty-one trappers under Charles Kemp all met death at the hands of Apaches.[40]

The killing of Juan José and the resultant Apache hostility toward Americans may have ended trapping on the Gila for the next few years. New Mexico officials may also have tightened their

[39] See the papers relating to José María Crespín, and "Carpio," September 23, 1836, El Paso, MANM.

[40] "Benjamin David Wilson's Observations on Early Days in California and New Mexico," foreword and notes by Arthur Woodward, *Publications, His-torical Society of Southern California*, Vol. XVI, No. 1 (1934), 77, 78, 81; J. J. Johnson to the Comandante General y Gobernador del Departamento de Chi-huahua, April 24, 1837, in *El Noticioso de Chihuahua*, May 5, 1837. Professor Rex W. Strickland, of the University of Texas at El Paso, first called this item to my attention. Arthur Woodward deals with the long-range consequences of the death of Juan José in "Sidelights on Fifty Years of Apache Warfare, 1836–1886," *Arizoniana*, Vol. II, No. 3 (Fall, 1961), 3–14.

security against foreign trappers.[41] Kirker and his cronies, however, continued to hunt there, hired by the governor of Chihuahua to seek Apache scalps instead of beaver.[42]

Foreigners who shied away from the Apache-controlled Gila could still trap to the south of the New Mexico settlements along the Río Grande Valley. In January, 1838, for example, a small trapping party of "civilized Indians"—Delawares and Shawnees— were camped at Robledo, a stopping place north of El Paso. They intended to continue trapping down the Río Grande to the Pecos, then follow that river back to Taos where they would join others who had come to New Mexico with them. The Indians, some of whom spoke English, were denied a license to trap by officials at El Paso and told to turn back. They went ahead anyway, showing up at Presidio del Norte, below El Paso, in late February, where the comandante imprisoned seventeen of their men and three of their women. A month later two Indians fled during the night, taking some of the presidio's horses and mules for good measure. The fate of the other Indians is not known.[43]

Even had these Indian trappers eluded capture, they probably would have returned to Taos with very few beaver skins. That same year of 1838, El Paso officials advised the departmental junta of Chihuahua that, due to indiscriminate trapping, the beaver and otter along the banks of the Río Grande were in danger of becoming extinct. Chihuahua officials responded by prohibiting trapping for

[41] Borrador of Comandante General of Chihuahua and Sonora, May 5, 1837, and Ministro de Guerra y Marina to the Governor of New Mexico, October 31, 1837, in Archivo de Justicia, Vol. 185, AGN.

[42] Kirker's despicable methods are described in Hafen, *Ruxton of the Rockies*, 148–149. Some new material appears in Minge's dissertation, "Frontier Problems" (University of New Mexico, 1965), 58–60. Two articles by Ralph A. Smith shed light on Kirker's later years: "The Scalp Hunter in the Borderlands, 1835–1850," *Arizona and the West*, Vol. VI, No. 1 (Spring, 1964), 5–22; and "The 'King of New Mexico' and the Doniphan Expedition," *New Mexico Historical Review*, Vol. XXXVIII, No. I (January, 1963), 29–55.

[43] Guadalupe Miranda to the Governor of Chihuahua, El Paso, January 10, 1838, in *El Noticioso de Chihuahua*, February 22, 1838, and papers regarding the "Imprisonment and escape of Indians. . . . " in Relaciones Exteriores, Doc. H/240(72:73)/21, Legajo 6-9-86.

the next six years and empowering muncipal authorities to enforce the law.[44]

The activities of Wilson, Kirker, and the others who trapped and traded on the Gila and in southern New Mexico during the mid-1830's seem to have been sporadic and of little economic consequence. By the end of the decade, at least, no significant trapping seems to have occurred in New Mexico. Nevertheless, some beaver pelts continued to find their way over the Santa Fe Trail to Missouri in the early 1840's. In 1842, for example, Ramsay Crooks informed Pierre Chouteau, Jr., that "the Santa Fe beaver is in store, and I will see ere long whether a buyer can be found here for it—there is 2478 [pounds]."[45] But statistics for this period are almost nonexistent. Missouri newspapers rarely mention furs among the exports from Santa Fe, and when they do, specific types or amounts are not indicated. On September 27, 1844, for example, the *Daily Missouri Republican* at St. Louis noted that the Santa Fe merchants brought back an estimated $50,000 worth of buffalo robes and "furs."

Most of the beaver pelts that entered New Mexico markets in the 1840's were obtained through trade rather than through trapping. By 1846, when the English traveler George Frederick Ruxton passed through New Mexico, he noted that "beaver has so depreciated in value within the last few years that trapping has been almost abandoned." By that time beaver was commanding all of ninety cents a pound in the southern Rockies.[46] A number of Americans and former mountain men had turned to trading for furs in the 1840's, using "Taos lightning" as their chief bartering item. This New Mexico–made whisky enjoyed a unique market, wherein the United States government unconsciously did its best to discourage competitors. Liquor was a forbidden trade item to

[44] Secretaría de la Junta Departamental de Chihuahua to the Governor of Chihuahua, September 27, 1838, in *El Noticioso de Chihuahua*, October 4, 1838.

[45] Crooks to Chouteau, July 10, 1842, Chouteau Collection. Reference through the kindness of Janet Lecompte.

[46] Hafen, *Ruxton of the Rockies*, 225; diary of Alexander Barclay, entry of August 31, 1846, in Barclay Papers, Bancroft Library, Berkeley, California.

the Indians in the territories to the north of New Mexico. Although imaginative traders managed to smuggle whisky in from the United States,[47] it was sometimes easier to obtain it from distillers at Taos. This was especially true after 1842, when the United States made strong efforts to contain the whisky trade along its border. Thus, in 1843, Manuel Alvarez, who had by then become the United States consul at Santa Fe, told the secretary of state that even though United States agents along the Missouri had stopped traders from smuggling liquor into Indian territory, "the amount consumed is much the same, as the deficiency from our country is made up from the valley of Taos and large parties of Mexicans are daily selling it to the tribes within our borders."[48]

The most direct sources of the liquor about which Alvarez and others complained were two new settlements on the Arkansas, Pueblo and Hardscrabble, founded in 1843 and 1844 respectively. Although only Hardscrabble was located on the Mexican side of the river, both communities were more Mexican than American and looked to Taos to supply the amenities of life. These communities, where many former mountain men had settled down to a life of farming and trading, became way stations in the exchange of Taos whisky for furs.[49] When George Ruxton visited Pueblo early in 1847, he saw two of the local residents starting for Taos "with some packs of peltries, intending to bring back Taos whiskey." At Taos, Ruxton had noted that most of the distilleries belonged "to Americans who are generally trappers and hunters, who having married Taos women have settled here." Their whisky, Ruxton said, had "a ready market" among Indian traders "who find the 'firewater' the most profitable article of trade with the aborigines, who ex-

[47] Chittenden, *American Fur Trade*, II, 669–74, provides examples, as do numerous other sources.

[48] Alvarez to the Secretary of State, Independence, Missouri, July 1, 1843, in Despatches from United States Consuls in Santa Fe, 1830–46, National Archives, Washington, D.C. A number of sources illustrate this trade in liquor from New Mexico. See, for example, Chittenden, *American Fur Trade*, II, 269.

[49] These settlements and their inhabitants are treated in Janet Lecompte, "The Hardscrabble Settlement, 1844–1848," *Colorado Magazine*, Vol. XXXI, No. 2 (April, 1954), 81–98, and in her forthcoming book, *Fort Pueblo*, which also treats the liquor trade in detail.

change for it their buffalo robes and other peltries at a 'tremendous sacrifice.' "[50] One of these distillers was Simeon Turley, whose still at Arroyo Hondo, just above Taos, "makes a great many drunkards," as Reverend Joseph Williams observed. Turley also made profits from furs. In the spring of 1843 he shipped some buffalo robes and beaver to Missouri. He told his brother that there would be more to come in the fall, at which time he expected to send one wagon "which will be mostly beaver, What I send you will be 15 to 1700$ I suppose."[51]

By the mid-1840's, as war with Mexico loomed, the fur trade from New Mexico had come the full circle. As in the Spanish period, trapping had ceased to be of consequence, and coarse furs again dominated the trade, although beaver fur was still to be found. Two and one-half decades of exposure to American trappers and traders had made an indelible impression on New Mexico. Ruxton thought that "from association with the hardy trappers and pioneers of the Far West, the New Mexicans have in some degree imbibed a portion of their enterprise and hardihood."[52] Actually, by having survived in a rugged and hostile frontier environment for over two centuries before the arrival of Americans, the New Mexicans had already demonstrated their "enterprise and hardihood." Perhaps the clearest manifestation of American influence on New Mexico was in conditioning the area for the military conquest of 1846. Living and working within sight of Americans had taught many New Mexicans that though the foreigners might be unpleasant and un-likable, at least they were not demons to be resisted at the cost of one's own life.

At Taos, however, where American trappers had gathered in greatest numbers before the Mexican War, the conquest was not destined to be bloodless. In January, 1847, less than five months after Kearny had seemingly subdued New Mexico, Taos Indians,

[50] Hafen, *Ruxton of the Rockies*, 219, 190–91.

[51] S. Turley to Jesse Turley, Taos, April 18, 1843, Turley Papers, Missouri Historical Society; Williams, *Tour to Oregon*, 84.

[52] Hafen, *Ruxton of the Rockies*, 181.

incited by disgruntled native New Mexicans, began a bloody revolt. It started early in the morning of January 19. One of the first to die was Charles Bent, newly appointed governor of New Mexico, who had reached Taos the night before after a wearying journey through deep snows from Santa Fe. Bent had come to be home with his family and had scoffed at reports of revolt: "Why should they want to kill me or my family? Have I not been their friend?" On the morning of January 19, Bent met a horrible death, killed in his own home by Taoseños, who spared his Mexican family. Before the day was over, Stephen Louis Lee, who had been appointed sheriff of Taos in December, and Narciso Beaubien, son of Charles, were also among the dead. The revolt spread from the village to nearby Arroyo Hondo, where Simeon Turley was killed and his home and mill left a smoldering ruin. At Río Colorado, farther up the river, trapper Mark Head and a man named Harwood died. At Mora a group of Santa Fe traders surrendered their arms only to be murdered.

As soon as news of the massacres reached Santa Fe on January 20, Colonel Sterling Price, who was military commander of the area, made preparations to end the insurrection. When he left Santa Fe for Taos on January 23, "Captain" Ceran St. Vrain rode at the head of a company of volunteers composed, it was said, of many former mountain men. By February 2 these avengers had fought their way to the valley of Taos. They spent much of the next day breaking a road through heavy snow to the village of San Fernando, where they discovered that the insurgents had taken refuge in the pueblo a few miles beyond. Inexorably, the pueblo was seiged and battered; the immense adobe walls of the church crumbled and one hundred fifty Indians died before the pueblo surrendered. In April, a trial was held at Taos. Charles Beaubien acted as presiding judge, Ceran St. Vrain served as an interpreter, and several former mountain men sat on the jury: Baptiste Chalifoux, Antoine Leroux, Manuel Laforet, Charles Autobees, Lucien Maxwell, Joseph Paulding, Charles Robidoux, William LeBlanc, Charles Town, and George Bent, a younger brother of the murdered governor, acted as foreman of the grand jury. Could the verdict ever be in doubt?[53]

Blood spilled and justice served, Americans shifted their attention from military matters to trying to dominate the area politically and economically. Toward these ends, former trappers such as Beaubien, St. Vrain, Carson, Leroux, Antoine Robidoux, and many lesser lights, would be exceedingly useful. Their familiarity with Spanish, their acquaintance with Mexican culture, and their connections with leading New Mexican families would help to soften the shock of the conquest; their unusual geographical knowledge and facility with Indian languages would serve to extend American control beyond the settlements and further American exploration of the Far Southwest.

Though the trapper as an occupational type had nearly disappeared in the Southwest by the time of the Mexican War, former trappers continued to exert influence in the region. And even after the last of them passed from the scene, stories of their adventures, true and otherwise, lived on for succeeding generations who would marvel at the trappers' daring, envy their freedom of movement, lament the shrinking of the wilderness which the trappers had beheld, and minimize the hardships and tedium the trappers had endured.

[53] This account is based on the official documents published in E. Bennett Burton, "The Taos Rebellion," *Old Santa Fe*, Vol I, No. 2 (October, 1913), 176–209. Court records are in Francis T. Cheetham, "The First Term of the American Court in Taos, New Mexico," *New Mexico Historical Review*, Vol. I, No. 1 (January, 1926), 23–41. Garrard, *Wah-to-yah*, 171–73.

BIBLIOGRAPHY

I. MANUSCRIPT MATERIALS

A. Archival and Library Collections

Alvarez Papers, State Records Center, Santa Fe, New Mexico.

Archivo de Gobernación, Archivo General de la Nación, Mexico, D.F.

Archivo de Justicia, Archivo General de la Nación, Mexico, D.F.

Archivo de la Secretaría de Relaciones Exteriores, Mexico, D.F.

Barclay (Alexander) Papers, Bancroft Library, University of California, Berkeley, California.

Bolton Transcripts, Bancroft Library, University of California, Berkeley, California.

Campbell Papers, Missouri Historical Society, St. Louis, Missouri.

Chouteau Collection, Missouri Historical Society, St. Louis, Missouri.

Cragin Collection, Pioneers' Museum, Colorado Springs, Colorado.

Despatches from U. S. Consuls in Santa Fe, 1830–46, National Archives, Washington, D.C.

Despatches From U. S. Consuls in Mexico City, 1822–1906, Vols. I and II, National Archives, Washington, D.C.

Documentos de la Ciudad de Juárez, Juárez, Mexico, microfilm copy at the University of Texas at El Paso.

Fur Trade Envelope, Missouri Historical Society, St. Louis, Missouri.

Gamble Papers, Missouri Historical Society, St. Louis, Missouri.

Hempstead Letterbooks, Coe Collection, Yale University Library, New Haven, Connecticut.

Mexican Archives of New Mexico, State Records Center, Santa Fe, New Mexico.

Miscellaneous File, State Records Center, Santa Fe, New Mexico.

New Mexico Land Grant Papers, Coronado Room, University of New Mexico Library, Albuquerque, New Mexico.

Notes from the Mexican Legation in the U. S. to the Department of State, Vol. I, National Archives, Washington, D. C.

Pinart, Alphonse Louis. Colección de manuscritos relativos a la región septentrional de Mexico, Series II, Bancroft Library, University of California, Berkeley, California.

Read Collection, State Records Center, Santa Fe, New Mexico.

Ritch Papers, Huntington Library, San Marino, California.

Santa Fe Ayuntamiento Journal, 1829–36, Coronado Room, Zimmerman Library, University of New Mexico, Albuquerque, New Mexico.

Santa Fe Envelope, Missouri Historical Society, St. Louis, Missouri.

Santa Fe Trail Papers, Abiel Leonard Collection, Western Historical Manuscripts Collection, State Historical Society of Missouri, Columbia, Missouri.

Smith [Peter] Papers, Bancroft Library, University of California, Berkeley, California.

Spanish Archives of New Mexico, State Records Center, Santa Fe, New Mexico.

Stearns [Abel] Papers, Huntington Library, San Marino, California.

Sublette Papers, Missouri Historical Society, St. Louis, Missouri.

Turley Papers, Missouri Historical Society, St. Louis, Missouri.

Vallejo [Mariano G.]. Documentos para la historia de California. Bancroft Library, University of California, Berkeley, California.

Wolfskill Ledger, 1830–31, Huntington Library, San Marino, California.

Year of 1847, First Book (A), Record of Land Established by Law, Federal Bureau of Land Management, Santa Fe, New Mexico.

B. *Unpublished Theses and Manuscripts*

Engelson, Lester Gordon. "Interests and Activities of the Hudson's

Bay Company in California, 1820–1846," M. A. thesis, University of California, Berkeley, 1939.

Lecompte, Janet. "Fort Pueblo," unpublished manuscript in possession of author, Colorado Springs, Colorado.

Minge, Ward Alan. "Frontier Problems in New Mexico Preceding the Mexican War, 1840–1846," Ph.D. dissertation, University of New Mexico, 1965.

Nuttall, Donald A. "The American Threat to New Mexico, 1804–1821," M.A. thesis, San Diego State College, 1959.

Ruiz, Ramón. "For God and Country: A Brief History of Spanish Defensive Efforts Along the Northeastern Frontier of New Mexico to 1820," M.A. thesis, Claremont Graduate School, 1948.

Wesley, Edgar B. "The Fur Trade of the Southwest," M.A. thesis, Washington University, 1925.

II. GOVERNMENT DOCUMENTS

Message from the President of the United States in compliance with a resolution of the Senate concerning the Fur Trade and Inland Trade to Mexico, February 8, 1832, U. S. Cong., 1 sess., *Sen. Doc. 90* (Ser. 213).

Petition of Sundry Inhabitants of Missouri, upon the Subject of a Communication Between the Said State and the Internal Province of Mexico, with a Letter from Alphonso Wetmore upon the Same Subject. February 14, 1825, 18 Cong., 1 sess., *House Doc. 79* (Ser. 116), in *Santa Fé Trail First Reports: 1825* (Houston, 1960), 47–69.

Relief to Citizens U. S. for Indian Depredations. U. S. 22 Cong., 1 sess., *House Doc. 38* (Ser. 217).

Storrs, Augustus. *Answers of Augustus Storrs of Missouri to Certain Queries upon the Origin, Present State, and Future Prospect, of Trade and Intercourse Between Missouri and the Internal Provinces of Mexico, Propounded by the Hon. Mr. Benton, November, 1825.* 18 Cong., 2 sess., *Sen. Doc. 7* (Ser. 108), in *Santa Fé Trail First Reports: 1825* (Houston, 1960) 1–45.

III. NEWSPAPERS

El Fanal de Chihuahua.
Independent Patriot (Jackson, Missouri).
Missouri Gazette (St. Louis).

Missouri Intelligencer (Franklin, Fayette, and Columbia).

Missouri Republican (St. Louis).

"The Mormons and the Far West." Ed. by Dale L. Morgan. Transcripts of newspaper articles which reflect Morgan's broad interest in the West. One copy of these transcripts is at the Huntington Library, San Marino, California.

El Noticioso de Chihuahua.

Niles' Weekly Register (Washington D.C.).

St. Louis Enquirer.

St. Louis *Times.*

El Sol (Mexico, D.F.).

IV. OTHER PRIMARY SOURCES

A. Books

Abert's New Mexico Report. 1846–1847. Albuquerque, 1962.

Anderson, William Marshall. *The Rocky Mountain Journals of William Marshall Anderson: The West in 1834.* Ed. by Dale L. Morgan and Eleanor Townes Harris. San Marino, California, 1967.

Barreiro, Antonio. *Ojeada sobre Nuevo Mejico,* in H. Bailey Carroll and J. Villasana Haggard, trans. and eds., *Three New Mexico Chronicles, q.v.*

Bolton, Herbert E. *Pageant in the Wilderness: The Story of the Escalante Expedition to the Interior Basin, 1776.* Vol. XVII of *Utah Historical Quarterly.* 1950.

Bonner, T. D. *The Life and Adventures of James P. Beckwourth.* Ed. by Bernard DeVoto. New York, 1931.

Carroll, H. Bailey, and J. Villasana Haggard, trans. and eds. *Three New Mexico Chronicles.* Albuquerque, 1942.

Carter, Clarence Edward, comp. and ed. *The Territorial Papers of the United States: The Territory of Louisiana-Missouri, 1815–1821.* Vol. XV: Washington, D.C., 1951.

Carter, Harvey L. *'Dear Old Kit': The Historical Christopher Carson.* Norman, 1968.

Clyman, James. *James Clyman, Frontiersman: The Adventures of a Trapper and Covered-Wagon Emigrant as Told in His Own Reminiscences and Diaries.* Ed. by Charles L. Camp. Portland, Oregon, 1960.

Coues, Elliott, ed. *New Light on the Early History of the Far West:*

The Manuscript Journals of Alexander Henry and David Thompson. 3 vols. New York, 1897.

Documentos para la historia de Mexico. Series IV. 7 vols. Mexico, 1856.

Domínguez, Fray Francisco Atanasio. *The Missions of New Mexico, 1776.* Trans. and annot. by Eleanor B. Adams and Fray Angélico Chávez. Albuquerque, 1956.

Dublán, Manuel, and José María Lozano. *Legislación Mexicana ó colección completa de las disposiciones legislativas expedidas desde la independencia de la republica.* 19 vols. Mexico, 1876–90.

Dye, Job Francis. *Recollections of a Pioneer, 1830–1853.* Los Angeles, 1951.

Ellison, William Henry, ed. *The Life and Adventures of George Nidever, 1802–1883.* Berkeley, 1937.

Ferris, Warren A. *Life in the Rocky Mountains: A Diary of Wanderings on the Sources of the Rivers Missouri, Columbia, and Colorado from February, 1830, to November, 1835.* Ed. by Paul C. Phillips. Denver, 1940.

Field, Matthew C. *Matt Field on the Santa Fe Trail.* Collected by Clyde and Mae Reed Porter and ed. by John E. Sunder. Norman, 1960.

Fowler, Jacob. *The Journal of Jacob Fowler.* Ed. by Elliott Coues. New York, 1898.

Garrard, Lewis H. *Wah-to-yah and the Taos Trail.* Introduction by A. B. Guthrie, Jr. Norman, 1955.

Gregg, Josiah. *Commerce of the Prairies.* Ed. by Max L. Moorhead. Norman, 1954.

Hackett, Charles Wilson, ed. *Historical Documents Relating to New Mexico, Nueva Vizcaya, and Approaches Thereto, to 1773.* 3 vols. Washington, D.C., 1937.

Hafen, LeRoy R., and Ann W. Hafen, eds. *Rufus B. Sage: His Letters and Papers, 1836–1847, with an Annotated Reprint of his "Scenes in the Rocky Mountains . . . ."* 2 vols. Glendale, 1956.

Hammond, George P., and Agapito Rey, trans. and eds. *Don Juan de Oñate, Colonizer of New Mexico, 1595–1628.* 2 vols. Albuquerque, 1953.

———, trans. and eds. *Expedition into New Mexico made by Antonio de Espejo, 1582–1583, as Revealed in the Journal of Diego Pérez de Luxán.* Los Angeles, 1929.

———, trans. and eds. *The Gallegos Relation of the Rodríquez Expedition to New Mexico.* Santa Fe, 1927.

———, trans. and eds. *Narrative of the Coronado Expedition, 1540–1542.* Albuquerque, 1940.

———, trans. and eds. *The Rediscovery of New Mexico, 1580–1594. The Explorations of Chamuscado, Espejo, Castaño de Sosa, Morlete, and Leyva de Bonilla and Humaña.* Albuquerque, 1966.

Hardy, R. W. H. *Travels in the Interior of Mexico in 1825, 1826, 1827, and 1828.* London, 1829.

Hodge, Frederick Webb, George P. Hammond, and Agapito Rey, trans. and eds. *Fray Alonso de Benavides' Revised Memorial of 1634.* Albuquerque, 1945.

Hulbert, Archer Butler, ed. *Southwest on the Turquoise Trail.* Denver, 1933.

Humbolt, Alexander de. *Political Essay on the Kingdom of New Spain.* 4 vols. London, 1811.

James, Edwin. *James's Account of S. H. Long's Expedition, 1819–1820.* Vol. XIV–XVII in Reuben Gold Thwaites, ed., *Early Western Travels.* 4 vols., Cleveland, 1905.

James, Thomas. *Three Years among the Mexicans and the Indians.* St. Louis, 1916.

Lafora, Nicolas de. *The Frontiers of New Spain: Nicolas de Lafora's Description, 1766–1768.* Trans and ed. by Lawrence Kinnaird. Berkeley, 1958.

Leonard, Zenas. *The Adventures of Zenas Leonard, Fur Trader.* Ed. by John C. Ewers. Norman, 1959.

Loomis, Noel M., and Abraham P. Nasatir. *Pedro Vial and the Roads to Santa Fe.* Norman, 1967.

Luttig, John C. *Journal of a Fur-Trading Expedition on the Upper Missouri, 1812–1813.* Ed. by Stella M. Drumm, with preface and notes by Abraham P. Nasatir. New York, 1964.

Meriwether, David. *My Life in the Mountains and on the Plains: The Newly Discovered Autobiography of David Meriwether.* Ed. by Robert A. Griffen. Norman, 1965.

Morgan, Dale L., ed. *The West of William H. Ashley, 1822–1838.* Denver, 1964.

Nasatir, Abraham P., ed. *Before Lewis and Clark: Documents Illustrating the History of the Missouri, 1785–1804.* 2 vols. St. Louis, 1952.

Ogden, Peter Skene. *Peter Skene Ogden's Snake Country Journals, 1824–1825 and 1825–1826.* Ed. by E. E. Rich. London, 1950.

Pattie, James Ohio. *The Personal Narrative of James Ohio Pattie of Kentucky.* Ed. by Timothy Flint. Philadelphia, 1962.

Pike, Albert. *Prose Sketches and Poems Written in the Western Country (with Additional Stories).* Ed. by David J. Weber. Albuquerque, 1967.

Pike, Zebulon Montgomery. *The Journals of Zebulon Montgomery Pike, with Letters and Related Documents.* Ed. and annot. by Donald Jackson. 2 vols. Norman, 1966.

Ruschenberger, W. S. W. *A Voyage Around the World, 1835, 1836, 1837.* 2 vols. Philadelphia, 1838.

Ruxton, George Frederick. *Ruxton of the Rockies.* Collected by Clyde and Mae Reed Porter, ed. by LeRoy R. Hafen. Norman, 1950.

Sibley, George Champlin. *The Road to Santa Fe: The Journal and Diaries of George Champlin Sibley.* Ed. by Kate L. Gregg. Albuquerque, 1952.

Simmons, Marc, trans. and ed. *Border Comanches: Seven Spanish Colonial Documents, 1785–1819.* Santa Fe, 1967.

Simpson, George. *Fur Trade and Empire: George Simpson's Journal.* Ed. by Frederick Merk. Rev. ed. Cambridge, 1968.

Simpson, Lieutenant James H. *Navaho Expedition: Journal of a Military Reconnaissance from Santa Fe, New Mexico, to the Navaho Country, Made in 1849.* Ed. and annot. by Frank McNitt. Norman, 1964.

Storrs, Augustus, and Alphonso Wetmore. *Santa Fé Trail, First Reports: 1825.* Houston, 1960.

Stuart, Robert. *On the Oregon Trail: Robert Stuart's Journal of Discovery.* Ed. by Kenneth A. Spaulding. Norman, 1953.

Thomas, Alfred Barnaby, trans. and ed. *After Coronado: Spanish Exploration Northeast of New Mexico, 1696–1727.* Norman, 1935.

———, trans. and ed. *Forgotten Frontiers: A Study of the Spanish Indian Policy of Don Juan Bautista de Anza, Governor of New Mexico, 1777–1787.* Norman, 1932.

———. *The Plains Indians and New Mexico, 1751–1778: A Collection of Documents Illustrative of the History of the Eastern Frontier of New Mexico.* Albuquerque, 1940.

Tamarón y Romeral, Bishop Pedro. *Bishop Tamarón's Visitation of New Mexico, 1760.* Ed. by Eleanor B. Adams, Albuquerque, 1954.

Twitchell, Ralph Emerson. *The Spanish Archives of New Mexico.* 2 vols. Cedar Rapids, Iowa, 1914.

Walker, Joel P. *A Pioneer of Pioneers, Narrative of Adventures thro' Alabama, Florida, New Mexico, Oregon, California, etc.* Los Angeles, 1953.

Warner, J. J., Benjamin Hayes, and J. P. Widney. *An Historical Sketch of Los Angeles County, California.* Los Angeles, 1936.

Weber, David J., trans. and ed. *The Extranjeros: Selected Documents from the Mexican Side of the Santa Fe Trail, 1825–1828.* Santa Fe, 1967.

Wetmore, Alphonso. *Gazetteer of the State of Missouri.* St. Louis, 1837.

Wheat, Carl I. *Mapping the Transmississippi West.* 5 vols. in 6. San Francisco, 1957–63.

Williams, Joseph. *Narrative of a Tour from the State of Indiana to the Oregon Territory in the Years 1841–1842.* Introduction by James C. Bell, Jr. New York, 1921.

Wislizenus, A. *Memoir of a Tour to Northern Mexico.* Washington, D.C., 1848.

Young, F. G., ed. *The Correspondence of Captain Nathaniel J. Wyeth, 1831–1836.* Eugene, Oregon, 1899.

Yount, George C. *George C. Yount and His Chronicles of the West.* Ed. by Charles L. Camp. Denver, 1966.

B. Articles

Allison, W. H. H. "Santa Fe as it Appeared During the Winter of the Years 1837 and 1838," *Old Santa Fe,* Vol. II, No. 2 (October, 1914), 170–83.

[Barrows, H. D] "The Story of an Old Pioneer [WilliamWolfskill]," *Wilmington* (California) *Journal,* October 20, 1866.

Becknell, William. "Journal of Two Expeditions from Boone's Lick to Santa Fe," in Archer B. Hulbert, ed., *Southwest on the Turquoise Trail* (*q.v.*), 56–68.

Bloom, Lansing B. "The Death of Jacques D'Eglise," *New Mexico Historical Review,* Vol. II, No. 4 (October, 1927), 369–79.

———. "A Trade-Invoice of 1638," *New Mexico Historical Review,* Vol. X, No. 3 (July, 1935), 242–48.

Camp, Charles L., ed. "The Journal of a 'Crazy Man,'" *California Historical Society Quarterly*, Vol. XV, Nos. 2 and 3 (June and September, 1936), 103–38, 224–41.

"Captain Don Santiago Kirker, the Indian Fighter, His Warring Against the Apaches From 1836 to 1847," *Santa Fe Republican*, November 20, 1847.

Chávez, Fray Angélico. "Addenda to New Mexico Families," published serially in *El Palacio*, Vols. 62–64.

———. "New Names in New Mexico, 1820–1850," *El Palacio*, Vol. LXIV, Nos. 9–12 (September–December 1957), 291–318, 367–80.

Cheetham, Francis T. "The First Term of the American Court in Taos, New Mexico," *New Mexico Historical Review*, Vol. I, No. 1 (January, 1926), 23–41.

Covington, James W. "Correspondence Between Mexican Officials at Santa Fe and Officials in Missouri: 1823–1825," *Missouri Historical Society Bulletin*, Vol. XVI, No. 1 (October, 1959), 20–32.

Day, Mrs. F. H. "Sketches of the Early Settlers of California, Isaac J. Sparks," *The Hesperian*, Vol. II, No. 5 (July, 1859), 193–200.

———. "Sketches of the Early Settlers of California, Jacob P. Leese," *The Hesperian*, Vol. II, No. 4 (June, 1859), 147–48.

[Douglas, Walter B.] "Ezekiel Williams' Adventures in Colorado," *Missouri Historical Society Collections*, Vol. IV, No. 2 (1913), 194–208.

Foster, Stephen C. "A Sketch of Some of the Earliest Kentucky Pioneers of Los Angeles," *Historical Society of Southern California* (1887), 30–35.

Goodwin, Cardinal. "John H. Fonda's Explorations in the Southwest," *Southwestern Historical Quarterly*, Vol. XXIII, No. 1 (July, 1919), 39–46.

Jones, Charles Irving. "William Kronig, New Mexico Pioneer, from His Memoirs of 1849–1860," *New Mexico Historical Review*, Vol. XIX, No. 3 (July, 1944), 199–224.

"M. M. Marmaduke Journal," in A. B. Hulbert, ed., *Southwest on the Turquoise Trail* (*q.v.*), 69–77.

Marshall, Thomas Maitland, ed. "Journals of Jules de Mun," reprinted from the *Missouri Historical Society Collections*, Vol. V, No. 3 (1928), 1–58.

Merk, Frederick, "Snake Country Expedition, 1824–25," *Oregon Historical Society Quarterly*, Vol. XXXV, No. 2 (June, 1934), 93–122.

"Peg-Leg Smith—A Short Sketch of His Life, *Daily Alta California* (San Francisco), March 8, 1858.

"Reports of the Fur Trade and Inland Trade to New Mexico, 1831," *Missouri Historical Society Glimpses of the Past*, Vol. IX, Nos. 1 and 2 (January–June, 1942), 3–39.

"Sketches from the Life of Peg-leg Smith," published serially in *Hutchings' Illustrated California Magazine*, Vol. V, Nos. 4–9. (October–March, 1860–61).

"The Story of an Old Trapper, Life and Adventures of the late Peg-Leg Smith," *San Francisco Evening Bulletin*, October 26, 1866.

Thomas, Alfred B. "An Anonymous Description of New Mexico in 1818," *Southwestern Historical Quarterly*, Vol. XXXIII, No. 1 (July, 1929), 50–74.

———. "Documents Bearing Upon the Northern Frontier of New Mexico, 1818–1819," *New Mexico Historical Review*, Vol. IV, No. 2 (April, 1929), 146–64.

———. "The Yellowstone River, James Long, and Spanish Reaction to American Intrusion into Spanish Domains, 1818–1819," *New Mexico Historical Review*, Vol. IV, No. 2 (April, 1929), 164–77.

Waldo, William. "Recollections of a Septuagenarian," *Missouri Historical Society Glimpses of the Past*, Vol. V, Nos. 4–6 (April–June, 1938) 59–94.

Warner, J. J. "Reminiscences of Early California, 1831 to 1846," *Publications, Historical Society of Southern California*, Vol. VIII (1907–1908), 176–93.

Weber, David J. "A Letter from Taos, 1826: William Workman," *New Mexico Historical Review*, Vol. XLI, No. 2 (April, 1966), 155–64.

Wesley, Edgar B., ed. "Diary of James Kennerly, 1823–1826," *Missouri Historical Society Collections*, Vol. VI, No. 1 (October, 1928), 41–97.

"Benjamin David Wilson's Observations on Early Days in California and New Mexico," Foreword and Explanatory Notes by Arthur Woodward, *Historical Society of Southern California Annual Publications*, Vol. XVI, No. 1 (Los Angeles, 1934), 74–150.

A. Books

Bailey, L. R. *Indian Slave Trade in the Southwest.* Los Angeles, 1966.

Bancroft, Hubert Howe. *History of California.* 7 vols., San Francisco, 1884–90.

Billington, Ray Allen. *The Far Western Frontier, 1830–1860.* New York, 1962.

Billon, Frederick. *Annual of St. Louis in its Territorial Days from 1804 to 1820.* St. Louis, 1888.

Bolton, Herbert E. *Bolton and the Spanish Borderlands.* Ed. and intro. by John Francis Bannon. Norman, 1964.

———. *Coronado, Knight of Pueblos and Plains.* Albuquerque, 1964.

Bork, Albert William. *Nuevos aspectos del comercio entre Nuevo México y Misuri, 1822–1846.* Mexico, D.F., 1944.

Bosch García, Carlos. *Historia de las relaciones entre México y los Estados Unidos, 1819–1848.* Mexico, D.F., 1961.

Broadus, J. Morgan. *The Legal Heritage of El Paso.* El Paso, 1963.

Chittenden, Hiram Martin. *The American Fur Trade of the Far West.* 2 vols. Stanford, 1954.

Cleland, Robert Glass. *This Reckless Breed of Men: The Trappers and Fur Traders of the Southwest.* New York, 1950.

Coyner, David H. *The Lost Trappers.* New York, 1847.

Dale, Harrison Clifford. *The Ashley-Smith Explorations and the Discovery of a Central Route to the Pacific, 1822–1829.* Glendale, 1941.

Douglas, Walter B. *Manuel Lisa.* Ed. and annot. by Abraham P. Nasatir. New York, 1964.

Duffus, Robert. *The Santa Fe Trail.* New York, 1934.

Espinosa, J. Manuel. *Crusaders of the Rio Grande.* Chicago, 1942.

Favour, Alpheus H. *Old Bill Williams, Mountain Man.* Norman, 1962.

Folmer, Henry. *Franco-Spanish Rivalry in North America, 1524–1763.* Glendale, 1953.

Forbes, Jack D. *Apache, Navaho, and Spaniard.* Norman, 1960.

———. *Warriors of the Colorado: The Yumas of the Quechan Nation and their Neighbors.* Norman, 1965.

Gerhard, Peter, and Howard E. Gulick. *Lower California Guidebook.* 4th ed. Glendale, 1967.

Gibson, Charles. *The Aztecs under Spanish Rule: A History of the*

Indians of the Valley of Mexico 1519–1810. Stanford, 1964.

Goetzmann, William H. *Exploration and Empire: The Explorer and the Scientist in the Winning of the American West.* New York, 1966.

Hafen, LeRoy R., ed. *The Mountain Men and the Fur Trade of the Far West: Biographical Sketches of the Participants by Scholars of the Subjects.* Introduction by LeRoy R. Hafen. 8 vols. Glendale, 1965–.

Volume I:
  Beckman, Margaret E., and William H. Ellison. "George Nidever," pp. 337–54.
  Cline, Gloria Griffen. "Job Francis Dye," pp. 259–71.
  Dunham, Harold H. "Manuel Alvarez," pp. 181–97.
  Rolle, Andrew F. "Isaac Slover," pp. 367–72.
Volume II:
  Baur, John E. "Francis Ziba Branch," pp. 55–60.
  ———. "Isaac Sparks," pp. 317–19.
  Dunham, Harold H. "Charles Bent," pp. 27–48.
  Rolle, Andew F. "William Pope," pp. 275–76.
  Settle, Raymond W. "Nathaniel Miguel Pryor," pp. 277–88.
  Stevens, Harry R. "Hugh Glenn," pp. 161–74.
Volume III:
  Baur, John E. "Richard Campbell," pp. 69–70.
  Cline, Gloria Griffen. "Jacob Primer Leese," pp. 189–96.
  Lecompte, Janet. "Antoine and Abraham Ledoux," pp. 173–79.
  Oglesby, Richard E. "William Morrison," pp. 197–203.
  Strickland, Rex W. "James Baird," pp. 27–37.
  Weber, David J. "Stephen Louis Lee," pp. 181–88.
Volume IV:
  Hafen, Ann W. "James Ohio Pattie," pp. 231–50.
  Humphreys, Alfred Glen. "Thomas L. (Peg-leg) Smith," pp. 311–30.
  Lecompte, Janet, "Alexander Branch," pp. 61–67.
  McDermott, John Dishon. "Joseph Bissonette," pp. 49–60.
  Nunis, Doyce B. "Milton Sublette," pp. 331–39.
  Voelker, Frederick E. "Thomas James," pp. 153–67.
  Weber, David J. "Gervais Nolan," pp. 225–29.
  ———. "John Rowland," pp. 275–81.

Volume V:

Carter, Harvey L. "John Gantt," pp. 101–15.

Cutter, Donald C., and David J. Weber. "Cyrus Alexander," pp. 23–30.

Dunham, Harold H. "Ceran St. Vrain," pp. 297–316.

McGaw, William Cochrane. "James Kirker," pp. 125–43.

Volume VI:

Haines, Aubrey. "Hugh Glass," pp. 161–71.

Lecompte, Janet. "John Poisel," pp. 353–58.

———. "Pierre Lesperance," pp. 241–46.

———. "Maurice LeDuc," pp. 227–40.

Murphy, Lawrence R. "Charles H. Beaubien," pp. 23–35.

Oglesby, Richard E. "Baptiste LaLande," pp. 219–22.

Weber, David J. "Francisco Laforet," pp. 213–18.

———. "Sylvestre S. Pratte," pp. 359–70.

Volume VII:

Lecompte, Janet. "Jean Baptiste Chalifoux," pp. 57–74.

Weber, David J. "John Harris," pp. 155–59.

———. "William Workman," pp. 382–92.

Volume VIII:

Weber, David J. "Louis Robidoux." (forthcoming)

Hafen, LeRoy R., and Ann W. Hafen, *Old Spanish Trail, Santa Fé to Los Angeles*. Glendale, 1954.

Hafen, LeRoy R., Ann W. Hafen, and W. J. Ghent. *Broken Hand: The Life of Thomas Fitzpatrick, Chief of the Mountain Men*. Denver, 1931.

Hammond, George P. *Don Juan de Oñate and the Founding of New Mexico*. Santa Fe, 1927.

Haring, Clarence H. *Trade and Navigation Between Spain and the Indies in the Time of the Hapsburgs*. Cambridge, Massachusetts, 1918.

Holmes, Kenneth L. *Ewing Young: Master Trapper*. Portland, Oregon, 1967.

Jones, Oakah L., Jr. *Pueblo Warriors and Spanish Conquest*. Norman, 1966.

Kelly, Charles, and Dale L. Morgan. *Old Greenwood: The Story of Caleb Greenwood, Trapper, Pathfinder, and Early Pioneer*. Rev. ed. Georgetown, California, 1965.

Lamar, Howard Roberts. *The Far Southwest, 1846–1912: A Territorial History*. New Haven, 1966.

Lavender, David. *Bent's Fort*. New York, 1954.

———. *The Fist in the Wilderness*. New York, 1964.

McNitt, Frank. *The Indian Traders*. Norman, 1962.

Manning, William R. *Early Diplomatic Relations Between the United States and Mexico*. Baltimore, 1916.

Moorhead, Max L. *New Mexico's Royal Road*. Norman, 1958.

Morgan, Dale L. *Jedediah Smith and the Opening of the West*. New York, 1953.

———, and Carl I. Wheat. *Jedediah Smith and His Maps of the American West*. San Francisco, 1954.

Myers, John Myers. *Pirate, Pawnee, and Mountain Man: The Saga of Hugh Glass*. Boston, 1963.

Ogden, Adele. *The California Sea Otter Trade, 1784–1848*. Berkeley, 1941.

Oglesby, Richard E. *Manuel Lisa and the Opening of the Missouri Fur Trade*. Norman, 1963.

Palencia, Isabel de. *The Regional Costumes of Spain*. London, 1926.

Parkhill, Forbes. *The Blazed Trail of Antoine Leroux*. Los Angeles, 1965.

Pearce, T. M. *New Mexico Place Names: A Geographical Dictionary*. Albuquerque, 1965.

Phillips, Paul Chrisler. *The Fur Trade*. 2 vols. Norman, 1961.

Reeve, Frank D. *History of New Mexico*. 3 vols. New York, 1961.

Richardson, Rupert Norval. *The Comanche Barrier to South Plains Settlement*. Glendale, 1933.

Riva Palacio, Vicente. *México a través de los siglos*. 5 vols. Mexico, 1887–89.

Robidoux, Orral M. *Memorial to the Robidoux Brothers*. Kansas City, 1924.

Robinson, Cecil. *With the Ears of Strangers: The Mexican in American Literature*. Tucson, 1963.

Russell, Carl P. *Firearms, Traps, and Tools of the Mountain Men*. New York, 1967.

Scharf, Thomas J. *History of Saint Louis City and County*. 2 vols. Philadelphia, 1883.

Scholes, France V. *Church and State in New Mexico, 1610–1650*. Albuquerque, 1937.

———. *Troublous Times in New Mexico, 1659–1670*. Albuquerque, 1942.

Simmons, Marc. *Spanish Government in New Mexico*. Albuquerque, 1968.

Sunder, John E. *Bill Sublette, Mountain Man*. Norman, 1959.

Templeton, Sardis W. *The Lame Captain: The Life and Adventures of Pegleg Smith*. Los Angeles, 1965.

Wallace, William S. *Antoine Robidoux, 1794–1860*. Los Angeles, 1953.

Watson, Douglas. *West Wind: The Story of Joseph Reddeford Walker, Knight of the Golden Horseshoe*. Los Angeles, 1934.

Wilson, Iris Higbie. *William Wolfskill, 1798–1866: Frontier Trapper to California Ranchero*. Glendale, 1965.

B. Articles

Binkley, William C. "New Mexico and the Texan Santa Fe Expedition," *Southwestern Historical Quarterly*, Vol. XXVII, No. 2 (October, 1923), 85–107.

Bloom, Lansing Bartlett. "New Mexico under Mexican Administration, 1821–1846," *Old Santa Fe*, published serially throughout Vols. I and II (1913–15).

Bolton, Herbert E. "The Spanish Occupation of Texas, 1519–1690," in John Francis Bannon, ed., *Bolton and the Spanish Borderlands* (q.v.), 96–122.

———. "French Intrusions into New Mexico, 1749–1752," in John Francis Bannon, ed., *Bolton and the Spanish Borderlands* (q.v.), 150–71.

———. "New Light on Manuel Lisa and the Spanish Fur Trade," *Southwestern Historical Quarterly*, Vol. XVII, No. 1 (July, 1913), 61–66.

Brugge, David M. "Vizcarra's Navaho Campaign of 1823," *Arizona and the West*, Vol. VI, No. 3 (Autumn, 1964), 233–44.

Burton, E. Bennett. "The Taos Rebellion," *Old Santa Fe*, Vol. I, No. 2 (October, 1913), 176–209.

Carroll, H. Bailey. "Some New Mexico–West Texas Relationships, 1541–1841," *West Texas Historical Association Year Book*, Vol. XIV, (October, 1938), 92–102.

Clayton, James L. "The Growth and Significance of the American

Fur Trade, 1790–1890," *Minnesota History*, Vol. XL, No. 4 (Winter, 1966), 210–20.

Cleland, Robert Glass. "The Early Sentiment for the Annexation of California; An Account of the Growth of American Interest in California, 1835–1846," *Southwestern Historical Quarterly*, Vol. XVIII, No. 1 (July, 1914), 1–40.

Creer, Leland Hargrave. "Spanish-American Slave Trade in the Great Basin, 1800–1853," *New Mexico Historical Review*, Vol. XXIV, No. 3 (July, 1949), 171–83.

Ellis, Florence Hawley and J. J. Brody. "Ceramic Stratigraphy and Tribal History at Taos Pueblo," *American Antiquity*, Vol. XXIX, No. 3 (January, 1964), 316–27.

Estep, Raymond. "The Le Grand Survey of the High Plains: Fact or Fancy," *New Mexico Historical Review*, Vol. XXIX, No. 2 (April, 1954), 81–96.

Folmer, Henri. "Contraband Trade Between Louisiana and New Mexico in the 18th Century," *New Mexico Historical Review*, Vol XVI, No. 3 (July, 1941), 249–74.

Foreman, Grant. "Antoine Leroux, New Mexico Guide," *New Mexico Historical Review*, Vol. XVI, No. 4 (October, 1941), 367–78.

Golley, Frank B. "James Baird, Early Santa Fe Trader," *Missouri Historical Society Bulletin*, Vol. XV, No. 3 (April, 1959), 171–93.

Hackett, Charles Wilson. "Policy of the Spanish Crown Regarding French Encroachments from Louisiana, 1721–1762," in Charles Wilson Hackett, ed., *New Spain and the Anglo American West*: *Historical Contributions Presented to Herbert Eugene Bolton*, 2 vols. Lancaster, Pennsylvania, 1932, I, 107–45.

Hafen, LeRoy R. "The Bean-Sinclair Party of Rocky Mountain Trappers, 1830–1832," *Colorado Magazine*, Vol. XXXI, No. 3 (July, 1954), 161–71.

———. "The Early Fur Trade Posts on the South Platte," *Mississippi Valley Historical Review*, Vol. XII, No. 3 (December, 1925), 334–41.

———. "Etienne Provost, Mountain Man and Utah Pioneer," *Utah Historical Quarterly*, Vol. XXXVI, No. 2 (Spring, 1968), 99–112.

———. "Fort Jackson and the Early Fur Trade on the South Platte," *Colorado Magazine*, Vol. V, (February, 1928), 9–17.

———. "Fort St. Vrain," *Colorado Magazine*, Vol. XXIX, No. 4 (October, 1952), 241–55.

———. "Old Fort Lupton and its Founders," *Colorado Magazine*, Vol. VI, No. 6 (November, 1929), 220–26.

———. "When Was Bent's Fort Built?" *Colorado Magazine*, Vol. XXXI, No. 2 (April, 1954), 105–19.

Hill, Joseph J. "Antoine Robidoux, Kingpin in the Colorado River Fur Trade," *Colorado Magaine*, Vol. VII, No. 4 (July, 1930), 125–32.

———. "Ewing Young in the Fur Trade of the Far Southwest, 1822–1834," *The Oregon Historical Society Quarterly*, Vol. XXIV, No. 1 (March, 1923), 1–35.

———. "New Light on Pattie and the Southwest Fur Trade," *Southwestern Historical Quarterly*, Vol. XXVI, No. 4 (April, 1923), 243–54.

———. "Spanish and Mexican Exploration and Trade Northwest from New Mexico into the Great Basin, 1765–1853," *Utah Historical Quarterly*, Vol. III, No. 1 (January, 1930), 3–23.

———. "An Unknown Expedition to Santa Fe in 1807," *Mississippi Valley Historical Review*, Vol. VI, No. 4 (March, 1920), 560–62.

Holmes, Kenneth L. "The Benjamin Cooper Expeditions to Santa Fe in 1822 and 1823," *New Mexico Historical Review*, Vol. XXXVIII, No. 2 (April, 1963), 139–50.

Jenkins, Myra Ellen. "Taos Pueblo and Its Neighbors, 1540–1847," *New Mexico Historical Review*, Vol. XLI, No. 2 (April, 1966), 85–114.

Kroeber, Clifton B., ed. "The Route of James O. Pattie on the Colorado in 1826: A Reappraisal by A. L. Kroeber," *Arizona and the West*, Vol. VI, No. 2 (Summer, 1964), 119–36.

Lacy, James M. "New Mexico Women in Early American Writings," *New Mexico Historical Review*, Vol. XXXIV, No. 1 (January, 1959), 41–51.

Lecompte, Janet. "Gantt's Fort and Bent's Picket Post," *Colorado Magazine*, Vol. XLI, No. 2 (Spring, 1964), 111–25.

———. "The Hardscrabble Settlement, 1844–1848," *Colorado Magazine*, Vol. XXXI, No. 2 (April, 1954), 81–98.

Maloney, Alice B. "John Gantt, 'Borderer,'" *California Historical Society Quarterly*, Vol. XVI, No. 1 (March, 1937), Pt. 1, 48–60.

———. "The Richard Campbell Party of 1827," *California Historical Society Quarterly*, Vol. XVII, No. 4 (December, 1939), 347–54.

Marshall, Thomas Maitland. "St. Vrain's Expedition to the Gila in

1826," *Southwestern Historical Quarterly*, Vol. XIX, No. 3 (January, 1916), 251–60.

Monahan, Forrest D. Jr., "The Kiowas and New Mexico, 1800–1845," *Journal of the West*, Vol. VIII, No. 1 (January, 1969), 67–75.

Morgan, Dale L. "New Light on Ashley and Jedediah Smith," *The Pacific Historian*, Vol. 12, No. 1 (Winter, 1968), 14–22.

Nasatir, A. P. "Jacques Clamorgan: Colonial Promoter of the Northern Border of New Spain," *New Mexico Historical Review*, Vol. XVII, No. 1 (January, 1942), 101–12.

Nute, Grace Lee. "The Papers of the American Fur Company: A Brief Estimate of Their Significance," *American Historical Review*, Vol. XXXII, No. 3 (April, 1927), 519–38.

Porter, Kenneth W. "Roll of Overland Astorians," *Oregon Historical Quarterly*, Vol. XXXIV, No. 2 (June, 1933), 103–12.

Reeve, Frank D. "Navaho-Spanish Diplomacy, 1770–1790," *New Mexico Historical Review*, Vol. XXXV, No. 3 (July, 1960), 200–35.

Richie, Eleanor L. "Background of the International Boundary Line of 1819 along the Arkansas River in Colorado," *Colorado Magazine*, Vol. X, No. 4 (July, 1933), 145–56.

Smith, Ralph A. "Apache 'Ranching' Below the Gila, 1841–1845," *Arizoniana*, Vol. III, No. 4 (Winter, 1962), 1–15.

———. "The 'King of New Mexico' and the Doniphan Expedition," *New Mexico Historical Review*, Vol. XXXVIII, No. 1 (January, 1963), 29–55.

———. "The Scalp Hunter in the Borderlands, 1835–1850," *Arizona and the West*, Vol. VI, No. 1 (Spring, 1964), 5–22.

Stephens, F. F. "Missouri and the Santa Fe Trade," *Missouri Historical Review*, Vol. XI, No. 4 (July, 1917), 291–94.

Thomas, Alfred Barnaby. "The First Santa Fe Expedition, 1792–1793," *Chronicles of Oklahoma*, Vol. IX, No. 2 (June, 1931), 195–208.

———. "Spanish Expeditions into Colorado," *Colorado Magazine*, Vol. I, No. 7 (November, 1924), 289–300.

Tittman, Edward D. "By Order of Richard Campbell," *New Mexico Historical Review*, Vol. III, No. 4 (October, 1928), 390–98.

Tyler, S. Lyman. "The Spaniard and the Ute," *Utah Historical Quarterly*, Vol. XXII, No. 4 (October, 1954), 343–61.

Ulibarri, George S. "The Chouteau-Demun Expedition to New Mexico, 1815–1817," *New Mexico Historical Review*, Vol. XXXVI, No. 4 (October, 1961), 263–73.

Voelker, Frederic E. "Ezckiel Williams of Boon's Lick," *The Missouri Historical Society Bulletin*, Vol. VIII, No. 1 (October, 1951), 17–51.

Weber, David J. "Spanish Fur Trade From New Mexico, 1540–1821," *The Americas*, Vol. XXIV, No. 2 (October, 1967), 122–36.

Woodward, Arthur. "Sidelights on Fifty Years of Apache Warfare, 1836–1886," *Arizoniana*, Vol. II, No. 3 (Fall, 1961), 3–14.

INDEX

The paper on which this book is printed bears the watermark of the University of Oklahoma Press and has an effective life of at least three hundred years.